Whatever became of...?

TENTH SERIES

Also by the Author

Lamparski's Hidden Hollywood: Where the
    Stars Lived, Loved, and Died
Whatever became of . . . ? EIGHTH SERIES
Whatever became of . . . ? NINTH SERIES

Whatever became of...?

ALL NEW TENTH SERIES
100 profiles of the most-asked-about movie stars and TV personalities. Hundreds of never-before-published facts, dates, etc., on celebrities.

OVER 200 THEN-AND-NOW PHOTOGRAPHS

RICHARD LAMPARSKI

CROWN PUBLISHERS, INC.

NEW YORK

For Frank Christi
1929–1982

Richard Fletcher
1946–1984
Memories that lift the heart

Published by Crown Publishers, Inc., 225 Park
Avenue South, New York, New York 10003
and represented in Canada by the
Canadian MANDA Group
CROWN is a trademark of Crown Publishers, Inc.
Manufactured in the United States of America
Library of Congress Cataloging in Publication Data
Lamparski, Richard.
Whatever became of—? All new tenth series.
1. Television personalities—United States—
Biography.   2. Moving-picture actors and
actresses—United States—
Biography.   I. Title.
PN1992.4.A2L32   1986   791.43′028′0922
[B]   86-8887
ISBN 0-517-56228-6
0-517-56229-4 (paper)
10 9 8 7 6 5 4 3 2 1
First Edition

Contents

NOTE: The superscript [8] and [9] with names in the text indicate that this personality is profiled in *Whatever Became of. . .? EIGHTH SERIES or NINTH SERIES* by Richard Lamparski.

Acknowledgments

The author gratefully acknowledges those who have helped to make this book possible:

Deborah Davis-Lipson
Wayne Martin
David Del Valle
Bob Satterfield
Phil Boroff
Chris Dietrich
Ronnie Britton
Wayne Clark
Lester Glassner
Dewitt Bodeen
Collectors Book Store
Robert F. Slatzer
Jim Brennan
Jim Janisch
Jim Jeneji
Deborah Davis
Copy King of Hollywood
Patrick Lobo
Doug Hart's Back Lot
Critt Davis
Gregory William Mank
Gary H. Grossman
Norman Lobo
Wayne Parks
Amaryllis Bierne-Keyt
Gawain Bierne-Keyt
Paul Adrian
Allied Artists Corp.
Paramount Pictures
Steven Arnold
Michael Back
Virginia Reidy
Roy Bishop
Beverly Hills Public Library
Eddie Brandt's Saturday Matinee
Mathew Tombers
Don Schneider of the Electric Theatre
    Museum
Donna Schaeffer

Paul Schaeffer
Peter Schaeffer
Richard Schaeffer
Anne Schlosser and the staff of the Library of
    the American Film Institute
Tony Slide
Sons of the Desert
Twentieth Century-Fox Corp.
United Artists
Jon Virzi
Marc Wanamaker of the Bison Archives
United Press International Photos
World Wide Photos
Morgan Amber Neiman
Francie Neiman
Chapman's Picture Palace
Frank Buxton
Diana Serra Cary
R. T. Brier
Cinemabilia
Columbia Pictures Corp.
Warner Brothers
Bob Cushman
Shelly Davis
Samson DeBrier
Walt Disney Prods.
Tim Doherty
George Eells
Leatrice Fountain
Hal Gefsky
Aurand Harris
Michael R. Hawks
Howard W. Hays
Terry Helgesen
Charles Higham
Herman Hover
Corinne Lobo
Michael Knowles
Don Koll

Anton LaVey
Los Angeles Times
Dick Lynch
Bobby Downey
Luther Hathcock
Mike Marx
Metro-Goldwyn-Mayer
Iris Adrian
National Screen Service
Sloan Nibley
R. C. Perry
Dorothy Revier
Sarah Richardson
Linda Mehr and the staff of the Motion Picture
    Academy of Arts and Sciences
Bill Tangeman
Art Ronnie
Donovan Brandt
Nick Bougas
Lloyd Douglas
Milton T. Moore, Jr.
Chuck Williamson
Gerald Bastable
Ian Grant
Adam O. Robertson
Paul Taylor
Bryan Ough
Tony Hawes
Jim Yousling
Dave Singer
Shulman Photo Lab
Beverly Churchill

Kirk Crivello
Jack Mathis
"Republic Confidential"
Jerry Siegan
Heidi Brandt
Dan Pattarson
Roy Moseley
IMP/GEH Still Collection
Harold Jacobs
Aljean Harmetz
Ken Septon
Hamilton Meserve
Colin Williamson
David Quinlan
Howard Prouty
Sue Ellen Picker
William W. Granger
Chris Dietrich
Joe Lynch
Doug Warren
Robert F. Slatzer
Kenny Parker
Raymond Schnitzer
George Putnam
Doug Hoerth
Movie World
Lynn Wood
Cary Schwartz
Jan-Christopher Horak
George Eastman House
Marty Jackson
Malcolm "Stuff" Leo

TENTH SERIES

Walter Abel was always perfectly groomed, whether he was playing Bette Davis's suitor, "D'Artagnan," or Shirley Temple's father. Forty years after posing for this portrait he looked at it and said, "That is store hair."

Walter Abel

The leading man and character actor of stage, screen, radio, and television was born in St. Paul, Minnesota, on June 6, 1898. His family had no connection with the theatre and disapproved of Walter's early choice of career. But, they did not forbid him to act in high school plays and after his father realized how serious his son was, he became more supportive.

Abel came to New York City in 1916. He acted in a few early silent pictures and in vaudeville while he was studying at the American Academy of Dramatic Arts. He had appeared in over half a dozen Broadway plays before becoming a member of the famed Provincetown Playhouse, where he got what he considers to be his big break. Eugene O'Neill, the leading playwright in the world at the time, cast him in *Desire Under the Elms* (1924). "And then," as the actor puts it, "he gave me a part in *Mourning Becomes Electra*. No role, no review has ever done for me what those two did. To please O'Neill was, to my generation of actor, the ultimate creative accomplishment."

Abel had contracts with Paramount Pictures and RKO. However, he continued throughout his career to intersperse screen work with Broadway appearances, giving him an independence and mobility. During the thirties he appeared in a play in London's West End and in 1949 he played "Hamlet" at Elsinore. Theatrical producers, well aware that films had made Walter's name and face well known to most Americans, were eager to have him in their shows. *When Ladies Meet* (1932), *Merrily We Roll Along* (1934), and *The Wisteria Trees* (1950) were three of his stage successes.

His beautifully modulated voice and splendid diction won him many parts on such prestigious radio programs as *Theatre Guild on the Air* and *Lux Radio Theatre*.

Especially skilled at farce, the slow-take and genteel exasperation were his trademarks. Yet he was never typecast.

Ann Harding had him in two of her screen

vehicles and he was with Claudette Colbert in three of hers. Walter supported Spencer Tracy in *Fury* (1936), Errol Flynn in *Green Light* (1937), Frieda Inescourt in *Portia on Trial* (1937), Charles Boyer in *Hold Back the Dawn* (1941), Danny Kaye in *The Kid from Brooklyn* (1946), and James Cagney in *13 Rue Madeleine* (1947). He played Fred Astaire and Bing Crosby's agent in *Holiday Inn* (1942) and the studio head in *Star Spangled Rhythm* (1942).

Among his other movies are: *The Three Musketeers* (1935); *Michael Shayne, Private Detective* (1940) with Marjorie Weaver; *Beyond the Blue Horizon* (1942) with Richard Denning;* *Fired Wife* (1943) with Robert Paige;* *Mr. Skeffington* (1944); *Kiss and Tell* (1945); *Island in the Sky* (1953) with Lloyd Nolan;* *Night People* (1954) with Rita Gam; *Bernardine* (1957); *Raintree County* (1957); *Mirage* (1965); *Quick, Let's Get Married* (1971); and *Silent Night, Bloody Night* (1974) with John Carradine and Candy Darling.

In 1926 Walter married Marietta Bitter, the daughter of the sculptor Karl Bitter, who was a member of Carlos Salzedo's quintet. She later played the harp in the pit at Broadway shows.

Widowed in 1978, Walter receives regular visits from his two sons and their children. None of his family has gone into acting or music.

Abel does not consider himself to be retired. His first movie appearance in some time was *Grace Quigley* (1985), in which he played one of the senior citizens whose life is ended with their approval and Katharine Hepburn's assistance.

Shortly after *Aren't We All?* opened in New York City in 1985, Walter had a joyful reunion with his favorite screen partner, Claudette Colbert. Ordinarily, however, he does not see any of those he has acted with. His explanation: "Either they're dead or they believe I am."

Ronnie Britton

Walter Abel has lived by himself on Manhattan's East Side since his wife died in 1978. The works of his father-in-law, sculptor Karl Bitter, are throughout the Abel brownstone and its garden.

3

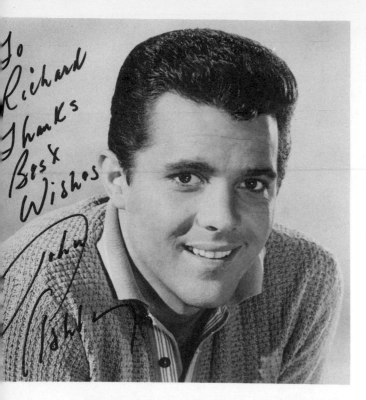

To Richard
Thanks &
Best
Wishes

John
Ashley

John Ashley starred in teenage exploitation, horror, and beach movies from the late fifties until the mid-sixties.

John Ashley

The teen idol was born on Christmas Day, 1934, in Kansas City, Missouri. He was adopted and raised in Tulsa, Oklahoma, by a gynecologist and his wife.

After getting a degree in business administration from Oklahoma State University, he came to Los Angeles, in the summer of 1955, where he planned to continue his schooling at UCLA. One of his fraternity brothers, who had become a press agent, brought Ashley on to the set of *The Conqueror* to meet John Wayne, another member of Sigma Chi. Wayne queried the young man about acting, something John had never considered as a profession. When the star offered to set up an appointment for him

with a producer at Ziv Television he agreed to the interview.

John Ashley appeared on several segments in *Men of Annapolis,* a series produced at Ziv, but was not serious about an acting career. Shortly thereafter he dropped by to American–International Pictures to pick up his date, the starlet Kathleen Case, who was being auditioned by the producers. While waiting for her he struck up a conversation with a writer who insisted John read a scene from a script that was about to go into production. He left the studio that day with a contract to appear in three features.

Just as soon as Ashley finished making his feature film debut in *Dragstrip Girl* (1957) with the late Fay Spain he was drafted into the U.S. Army. Upon his release six months later he was cast as the lead in *Motorcycle Gang* (1957).

It was at that point that he had an opportunity to take a major step toward becoming a serious dramatic actor. The part he was offered on TV's *Matinee Theatre* was, he admits, the only one he ever really yearned to play. Entitled *The Alleyway,* John was to be cast as an inexperienced young man opposite Janis Paige who was to portray a mature woman who becomes attracted to him. But because the shooting schedule of the third film on his contract conflicted, he was enjoined from doing the show. His disappointment was so deep he refused to honor his commitment to American–International and was suspended.

He looked on the remainder of his acting career as merely a series of jobs in front of a camera. The only motion picture of the many he made that was a quality product was *Hud* (1963).

For a while he had a running part on the series *The Beverly Hillbillies* playing one of Donna Douglas's suitors. He was the costar of *Straightaway,* a series that ran on ABC-TV during the 1961-62 season.

John Ashley's 1962 marriage to Deborah

Walley, which took place aboard an Acapulco-bound yacht, was given the kind of coverage in the press that was once accorded only to major stars. But to young moviegoers the couple was one of the most glamorous of the era. Fanzines regarded him as a teenage heartthrob and his wife, probably because she had portrayed "Gidget," had an even larger following. The newlyweds told Louella O. Parsons, among other media people, that they would never allow either career to affect their marriage. They received another surge of publicity when the fanzines interviewed and photographed them together with their baby son, Anthony. "The House of Happiness" was what one feature article on the Ashleys was called.

In 1965 John and Deborah were paired in *Beach Blanket Bingo.* When they separated the August of that following year, he moved out of their home and took up temporary residence with his friend Nick Adams. The Ashleys were divorced in 1966.

John Ashley has appeared in over three dozen movies, usually as the lead. Among them were: *Woman Hunt* (1962); *Beach Party* (1963) with Bob Cummings;[9] *High School Caesar* (1960); *Muscle Beach Party* (1964); *How to Make a Monster* (1958) with Walter Reed;* *Frankenstein's Daughter* (1958) with Donald Murphy;* *Suicide Battalion* (1958); *Mad Doctor of Blood Island* (1969); and *The Beast of the Yellow Night* (1970).

He began producing films, at first for American–International, then on his own. Some, such as *Woman Hunt* (1962), *Twilight People* (1972), *Beyond Atlantis* (1973), and *Sudden Death* (1977), he acted in as well. He moved back to Oklahoma to oversee the chain of theatres he had bought, but spent much of his time in the Philippines where he produced low-budget features. *Black Mama, White Mama* (1973), *The Big Doll House* (1971), *Savage Sisters* (1974), and *Beyond Atlantis* (1973) were among them.

John Ashley in his office at Stephen J. Cannell Productions where he produces the TV series **The A-Team.**

In 1979 Ashley, his second wife, and their son moved back from Oklahoma to a home in the San Fernando Valley. His boy by Deborah Walley has lived with John since he was eight years old.

He has produced two made-for-television movies that starred his old friend Robert Conrad.

When actors he knows are up for parts on *The A-Team*, the TV show he produces, John does not attend the readings and leaves the decisions on such castings to his staff. He does not miss acting and did a small part on his own program once only at the urgings of its cast.

He has explained his attitude thusly: "Even as a little boy I loved movies, but acting was something I fell into. I never worked at it or had a burning desire to be a star. I much prefer the other side of the camera."

5

Mary Badham made her professional acting debut in To Kill a Mockingbird, *the screen version of the best-selling novel by Harper Lee.* Gregory Peck won the Best Actor Oscar of 1962 for his portrayal of her father. Mary was nominated as Best Supporting Actress.*

Mary Badham

The Oscar nominee was born in Birmingham, Alabama, on October 7, 1952. Her father, after retiring from the U.S. Air Force as a general, became president of the Bessemer Coal, Iron, and Land Company.

The novel *To Kill a Mockingbird,* a best seller when it was first published in 1960, won the Pulitzer Prize in fiction in 1960. After screen rights were acquired, over two thousand girls were interviewed, auditioned, and tested for the key role of "Scout," a girl still in grammar school.

The producers were hoping to find a total unknown for the part. A casting agent, sent to look at girls in southern states, received a phone call when she reached Birmingham. The caller, who has never been identified, advised her to audition Mary Badham.

In interviews after she had been signed to play in the picture opposite Gregory Peck, Mary was quoted as stating: "I used to lie in bed and pretend I was in movies. Now it's as though my dreams have come true." In 1986 she said, "Like most little girls where I come from, I had taken ballet. A few times, I had taken part in skits we performed at grown-up functions. But acting was something that had never crossed my mind."

Mrs. Badham, who was English and had acted briefly in her youth, was more receptive to the offer of a screen test than her husband. Mr. Badham felt the experience of playing an important part in a major motion picture might have a negative effect on his daughter, but allowed his wife and Mary to go to Hollywood.

Mary was in the audience when the Academy Awards of 1962 were given out. She had been told that the odds that evening were heavily in favor of Patty Duke.

"I knew about her background," she said recently. "So, I wasn't surprised that she got it. But then, I was ten years old and wouldn't have been surprised if I'd gotten it. But I wasn't really upset, either."

Her only other A movie was *This Property is Condemned* (1966), which was based on the one-act play by Tennessee Williams. Mary played Natalie Wood's tomboy kid sister. The male star was Robert Redford. The film failed at the box office. In 1966, she also appeared in the quickly dismissed *Let's Kill Uncle.*

6

Mary appeared on a segment of the *Dr. Kild-are* and *Twilight Zone* TV series and then she and Mrs. Badham returned to Birmingham.

Her father was concerned about what his daughter was being exposed to. Over twenty years later Mary said, "I didn't want to come back to Alabama, but at the same time, I knew in my heart that I should. People were relating to me as an adult, and I was barely in my teens. It *was* confusing."

She attended high school in Phoenix, Arizona, and several times during those years flew to Los Angeles in connection with screen roles. Had her parents known of these trips, they would have forbidden them. Again in retrospect, Mary believes her parents were right. She recalls one reading for a part that turned into what she describes as a "total disaster."

Mary Badham is married to a sheep farmer. They live in Sandy Hook, Virginia. Only a few of their friends, neighbors, or customers know of her career. Along with her responsibilities as a wife and mother, she holds down two jobs in retail stores, working six days a week.

Although she has had no inquiries concerning her services for acting in a great many years, Mary Badham has not given up hope that "lightning might strike twice."

Mary's only connections with Hollywood are occasional telephone calls from Anna Lee,* who was a close friend of her mother's, Gregory Peck, and her brother, the movie director John Badham.

She was approached to play one of the southern girls menaced by Clint Eastwood in *The Beguiled* (1971). John Badham strongly advised her not to see the picture, she says. Her brother felt she would be offended by its content.

"My brother John tells me the profession has changed completely and that I should stay where I am," she has said. "He insists that I'd have to study acting, but I was told never to take lessons—that I was an instinctive actress.

Most of the performances I see on TV and in movies are so self-conscious and overacted. I would think a natural actress would be welcome."

Mary Badham lives with her husband and daughter on a farm in Sandy Hook, Virginia.

Vilma Banky was known to most European cinemagoers as "The Hungarian Rhapsody" before producer Samuel Goldwyn brought her to the United States in 1925. Her Hollywood films made her a major star of the silent screen throughout the world.

Vilma Banky

The star of European and Hollywood silent pictures was born in Budapest, Hungary, on January 9, 1898.

When Samuel Goldwyn signed her to a contract during a European trip in 1924 she was already well established in the Hungarian cinema. Having made thirteen features and played opposite such Continental stars as Max Linder and Ivan Petrovich, the name Vilma Banky was known to European moviegoers.

The producer spent lavishly to publicize "The Hungarian Rhapsody" and introduced her to Americans in *The Dark Angel* (1925). The movie was such a success that Vilma and her costar Ronald Colman became overnight the most popular love team on the screen. She played opposite Rudolph Valentino in both of her next two pictures. *The Eagle* (1925) and *Son of the Sheik* (1926). Both were smash hits, but fans clamored to see the exotic beauty reunited with Colman. Goldwyn cast them together in *The Winning of Barbara Worth* (1927), *The Night of Love* (1927), *The Magic Flame* (1927), and again in *Two Lovers* (1928).

If ever a couple had the good wishes of the film capital Vilma Banky and Rod LaRocque had it when their engagement was announced. Hollywood had taken to Vilma from the start for her humor about her own struggle with the English language. "Bankyisms" had been laugh-getters among her peers since her arrival. Professionally, Vilma and Rod LaRocque were equals. He had all the looks and dash of a star, but was well read and had good manners. Gloria Swanson, years after they had played together in a picture, admitted that of all her leading men, LaRocque was the most "fascinating." Aileen Pringle once said of LaRocque, "He could act, but he wasn't an actor, which of course made him so much more attractive."

Never before or since has Hollywood produced so glamorous and romantic a wedding. Goldwyn gave the bride away. Cecil B. DeMille was the best man and Louella O. Parsons was matron of honor. The ushers, headed by Donald Crisp, were Harold Lloyd, Jack Holt, Victor Varconi, and director George Fitzmaurice. Bebe Daniels, Frances Howard (Mrs. Samuel Goldwyn), Mildred Harris (Mrs. Harold Lloyd), and Constance Talmadge were bridesmaids. There were so many fans that day (January 27,

1927) in front of the church that four hundred policemen could barely control them, especially when the famed newlyweds emerged after the Roman Catholic ceremony. Tom Mix got the second loudest roar from the crowd when he arrived in a coach drawn by four horses.

The lavish reception for six hundred that Goldwyn hosted seemed to include every star in filmdom. But there was also another celebration, given by William Boyd and his wife Elinor Fair for fellow stars who, like them, had not been invited to the official doings. "It was like a public holiday," recalled the late Leatrice Joy[8] fifty years after the event.

"And then we lived happily ever after," said Vilma almost fifty years after her marriage. "Or at least until 1969 when Rod died in his sleep. Since then I've not really been unhappy, but I still miss him a great deal. He was such an interesting man. We always had things to talk about. And a gourmet cook!"

A Lady to Love (1930), the first screen version of the play They Knew What They Wanted and her second talkie, was reviewed by the New York Mirror with the headline "Vilma Banky's Accent Delights in New Talker." Variety called it "Surefire entertainment, and that includes Vilma Banky's accent." In the opinion of the New York Post, "The use of her speaking voice on the screen has added new fascinations to her familiar charms."

The knowledge that she could, if she chose, continue in sound films was gratifying, but Vilma did not feel comfortable in the new medium and had begun to tire of public life. In 1930 and 1931, the LaRocques toured in the play The Cherries Are Ripe, their only professional appearance together, and then left on an extended European vacation. While in Austria she costarred with Luis Trenker* in The Rebel (1932). She then announced that she would henceforth be known as "Mrs. Rod La-Rocque."

Vilma Banky's Los Angeles apartment overlooks the green of the Wilshire Country Club where she reigned in 1950 and 1951 as Women's Golfing Champion.

Rod LaRocque acted sporadically in pictures after his wife's retirement, but he was mainly concerned with the buying and selling of land in California's Ventura County, making millions of dollars in the process.

Vilma sold their Beverly Hills home to Richard Benjamin and Paula Prentiss and now lives in the same luxury apartment building she moved out of on the day of her famous wedding. She says that most of her time is spent "just thinking. I've had such good fortune in my life that I have many, many lovely memories."

The scenarist who wrote several of Vilma's pictures, the late Frances Marion, once said that the only two really happily married couples she had ever known in all of her many years in Hollywood were William Haines and his lover Jimmy Shields and the LaRocques.

Charlie Barnet (left) and his good friend Tommy Dorsey. He enjoyed the company and admired the music of both Dorsey brothers and appeared with them in their movie The Fabulous Dorseys *(1947).*

Charlie Barnet

The leader of one of the most renowned of the big bands was born Charles Daly Barnet in New York City. His birth date is October 26, 1913. He never knew his father, who was divorced from his mother in 1915. Charlie's maternal grandfather was a vice-president of the New York Central Railroad.

It was at the Riverdale Country School that he learned to play the piano. He was already a member of the school band when he began playing soprano saxophone as well.

Charlie Barnet has stated that he was "probably more enthralled with the life than the music—at first." But he soon developed an ear for the best that was being heard at that time.

Duke Ellington was his musical hero and it was his featured instrumentalist Johnny Hodges who was the chief influence on Barnet's playing the alto and soprano saxophones. On tenor sax it was Coleman Hawkins's technique that Charlie aspired to.

His schoolboy fantasies were more than fulfilled by the availability of liquor, marijuana, and willing young women. All three were a major part of each day of his life throughout his career.

It is difficult to describe the "Barnet sound," perhaps because he began and remained a student and admirer of innovative jazz. His band played homage to Ellington and Count Basie, but those great artists served merely as inspirations, not styles to be imitated. And Charlie Barnet's rendition of any work always added something fresh. For instance, his recording of

"Cherokee" is much better remembered today than that of Ray Noble, who wrote it.

Trumpeters Clark Terry and Doc Severinsen are among those who were longtime members of the Charlie Barnet Orchestra. Dave Lambert, long before Lambert, Hendricks and Ross was formed, and the Modernaires, years before their association with Glenn Miller, were his vocalists, as were Kay Starr and Lena Horne. Red Norvo, Neal Hefti, Dave Barbour, and Maynard Ferguson were among his sidemen, as was Billy May, who often did the arrangements.

In the late thirties and early forties when the Charlie Barnet Orchestra was really coming into its own, he hired black musicians. It was then called "breaking the color bar," something almost no other big band leader was willing to do. "I wasn't trying to prove anything," explains Barnet. "My bag was music, not civil rights. I just wanted the best men available. Often they happened to be black." This color-blind approach to hiring was very likely the reason his group never had its own commercial radio show and failed to get bookings in certain prestigious hotel rooms. He had a large following among urban blacks and he is especially proud of breaking the house record at the Apollo Theatre in Harlem, Christmas week, 1939. In his autobiography, Malcolm X, who early in his life worked in dance halls, credited Barnet with being the only white band to play for an all-black audience of dancers at the Roseland State in Boston.

Charlie Barnet and his orchestra appeared in such movies as *Syncopation* (1942); *Juke Box Jenny* (1942); *Freddie Steps Out* (1946) with Freddie Stewart; *Make Believe Ballroom* (1949) with Jerome Courtland;* *A Song is Born* (1948); *Music in Manhattan* (1944); and *The Big Beat* (1958).

His original recordings of his own composition "Skyliner," a smash hit of the forties, are much sought after by collectors. So is "The

Howard W. Hays

Barnet in the bar of his Palm Springs home. After many years of heavy drinking and marijuana smoking Charlie now abstains completely.

Wrong Idea," an earlier success that was a shameless send-up of such saccharine sounds as Guy Lombardo and Sammy Kaye.[9]

In *Those Swinging Years,* which he wrote with Stanley Dance, Charlie stated that he did not consider rock and roll to be music. In his opinion, rock is performed by "mental cases and untalented misfits." He believes it has had a "degenerative influence on the nation's youth."

Barnet refuses to disclose how many marriages, divorces, and annulments he has had. One of his contemporaries insists that Charlie is married to his thirteenth wife. He and the present Mrs. Barnet have been together for over twenty-five years. She is fully aware that her husband frequently sees a much younger woman. A few years ago when Charlie brought a young woman from France, his wife found an apartment for her and helped furnish it.

11

Claire (top) and Merna Barry were frequent guests on Ed Sullivan's long-running Sunday-evening television variety show.

The Barry Sisters

The popularizers of "Yiddish Swing" were born on the Lower East Side of Manhattan to a Russian father and an Austrian mother. Claire's birthday is October 17. Merna was born two years later on April 6.

Claire, who was then called "Clara," had no interest in a career and does not remember ever singing before her mother taught her the English and Yiddish lyrics of a popular song.

The little girl was then taken to radio station WEVD for an audition. Claire was picked to repeat the performance on the air and was paid a stipend.

"You might say it was an enjoyable first experience," says Claire. "I don't remember Momma once prodding me after that. My best friend was taking piano lessons. I used to sing as she practiced, which is how I learned to read music."

Soon Claire returned to the air on the same program. For over a year she was a regular. Then she became one of the trio "Lily, Silly, and Milly." The threesome sang in Yiddish for fifteen minutes weekly for a salary of $1 each per fifteen-minute program.

After that time their mother bought for $3 an upright piano and the girls, at Claire's insistence, began singing duets.

Like her sister, Merna took at once to performing and debuted on radio as part of "Lily, Silly, and Milly."

As "The Bagelman Sisters," their real surname, they were heard on various stations in the New York area. At one point they were paid twenty-five cents each for harmonizing on a sustaining program. "But," reasoned Claire, "it was exposure and with our combined salaries we could get Momma a lovely present every week."

When Claire appeared solo on the *Horn & Hardart Children's Hour* she realized she did not want to work again without Merna. The Bagelmans were appearing frequently as paid entertainers at "catered affairs" in Brooklyn, where they then lived.

They became "The Barry Sisters" when Molly Picon hired them for her Maxwell House radio show.

It was at this time that their act changed as well. They found that by singing popular songs in Yiddish and Yiddish songs in English they would widen their appeal. They began recording and, according to Claire, cut their version of

"Bei Mir Bist Du Schön" before the Andrews Sisters came to prominence with their hit recording. The band on one of their albums was led by Archie Bleyer.*

Sunday afternoons they were heard on the *Yiddish Swing* radio show done live from the Capitol Theatre on Broadway. Their billing was "featuring the Barry Sisters," and Harry Belafonte, Joey Bishop, and Vic Damone were among their guests.

Ed Sullivan, in addition to writing a nationally syndicated newspaper column, produced variety shows on Broadway. The Barry Sisters, who were often on the bill of those presentations, forged a working relationship with him at that time that lasted until his death. Their many appearances on his Sunday evening television show made them familiar to millions and promoted their records. They were among the troupe that Sullivan took to Europe for a five-week tour. The Barrys were astonished when some of the 20,000 Soviets who heard them sing in Gorky Park knew the lyrics from copies of their records that had been smuggled into the USSR.

"Russian Jews responded to us in a big way," says Claire. "To make one's Jewishness part of a performance got to them because ethnicity is strongly discouraged. We were so popular there we were officially reported as dead. Now I meet Russians who've come here and they're amazed that we didn't both die twenty-five years ago. It seems a Barry Sisters cult was forming and the government wanted to discourage it."

Claire and Merna worked steadily, appearing at the London Palladium and the Persian Room of New York's Plaza Hotel. In 1972 they gave a concert at Carnegie Hall.

In the fall of 1976 the Barrys had just returned from an engagement in Australia when Merna complained of a severe headache. On October 31, 1976, she died of brain cancer.

It was Claire's husband, a dentist who is also

Claire, the eldest of the Barry Sisters and the survivor. Claire and her husband, Robert A. Easton, D.D.S., live in the Murray Hill area of Manhattan.

a professional jazz pianist, who in recent years has coaxed her back into performing by herself.

The one sour note of the dual career was the occasional put-down by the nationally syndicated columnist Jack O'Brian. "They never stop a show, but they certainly can slow one down" was typical of his printed remarks. They ceased after Claire wrote him a note. "We always welcomed constructive criticism," says the singer. "But what he wrote was mean-spirited. Why? Neither of us ever met the man."

Some who saw them on *The Ed Sullivan Show* believe they remember the Barrys dedicating songs to their mother. Claire declares that they never did. "Of course," she explains, "'My Yiddish Momma' was one of our popular numbers, but we never spelled it out any more than I do now in my act when I sing 'You and Me Against the World.' My audience know it's for Merna, who I still miss terribly. I think it's just how we came over—as a couple of nice Jewish girls who were very close to their mother."

Don Beddoe played a wide variety of parts in over 150 motion pictures. When he is recognized today it is usually for his voice.

Don Beddoe

The character actor was born on July 1, 1903, in the Shadyside area of Pittsburgh. His father, a leading tenor of the day, sang at the coronation of England's George V. Both of his parents were born in Wales.

Don showed no aptitude for business, although that was his major at the University of Cincinnati. When he returned to get his B.A., he became active in the theatrical productions on campus.

It was Mrs. Beddoe, sensing how much her son loved to act, who brought him together with Stuart Walker, the founder of one of American's leading repertory companies.

"She was a real promoter, my mother," said Beddoe in 1986. "One night she had Walker and his current boyfriend to dinner. The outcome was that I was taken on as a member of his famous stock company. It provided excellent training and credentials."

After appearances in five Stuart Walker productions he made his debut on Broadway in support of Spencer Tracy in the comedy *Nigger Rich* (1929). The following year he was in *Penny Arcade,* the play that brought its stars, James Cagney and Joan Blondell, to Hollywood. In 1932 he played the poet Homer in *Warrior's Husband,* which starred Katharine Hepburn. In 1935 he was in the supporting cast of the Jane Cowl vehicle *First Lady.*

The influential midwestern critic Claudia Cassidy singled him out for a rave in *Father Malachy's Miracle* (1937). Then he got a very showy role in the London company of the 1935 Broadway hit *The Night of January 16.* Upon his return to the United States Beddoe played the same part in a production that he also directed in Syracuse, New York. Movie mogul Harry Cohn, in town for a horse race, saw his performance and a contract resulted.

He claims to have appeared in seventy-three of Cohn's productions, including *Three Sappy People* (1939) and *You Nazty Spy* (1940), "Three Stooges" shorts. The most notable pictures he made at Columbia were *Golden Boy* (1939), as William Holden's trainer; *The Face Behind the Mask* (1941), the Peter Lorre starrer in which Don was a kindly policeman; and *The Talk of the Town* (1942).

During the late thirties and into the forties Don Beddoe was one of the most familiar faces on the screen, especially in low-budget fare. He was in the serials *Flying G-Men* (1939) and *Mandrake the Magician* (1939); three "Lone Wolf" features; two of the "Blondie" series; and a "Wild Bill" Elliott picture. There was also a "Charlie Chan" movie and one with Abbott and Costello, *Buck Privates Come Home* (1947).

Boris Karloff fans know him for his support of the star in *The Man They Could Not Hang* (1939), *Before I Hang* (1940), and *The Boogie Man Will Get You* (1942).

Most students of the low-budget movie consider two of his, *Gun Crazy* (1949) and *The Narrow Margin* (1952), to be among the finest ever made during that period.

Among his A pictures are: *O.S.S.* (1946), *The Best Years of Our Lives* (1946), *The Farmer's Daughter* (1947), *Cyrano de Bergerac* (1950), *Carrie* (1952), *Don't Bother to Knock* (1952), *A Star Is Born* (1954), *The Night of the Hunter* (1955), and *Pillow Talk* (1959).

Of the filmed performances he has given, which number over 150, his favorite was in *The Enforcer* (1951), a Humphrey Bogart starrer.

By 1970 his wife, the member of a wealthy and socially prominent California family, was in poor health. He retired from acting and the couple began to take lengthy and frequent trips abroad. They were in the Canary Islands when she died. They had been married for thirty years.

When Beddoe remarried in 1974 it was to the travel agent who had booked the last cruise he took with his first wife. They had been wed for several weeks when he first became aware of her background. The present Mrs. Beddoe was known professionally as Joyce Mathews[8] and had been married to and divorced from Milton Berle twice. She had subsequently married and divorced millionaire impresario Billy Rose, also twice.

The Beddoes live in Mission Viejo, California, but travel much of the year in connection with her business.

In a recent interview Don Beddoe spoke of his career: "I knew from the very outset that I'd never get a part or hold an audience with my looks, so I learned to act. Often I was hired when a role was poorly defined and they didn't know how to cast it. Someone would say, 'Get Beddoe. He'll do something with it.' Acting, however, was all I really liked about the profession. I got along well with everyone I worked with but was never really friendly with any one of them. Never became a big name, but I got to play all sorts of men and that's what all actors hope to do."

Jim Brennan

The octogenarian actor Don Beddoe in his Mission Viejo, California, home with two of his three poodles.

15

Belita's photograph was on the cover of Life *magazine's issue of August 27, 1945.*

Belita

The skater-dancer-actress was born on October 21, 1923, in Hampshire, England. Her full name is Maria Belita Gladys Lynne Jepson-Turner. "Belita" was the name of the ranch her great-grandfather owned in Argentina.

Her mother, whose early theatrical ambitions had been thwarted, was determined that her daughter would be a star. Belita was barely able to walk when she made her debut playing a doll at a bazaar honoring the Royal Family. By age two years she and her two brothers had a dancing act. Her skating lessons began when she turned four years old.

She had been studying with Anton Dolin for about a year when they first danced together at a performance in Cannes. He was then a major figure in the world of dance and his partner was eleven years old. When Vera Zorina* left the Dolin company, Belita replaced her.

Before coming under Dolin's auspices her skating had brought her several awards. It was with his blessings that she competed in the 1936 Olympics on the British team. After coming in fifth in World Competition, Belita turned professional. Her mentor then choreographed her skating act. The two danced and skated together after that until she injured her back.

Belita and her mother went from doctor to doctor but her condition did not improve until on the advice of Peter Lorre she was successfully treated by a Los Angeles physician. By then World War II had broken out in Europe. She danced briefly with Ballet Theatre, but the salary was so low she accepted a more lucrative offer from Ice Capades. Publicized as the "Golden Girl," her specialty was the difficut and dangerous "split jump."

Skating was a rage in Hollywood at the time because of the success Sonja Henie was having in films for Twentieth Century–Fox. Vera Hruba Ralston,[8] who had been featured with Belita in the Ice Capades shows and movies, was pacted by Republic Pictures at the same time Belita was signed by Monogram Pictures.

In *Silver Skates* (1943) with the late Kenny Baker she skated to Beethoven's Fifth Symphony.

In most of her other movies she only acted or danced, both of which she preferred to skating. James Ellison[8] was her leading man in *Lady, Let's Dance* (1944). Some of her other movies were *The Gangster* (1947) with the late Fifi D'Orsay and Joan Lorring;* *The Hunted* (1948); *The Man on the Eiffel Tower* (1949) with Patricia Roc and Robert Hutton;[9] *Never Let Me Go* (1953) with Gene Tierney;[8] *Invitation to the Dance* (1957); and *Silk Stockings* (1957). Her last screen appearance was in *The Terrace* (1964) under the direction of Leopoldo Torre Nilsson. She is probably best remembered for the thriller *Suspense* (1946).

She was strongly influenced by Charles Laughton and acted with his theatrical company in *The Cherry Orchard* and *Twelfth Night*.

In spite of her $1,200 weekly salary, Belita never liked working or living in Hollywood. "It was like being in prison," was how she described it in a 1984 interview. She believes she would have been used by other, more prestigious studios if Monogram had not set her loan-out fee at a prohibitive $5,000 a week.

During the fifties she returned to England, where for a while she toured in her own ice revue and appeared in the West End production of *Damn Yankees!*

She appeared in the original off-Broadway production of *Ulysses in Nighttown* (1958), a success in which she later toured England and the Continent for two years. Another member of the cast was Ken Berwick, who acts in the United States under the name James Kenny. They have been married since 1966.

In 1968 Belita underwent a successful operation for cancer. Since then she and her husband have established and run a nursery on the grounds of their London home, which was built in 1763 near the Thames.

Jo Lynch

Belita owns and manages Crabtree Gardens, a nursery in the Fulham area of London.

Belita has studied mime with Marcel Marceau. She drew on that and her years of dancing and acting when in 1981 she donned skates for the first time in over two decades. The show was *Superskates* at Madison Square Garden. In it she stunned her audience and staggered one critic who, while admitting that he considers ice skating a sport rather than an art, said of her performance: "To the strains of Duke Ellington's 'In My Solitude' this woman showed me the metamorphosis of an alcoholic-derelict on ice—mind you! It was totally believable, and deeply moving. It was art on ice."

Joan Bennett starred on the screen, on stage, and in the television series Dark Shadows. *She was married to two of Hollywood's most glamorous men and was the central figure in a scandal that made headlines around the world.*

Joan Bennett

The actress described in the book *The Great Movie Stars* as "the epitome of the film star" was born in Palisades, New Jersey, on February 27, 1910. Her mother, Adrienne Morrison, acted on Broadway before and after her marriage to matinee idol Richard Bennett. Her older sister, Barbara Bennett, had a career as a dancer before retiring to marry singer Morton Downey. Her eldest sister, Constance Bennett, was the highest paid star in Hollywood for a brief period in the early thirties.

Joan left finishing school to elope while she was still in her teens. When the marriage ended a short time later she began acting to support herself and an infant daughter. After a few small stage and film roles she appeared on Broadway with her father in *Jarnegan* (1928) and drew some serious offers from Hollywood.

Her official movie debut was with Ronald Colman in *Bulldog Drummond* (1929). Joan made over thirty features after that in what fans consider to be the first and less interesting part of her Hollywood career. In most of them she was demure. In all of them she was a light blonde, a somewhat heightened shade of her natural color.

She played opposite George Arliss, Harry Richman, and John Barrymore, major stars of the time, as well as newcomer Spencer Tracy. Bing Crosby crooned to her in two of his films and she was paired with Cary Grant in two of his. Some of her pictures, such as *Little Women* (1934) and *Private Worlds* (1935), were important ones, but they did not make her a star.

It was producer Walter Wanger who saw her potential when he put her under personal contract in the mid-thirties. Joan was then married to screenwriter Gene Markey. With the release of *Trade Winds* (1939), which Wanger produced, her career and personal life changed considerably. For that film she became a brunette, a hair color she was to keep for the remainder of her career. Two years later, having divorced Markey, Joan became the wife of

Walter Wanger.

Always cool and usually classy, there was also the suggestion that she didn't take herself all that seriously. She needed those qualities along with all the goodwill that could be mustered among friends and fans when Walter Wanger shot her agent, Jennings Lang.* The producer served a brief prison term for the crime that was one of the big stories of 1951. The marriage survived for another eleven years. Joan's career, seemingly, was unharmed.

The second of her four daughters is by Gene Markey who later married Hedy Lamarr,* Myrna Loy, and then the owner of Calumet Farms. Two others are by Wanger. She has twelve grandchildren.

For all the advantages of blood and marriage her roles were seldom tailored to her talents. The only Joan Bennett pictures she considers worth watching are *Father of the Bride* (1950) and *Father's Little Dividend* (1951), in which she played opposite Spencer Tracy, and the three in which Fritz Lang directed her: *Scarlet Street* (1946), *The Woman in the Window* (1944), and *Secret Beyond the Door* (1948). *The Man in the Iron Mask* (1939), *The House Across the Bay* (1940), *Son of Monte Cristo* (1940), *Nob Hill* (1945), *The Macomber Affair* (1947), and *We're No Angels* (1955) are some of the others from her brunette period that are frequently shown on television or in revival programs.

Ms. Bennett and her present husband, retired newspaper publisher David Wild, whom she married in 1973, live in Scarsdale, New York, with her poodle and Lhasa Apso.

In an interview in her home in Scarsdale, Joan Bennett said: "I am retired. My husband and I take a lengthy cruise every year. I don't see new movies but sometimes I stroll into the den while David's watching one on cable or cassette and I can't believe the language in them. Mind you, I've certainly used most of

Richard Lamparski

Joan Bennett in her Scarsdale, New York, home in 1985. The portrait was done by Paul Clemens when she was a prime contender for the role of "Scarlett O'Hara."

those words—still do now and then—but not in a picture. He's a theatre buff but I always take a good book along and if the first act doesn't grab me I read in the ladies' lounge. Often it's a book by or about one of my contemporaries. So many of them seem to have had such a hard time of it. I don't think much of most of the films I made, but being a movie star was something I liked very much."

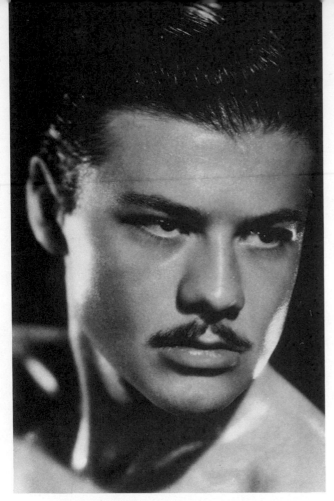

To the fans he was known as "The Turkish Delight." Among the stars he played with on screen and off Turhan Bey was considered "forbidden fruit." One of his costars recently recalled her experience with him: "Ecstasy, my dear! But not for every day."

Turhan Bey

The exotic star of the forties was born on March 30, 1922, in Vienna. His original name was Turhan Selahettin Schultavey. His mother's family was partly Jewish and owned large glass factories in Czechoslovakia. His father was the Turkish military attaché in Austria.

Turhan's parents divorced when he was very young, after which he traveled extensively with his mother. They left Vienna shortly after the Anschluss and came to the United States where they stayed for a while with his uncle, who was working with Albert Einstein.

Turhan drove his mother and grandmother from New York to Hollywood in the new Chrysler Saratoga he had been given for his eighteenth birthday. He had no acting aspirations, but joined a class in speech to improve his English. Nor was he especially interested in movies, aside from having what he calls "the kind of crush on Katharine Hepburn that only a teenage boy can have for a movie star." His speech teacher asked him to act in a play he was directing. Scouts from Warner Brothers picked him from the cast to do a small part in the Errol Flynn starrer *Footsteps in the Dark* (1941). Parts in four more pictures followed the same year.

As Turhan tells it: "It was quite wonderful in those years. One was young and good-looking, and it seems those were the very two things everyone was looking for. Everyone seemed to like us. We never made enormous sums, but we were able to live as though we did."

Pacted by Universal, Bey's accent and features were used to advantage in *Arabian Nights* (1942), *The Mummy's Tomb* (1942), and *White Savage* (1943), the serial *Adventures of Smilin' Jack* (1943), *Sudan* (1945), and *Ali Baba and the Forty Thieves* (1944). George Zucco pursued him in *The Mad Ghoul* (1943), and he saved Susanna Foster[8] from Boris Karloff in *The Climax* (1944).

He describes Katharine Hepburn as "very kind" when they played together in *Dragon Seed* (1944). "That is to say, she never once laughed," he says. "And think of how funny I must have seemed to her. I was twenty-two and quite agog over her. But there was Tracy, who was often on the set. I wasn't so young I didn't know what happens when it's a choice between Turhan Bey and Spencer Tracy."

The intense Turhan Bey–Lana Turner romance was the lead story of Louella O. Parsons's column and radio show quite a number of times. The journalist chided him publicly when he stopped calling the blonde siren after she spoke once too often of marriage.

"I never for a moment considered marriage to any of the women I have known," he said in 1985. "But, I wish to add that it was never only sex. In every affair I have ever had my heart was involved."

His reputation with other movieland beauties is part of Hollywood legend. Well into the eighties screen stars of the forties have been seen to become misty-eyed at the mention of his name. Decades after Turhan Bey left Hollywood, William Holden, speaking of his own exploits, allowed that he was the one man he would be most loath to follow in a relationship with a woman.

"But on the screen I was an ersatz lover," he has said, and points out that had so many male stars not gone into the services after 1941 he, most likely, would have remained relegated to playing "patent leather heavies" and ethnic roles. In his first screen appearance he had played an "Ahmed" and in his second he wore a turban. Then for a few years he was cast opposite Merle Oberon, Maria Montez, and the late Evelyn Ankers.* Some film historians maintain, however, that he never was allowed to kiss any of his leading ladies on the screen. Bey admits he has no recollection of ever having done so.

After spending a brief time in the army near the end of World War II, Turhan returned to Hollywood and was given his first assignment. He was to play a character described in the script as "a short, fat, oily Oriental with bulging eyes." When he objected his contract was sold to Eagle-Lion, where he made *Out of the Blue* (1947), *Adventures of Casanova* (1948), and *Parole, Inc.* (1949).

Gloria Grahame had just won the Oscar when Turhan was offered a part in her next pic-

Marlene Czernin

A bachelor and a Rosicrucian, Turhan Bey shares with his mother a home in the Grinzing area of Vienna.

ture. But it turned out to be a Sam Katzman cheapie, *Prisoners of the Casbah* (1953). As in his first he was "Ahmed," but this time he was a South Sea Islander with a flower behind his ear. "I was having enough troubles with my receding hairline without the worry of keeping hibiscus in it."

The play he did on the road with Gloria Vanderbilt never came to Broadway. Bey then returned to Europe where he produced the picture *Stolen Identity* (1952) with Francis Lederer[8] and Cornell Borchers.*

He is amused by memories of his career, which he has always considered a fluke. His recorded voice narrates the show at the Marionette Theatre in Salzburg and he has directed two of its English productions. The right part, however, such as an arch but subtle villain in a "James Bond" feature would interest him.

His only regrets, which have come about through an understanding of karma, are of the abortions that his lovers had—some at his insistence.

In his home in Vienna, Bey is preparing a book of the color photography he has done over the years. Much of it is erotic studies of beautiful young women.

U.S. audiences know Honor Blackman as the leather-clad lead in the early episodes of **The Avengers,** *an English-made TV series of the sixties that has developed a strong cult following. Her most important movie role to date was in the "James Bond" film* **Goldfinger** *(1964), playing "Pussy Galore."*

Honor Blackman

The English actress who has become a cult heroine was born in London to Cockney parents on August 22, 1925.

Honor had an older sister who could dance well and who was considered to have a beautiful voice. In her own words: "I would never have dreamed of performing. She seemed to be able to do splendidly all the things I believed I could never do at all. Then when I was fifteen, our dad suggested that I might get on much

better in life without a Cockney accent. So, I began diction lessons which eventually led to classes in acting and dancing. I worked very hard and, to my astonishment, gained confidence."

When her father read aloud a newspaper notice of an audition for a play, Honor did not hesitate to present herself. She was taken on as understudy to a principal and got to go on for her several times. On one occasion, a West End producer saw her and put her in one of his shows.

Her second legitimate engagement brought her a movie contract. She became a member of the Rank Charm School, which meant she was one of the starlets under contract to J. Arthur Rank.

She appeared in the features *Fame is the Spur* (1947) with Rosamund John;* *Daughter of Darkness* (1947); *Quartet* (1949); *Conspirator* (1950) with Elizabeth Taylor and Robert Taylor; *So Long at the Fair* (1950); *Diplomatic Passport* (1954) with Marsha Hunt; *A Night to Remember* (1958); and *A Matter of Who* (1962).

Honor Blackman first appeared as "Cathy Gale" on *The Avengers* TV show in 1963. With her leather gear and judo skills, the character proved again and again to be more than a match for even the most macho males. By the 1964 season, she had become the star of the series. Feeling she would be forever typecast if she stayed, the actress did not sign for a fourth season. By then she had played "Pussy Galore," the nemesis of "James Bond," in the movie *Goldfinger* (1964), a box office blockbuster.

It was the time of the Women's Movement and what has been called the Sexual Revolution. Her image of the strong, independent, sexually aggressive woman became to some a role model and to others a fantasy of the ideal dominatrix. The themes and tone of the fan mail that poured in from all over the world was, in her own words, "beyond all belief, darling!"

At the height of her celebrity, a London-based firm hired her to launch a line of pipes made for women. Honor appeared in public places and in advertising smoking their various colored and shaped pipes. The product never caught on, but the publicity only confirmed that she was the sort of woman who usurped what had been believed to be exclusively male prerogatives.

Although many of her efforts have not been seen in North America, Honor has never ceased to be active on TV, stage, and in features. In late 1985, she left *On Your Toes,* the revival in which she costarred for over a year at London's Palace Theatre. Among her later films are: *Life at the Top* (1965), *The Virgin and the Gypsy* (1970), *To the Devil a Daughter* (1976), and *The Cat and the Canary* (1978).

She felt she did some of her best work in *Agnes of God* as the Mother Superior. Because of negative reviews, the play, a Broadway import, closed during a try-out tour.

For the first thirty years of her career, Honor's goal was to be known and remembered for her portrayal of Saint Joan. "Had I believed for a moment that I might never play her, it would have broken my heart," she admitted in 1985. "But I never did and my heart is whole."

She is equally sanguine about being passed over repeatedly for roles in Shakespeare and Shaw. "I am thought of as a commercial actress," she says with a wry smile.

The one time Ms. Blackman has seemed to step out of character was in a London divorce court in 1975. She wept openly as she told judges that her thirteen-year marriage to actor Michael Kauffman was "an experience I could have done without."

The son and daughter the Kauffmans adopted during the marriage live with the actress in the Barnes area of London. Both children are discouraged by their mother from

Honor Blackman, an active member of Britain's Liberal Party, lives in the Barnes area of London with her two adopted children.

going into her profession because, "I believe that one has to have a very particular nature to be in the theatre successfully and with enjoyment. It is a terribly insecure business, and unless you get to the top, one's life is wasted." She believes, however, that had she done anything else other than act, "I would have gone quite mad."

The roles for which she is most widely recognized are not her favorites. The parts she has liked the best were in the company of *A Little Night Music* that toured the United Kingdom in the seventies and the heavies she plays in pantomimes performed for children at Christmastime. "My deep voice terrifies them," she says with obvious delight. "I've actually been recognized on the street, no costume or makeup, and had them hiss me. No applause will ever mean as much as those hisses."

23

Betsy Blair and Ernest Borgnine were both nominated for Oscars for their performances in Marty. *The film won the Academy Award as the Best Picture of 1955 and he was voted Best Actor. Betsy did not win and remained on the blacklist in Hollywood, but was chosen that year's Best Actress at the Cannes Film Festival.*

Betsy Blair

The blacklisted Oscar nominee was born in Cliffside, New Jersey, on December 11, 1923. Her baby photo won honorable mention in a *New York Daily News* contest for children with "charm and character." In grammar school she was an honor student and was considered the best in her dance class. Before she was in her teens Betsy was acting in amateur plays. Later she modeled for John Robert Powers as what she calls "your gawky fourteen-year-old as perceived by the ladies at *Vogue."*

After graduation from high school in 1939 she passed up a scholarship to Sarah Lawrence in favor of a job in a nightclub chorus line where she replaced Nora Kaye* at $35 a week. When she auditioned at Billy Rose's Diamond Horseshoe, Betsy met Gene Kelly.

"It was just like in the movies," she admitted forty-five years later. "As soon as I saw him I knew it was *him.* And, just like in the movies, he eventually came around, and we got mar-

ried. Gene and I arrived in Hollywood on December 7, 1941, he with a movie contract. The next year we had our daughter, Kerry."

Kelly had been a choreographer when they met and became a star when he created the title role in *Pal Joey.* Betsy was playing a few blocks away in Saroyan's *The Beautiful People* (1941). Later she understudied Julie Haydon* in *The Glass Menagerie,* but never got to go on.

To attend the star-studded, informal parties at the Kelly home was to be "in" among Hollywood's younger set. Her husband was one of M-G-M's most valuable properties. But his wife refused offers of long-term contracts. She even declined to test for the title role in *The Song of Bernadette,* because "I was much too left wing to promote Roman Catholicism and miracles."

She did try out for the leads in *Letter from an Unknown Woman* and *Rebecca,* losing both to Joan Fontaine. Two other roles for which she was seriously considered were in *He Ran All the Way* and *A Place in the Sun.* Both were played by Shelley Winters.

It was not until *Kind Lady* (1951) that she realized her beliefs had placed her on a blacklist. Signed for the role, Betsy received a call from a journalist advising that she would be fired because she had appeared along with Anne Revere and Lloyd Goff for a cause considered to be subversive.

After studio head Dore Schary vouched for her patriotism with the American Legion and Louis B. Mayer interrogated Betsy and Gene Kelly, she was put back on the picture. But it was her last screen role until independent producers hired her for *Marty* at the suggestion of author Paddy Chayefsky. Even when she received an Oscar nomination as the Best Supporting Actress of 1955 and won the Best Actress award at the Cannes Film Festival for her performance in *Marty,* there were no further offers.

As Betsy Blair now views that period: "To sit out the McCarthy era in a house on Rodeo Drive as Mrs. Gene Kelly is not so bad. But the atmosphere that prevailed eventually destroyed my marriage. My ideas ran against the political currents of the time. By 1957 we were divorced."

The next years were spent in Paris because "that's where the second man in my life happened to live. After that relationship ended, Lindsay Anderson introduced me to Karel Reisz. He lived in London, so I came here and we got married. I helped raise his three sons. In other words, the man in my life has always been the deciding factor. I don't know how I really feel about that because I've just recently figured it out."

Among European film makers she is known for the deeply moving performance she gave in *The Snake Pit* (1948) and as the wallflower in *Marty.* She had the lead in the Spanish-made *The Lovemaker* (1958), which was a success abroad, but is virtually unknown in the United States. Michelangelo Antonioni chose her for his picture *Il Grido* (1962).

Among her other screen credits are: *The Guilt of Janet Ames* (1947), *A Double Life* (1948), *Another Part of the Forest* (1948), *Mystery Street* (1951), *The Halliday Brand* (1957), *I Delfini* (1960), *Senilita* (1961), *All Night Long* (1962), *Marry Me! Marry Me!* (1969), and *A Delicate Balance* (1973).

For the BBC Betsy has appeared opposite Rod Steiger in the televised *Death of a Salesman* and with Martin Balsam in *Come Back, Little Sheba.* American audiences saw her again in the PBS production of *Summer and Smoke* and in *Spoon River Anthology.*

The highlights of her stage career have been playing "Desdemona" to Orson Welles's "Othello" and the title role of a West End production of *The Trial of Mary Dugan.*

For several years in the early eighties Betsy trained as a speech therapist with the intention of working full-time with handicapped children. But, when her husband signed to direct a Broadway show, she left her position to be with him.

She has three grandchildren by her daughter, who is a psychoanalyst married to a psychoanalyst. Her closest friend is Haya Harareet. *

Betsy Blair and her husband, producer-director Karel Reisz, have a Victorian house in London's Maida Vale district. Their tenant on the top two floors is the author John Lahr.

Richard Lamparski

In the April, 1951, issue of Ebony *magazine Hadda Brooks was featured as the first black woman to have her own TV show in California. She was sponsored on Channel 13 in Los Angeles and Channel 7 in San Francisco by the Kaiser-Frazer automobile dealers.*

Hadda Brooks

The "Queen of the Boogie" was born on October 29, 1916, in East Los Angeles, an area then known as Boyle Heights. Her father was a sheriff at the city's Hall of Justice. Mrs. Brooks was a physician.

In Hadda's words: "My sister and I never wanted for anything. We had lovely clothes, often nicer than our Jewish neighbors. We were both offered piano lessons, but I accepted. I was only four years old, but my daddy told me I could take them for as long as I wanted to. There was no pushing from either parent. They let me find my way. And there was no sense of living in a ghetto. I don't ever remember the color of my skin being mentioned."

Hadda had no ambitions to perform, in fact had never considered it until she was "discovered." After graduating from the University of Southern California, she took a job playing piano at a dance studio. The instructor asked her to play the "Poet and Peasant Overture," finding as many variations as possible. During one class, in which she "boogied" it, Jules Bi-Hari, musical entrepreneur, heard her.

As the artist remembers it: "This man, who I knew as someone who pushed jukeboxes, asked me how long it took me to turn things into a boogie. I told him ten minutes and the next thing I knew I was making a record."

"Swinging the Boogie," her first recording, was a hit on Bi-Hari's Modern Records of Hollywood label. It was he who gave her the title that she has never shaken when he produced the successful album *Hadda Brooks, Queen of the Boogie.* For fifteen years, he was also her manager.

She made her name with boogie, but that was never her preferred style. "Loud noises, and boogie is loud, annoy me," explains Hadda. "And most of the people who like it are loud. That annoys me even more."

During an engagement with Charlie Barnet at the Million Dollar Theatre in downtown Los Angeles, she began singing. He insisted, over her strong objections, that she do it. She sang a ballad and received an ovation. It was the beginning of a new career, singing what she calls "my soft sound."

Her hits were: "You Won't Let Me Go," "Don't Take Your Love From Me," "That's My Desire," "Don't You Think I Ought To Know," and "Trust In Me," all in the late forties.

She appeared in the feature *Out of the Blue* (1947) and starred in the musical soundie *The Joint Is Jumpin'*. Sarah Vaughan and Ella Fitzgerald both tested for the part that Hadda played in *In a Lonely Place* (1950), warbling "I Hadn't Anyone Till You" to Humphrey Bogart and Gloria Grahame. In *The Bad and the Beautiful* (1953), she sang "Temptation."

Musicologist Leonard Feather has written of her "deep resonant tones, jazz-rooted phrasing, and intelligent choice of ballads" and the "rakishly mordant tone that recalls Billie Holiday."

To others, Hadda's quasiconversational tones in torch songs are reminiscent of Mabel Mercer.

During one tour with the Harlem Globetrotters, which covered 86,000 miles, Hadda Brooks was given a private audience with Pope Pius XII, who baptized her. The door of her East Los Angeles home bears a prominent notice headed: "This is a Roman Catholic home."

Her husband, a journalist with the *Pittsburgh Courier,* died over a decade ago. She has no children.

Ms. Brooks considers herself "semiretired." If a charity that is to her liking asks her, she will perform, and she would consider a local engagement. Her concerns are the room's location, clientele, and how well it is managed.

She insists she does not miss performing and says many months go by in which she never touches the piano in her home. Foreign audiences, she believes, spoiled her. "They're more attentive, more appreciative," she said recently. "So many people in the States come not to be entertained, but to be seen."

The radio in her home is usually tuned to an "Easy Listening" station. Among her favorites

Michael Knowles

The queen of the "boogie" lives in East Los Angeles. She is now a widow and her companion is a dachsund.

are Nat "King" Cole, Perry Como, and Art Garfunkel. She has always much preferred the male voice, with the single exception of Dionne Warwick. Whenever Ms. Warwick performs in the L.A. area, the "Queen of the Boogie" is in her audience.

"So easy to open, even a child can do it" was the announcer's line as the four-year-old Bernadette Castro demonstrated her family's product. During the eight years that the original commercial was aired Bernadette became the subject of running gags by Milton Berle, Jack Paar, and Johnny Carson. Columnist Dorothy Kilgallen suspected Bernadette of being a midget because she wore nail polish. The child had refused to do the ad unless she was allowed to have her nails painted.

Bernadette Castro

Television's first child celebrity was born on July 10, 1944, in New York City.

Her parents owned and operated a small firm near their home that manufactured convertible sofas of Mr. Castro's design. He believed his product was superior to the others on the market because of its ease of operation. Then, as Castro family legend has it, their four-year-old, Bernadette, opened one of their sofas without help or prompting.

Bernadette's father did not think people would believe from a photo that a four-year-old girl could do such a thing. Since newspaper ads cost much more than television time in 1948, a commercial was filmed and New York City's Dumont-owned TV station, WABD, began running it at $25 per airing.

The response in the first few weeks was disappointing. Castro's spot was the first local ad ever to run and the public took a while to digest what they were watching. However, by the eleventh week of the thirteen-week contract, his business was booming. Many of Castro's customers came with their children who they would direct to "now open it—like the little girl on TV."

The original commercial ran 30,000 times. Bernadette was the most televised child in America and a "Bernadette Castro line" was part of the routine of every East Coast comic.

Since Castro Convertibles are sold only in New York, New Jersey, Connecticut, and Florida, television viewers in other parts of the country were often unable to get the jokes that were frequently made about her on network television.

When she was twelve the Castros used her in what they claim to be the first live television commercials in color ever done on a New York station. New ads with Bernadette were filmed or taped every few years through the sixties.

Bernadette has, in her own words, "never suffered from shyness," and very much enjoyed being recognized throughout childhood and adolescence. She remembers no negative reactions from other children, but claims there were continual complaints by their parents that she was being favored because she was famous. Her parents finally put her in a private school for child performers and children of celebrities.

During high school, with no encouragement from her parents, she formed her own band with herself as vocalist. Bernadette spent almost two years trying to establish herself as an entertainer. She was auditioned by Motown's Berry Gordy and signed to a contract with Col-Pix.

But after her Carnegie Hall concert failed to ignite her career, she withdrew for a few years while she was raising her four children.

Bernadette's husband, Dr. Peter Guida, heads a section of the New York Hospital of Cornell Medical Center. They live in "Panfield," a mansion built on six acres overlooking Long Island Sound and surrounded by walled gardens. Their home, which was built in 1915, houses seventeen Castro convertibles.

Speaking of her life today, she has said: "All I need do is look at what has and hasn't happened to many of my contemporaries and I thank God I left show business. I don't worry about getting older or having a hit because I have one." Very shortly Castro Convertibles will be selling in California, too. Since the retirement of her parents Bernadette has headed the firm.

If she has a regret it is that her younger brother, now deceased, was never used in the commercials. Her daughter and three sons have all been seen in ads for the family product.

Bernadette Castro, the executive vice-president of Castro Convertibles, giving a demonstration in one of the company's thirty showrooms.

Wes Spofford

George T. Simon wrote in The Big Bands: *"In repose Carmen Cavallaro had a face like a sad clown (without makeup, of course), but as soon as he started playing, his whole expression changed and he became the dynamic personality showman." The musicologist considered him "the best of all the flashy, society-music pianists."*

Carmen Cavallaro

"The Poet of the Piano" was born in New York City of Sicilian parents and baptized Carmelo Cavallaro. His birth date is May 6, 1913. He was raised in Harlem.

From a very early age Carmen showed a keen interest in the operatic records his father played on the family Victrola. Mrs. Cavallaro saved coupons from Octogon soap until she was able to get their son a toy piano. Although he was only three years old and the black keys on his little piano did not work, he was soon able to play along with the recordings. In a couple of years he started taking lessons. When in 1919 he lingered near death with the Spanish influenza that swept the country, Mr. Cavallaro, a barber, promised the boy that he would get him a real piano when he was well again.

"It cost seven hundred and fifty dollars," recalls Cavallaro. "Have you any idea how many haircuts that amounted to? It was years before I really appreciated what my parents had sacrificed."

Carmen was always inclined to improvise even though he was schooled in classical music. Being paid $5 for playing one night with a neighborhood jazz band was enough to decide him to turn professional when he was about eighteen years old.

He acquired experience and honed his style as a sideman with various groups. His first real break came as pianist with Al Kavelin's band on live radio broadcasts that emanated from the Hotel Lexington in Manhattan. Later in the thirties he was featured with the Abe Lyman and Enric Madriguera aggregations. His greatest exposure during this period was with Rudy Vallee on the *Fleischmann Hour,* a program popular nationally.

In late 1939, shortly after Cavallaro formed his own band, he was approached by executives of Decca Records. At their suggestion he recorded ten standards with the backing of a rhythm section. The album, *Dancing in the Dark,* was one of the label's biggest sellers of the time and has been reissued several times. His original contract, which called for a payment to him of a flat $1,000 fee, was renegotiated.

From that first hit Carmen Cavallaro was a major attraction. He is described in *The Complete Encyclopedia of Popular Music and Jazz* as "flashy, flowery but with excellent touch and technique and with beautiful chords." It was a style that brought him top billing whether he played the Hollywood nitery Ciro's or New York's Paramount Theatre. Sales of his recordings of Chopin's Polanaise in A-flat and the Warsaw Concerto earned him gold records at a time when a million seller was rare. Cavallaro's interpretations of those classics were the only ones many Americans ever knew.

He was pictured in advertisements for Rheingold Beer and endorsed the Thomas Scalp Treatment (but never had one).

At New York's Biltmore, Astor, and Waldorf-Astoria hotels Carmen Cavallaro played for dancing. At theatres such as the Strand the audiences came for the sheer listening pleasure of his renditions of "I'm Getting Sentimental Over You" and "I'll See You in My Dreams."

The career that brought him before audiences as diverse as Disney World and Prince Rainier and Princess Grace of Monaco slowed down considerably after his move a number of years ago to Columbus, Ohio, the hometown of his present wife. Its slow pace seems even more agreeable to the musician after he suffered a heart attack followed by triple bypass surgery in 1984.

Carmen Cavallaro concertizes each year in Japan, where his album of the sound track from *The Eddy Duchin Story* has remained in print since the movie was released in 1956. He usually works alone, as he did during an extended engagement at the Biltmore Hotel in Phoenix in 1985.

Early in his career as a soloist a reviewer in a Detroit newspaper wrote that he played "like a

Contracts with Carmen Cavallaro call for a Steinway piano to be provided for all of his engagements. This photograph was taken recently in the Manhattan showrooms of Steinway & Sons.

poet." His press agent insisted that his billing be henceforth, "The Poet of the Piano." Although it became one of the best known in the entertainment business, Cavallaro says he "cringes" whenever it is used in his presence. "On one hand I'm very grateful, because it clicked immediately with the press and public, but that's how Chopin was known. The pretentiousness!"

31

To movie fans George Chandler is probably best known as the cuckolded husband of Ginger Rogers in the comedy classic **Roxie Hart** *(1942). His most prominent part on TV was as "Uncle Petrie Martin" on the* **Lassie** *series.*

George Chandler

The actor sometimes referred to as "the most familiar, but nameless, face on the screen" was born in Waukegan, Illinois, on June 30, 1898. He always said that his acting ambitions began when he was twelve years old and wore the head of a donkey in a production of *A Midsummer Night's Dream.*

While earning a degree in business administration at the University of Illinois Chandler was the comical leader of the student band. He soon turned professional and paid his expenses by working on weekends and holidays at dances and parties.

For a few years he worked in stock companies, in speakeasies, and on the Chautauqua circuit. In vaudeville he was billed as "George Chandler, The Musical Nut." Using a violin and a saw as his props he developed the drollery that almost became his trademark on the screen.

On tour with a Fanchon Marco unit he was noticed by a studio talent scout and cast in the *Tenderfoot Thrillers* two-reelers being made by Universal. *Tenderfoot Courage* (1927), his first in the series, was directed by William Wyler. *The Fatal Glass of Beer* (1933), a W. C. Fields vehicle, had George in a bit part.

He made his first feature, *The Virginian* (1929), in support of Gary Cooper. The early credit that he believed really established him was the Marion Davies starrer, *The Floradora Girl* (1930).

Among his other films are: *In Gay Madrid* (1930) with Dorothy Jordan; * *Only Saps Work* (1930) with Mary Brian; [8] *Blessed Event* (1932); *Hi, Nellie!* (1934); *The Country Doctor* (1936) with John Qualen; * *Fury* (1936); *Three Men on a Horse* (1936); and *Woman Chases Man* (1937) with Joel McCrea. [8]

George believes his most important professional break came when he began a long association with William Wellman. The director was impressed with what Chandler was able to do with the very small part of a messenger in *A Star is Born* (1937). He used him the same year in *Nothing Sacred* and through the years in *Beau Geste* (1939), *The Great Man's Lady* (1942), *The Ox-Bow Incident* (1943), *Buffalo Bill* (1944), *This Man's Army* (1945), *Across the Wide Missouri* (1951), *My Man and I* (1952), and *The High and the Mighty* (1954). Wellman began calling the actor his "good luck piece." They worked so well together that when George claimed he could not play the part he was offered in *The Light That Failed*

(1939) because his English accent was not convincing, Wellman had the character changed to an English deaf-mute.

Among his later films are: *Jesse James* (1939), *The Return of Frank James* (1940), *Arizona* (1941), *Western Union* (1941), *Since You Went Away* (1944), *Lover Come Back* (1946), *Dead Reckoning* (1947), *Singing Guns* (1950) with Ella Raines,[9] *Hans Christian Andersen* (1952), *Spring Reunion* (1957), *Dead Ringer* (1954), *The Apple Dumpling Gang Rides Again* (1979), and *Every Which Way But Loose* (1978).

He became known to a new generation in his role on the *Lassie* television series. On it he played the uncle of Jon Provost.* Although it lasted only one season in 1961, *Ichabod Adams* contained some of George's best work on television. In the title role he played an old man who owned virtually the entire small town in which he lived.

When at university George was active as the business manager of the campus newspaper, a member of the drama society, and an officer of his fraternity. By 1946 he had been elected to the board of directors of the Screen Actors Guild. He was the union's treasurer from 1948 to 1960, when he succeeded Ronald Reagan as its president, a post he held until 1963.

The actor was widowed in 1963 after twenty-seven years of marriage. His eldest son, Gary, is an executive with Lorimar Productions. Bodie, the middle son, is the musical director of Columbia Television. The youngest, Michael, is the president of a national auto parts firm.

In 1968 staunchly conservative Republican Chandler met and married a Jewish widow who was politically liberal. They had met on a golf course. "He was golf's greatest enthusiast," says his widow. "He got a lot of the stars he supported interested in the game. Like everyone else, I thought I'd seen his face before, but I really didn't know who he was. All I

The late George Chandler and his wife, Helen, shortly before he died in 1985. The couple lived in a house in the hills overlooking the San Fernando Valley.

knew is I'd met a man who actually enjoyed the fact that I was a good golfer. Only another expert lady golfer would understand how rare this is with men."

It amused him that people often recognized him, but seldom knew his name. The book he never got around to writing was to be entitled *Your Face Looks Familiar*. Helen Chandler believes his talent, like his golf game, was founded on a secure ego. "George wasn't threatened by my game any more than he was when he worked with the biggest stars in Hollywood. We only made him better. My husband knew what he could do. He knew who he was."

His last time before the camera was in the 1976 made-for-TV movie *Griffin and Phoenix*. An octogenarian at the time, George portrayed a man celebrating his eightieth birthday and got a chance to play his fiddle. He was, however, already suffering from Alzheimer's disease. When he died on June 10, 1985, his family asked that donations go to organizations researching the illness.

Old friends Fritz Feld and Dana Andrews were among the mourners at his funeral. His casket was blanketed in the floral tribute sent by the President of the United States, Ronald Reagan, a man Chandler much admired.

When Peter Coe played with Maria Montez in Gypsy Wildcat *(1944), she described him to Louella Parsons as a "cross between Spencer Tracy and Charles Boyer." He may be best remembered for his appearances in the cult films* House of Frankenstein *(1944) and* The Mummy's Curse *(1945).*

Peter Coe

The film actor was born Peter Knego on Armistice Day, 1918, in Dubrovnik, a seaport in the Kingdom of the Serbs, Croats, and Slovenes, which shortly thereafter became known as Yugoslavia. His mother died in childbirth and he was taken to the mountains of Montenegro where he was raised by an aunt.

His passion was acting, despite the strong disapproval of his father, a sea captain. When he was a child Peter was picked to play Anton Walbrook as a boy in *Zigeunerbaron* (1935). It had served to confirm his ambitions. His heroes at the time were Ramon Novarro and Johnny Weissmuller.

He went to London as a teenager under the guardianship of a family friend who was England's leading speech therapist. Through his sponsor he met King George VI, whose stutter was being corrected, and Sir Oswald Moseley. The latter, who headed the Union of British Fascists, had a son with a speech impediment.

Peter trained at the Royal Academy of Dramatic Arts and appeared in several of the school's plays.

He came to the United States with a visa valid for two weeks, but two days before it was to expire he met Mrs. Sara Delano Roosevelt. The president's mother arranged for permanent residence and eventual citizenship.

While studying at the American Academy of Dramatic Arts he supported himself as a member of the chorus of Billy Rose's *Aquacade* at the World's Fair of 1939. He also understudied his idol Johnny Weissmuller and appeared in his stead when, according to Peter, "Johnny was too drunk to go on."

He has claimed to have won several swimming championships while he was in England, but his name does not appear in records of the period.

Peter's Broadway debut was in *The Fifth Column* (1940), a play based on the Hemingway short story. When it closed he played one of the Brazilian sailors in *My Sister Eileen* (1940).

After critics singled him out as the sexy sadist in *Men in Shadow* (1943), he was signed by a powerful theatrical agency.

Universal Pictures tested him opposite Lois

Collier* and placed him under contract. His name was changed and he debuted in the Walter Wanger production *Gung Ho!* (1944) playing a Polish immigrant Marine hero. (He and Sam Levene are killed during an attack on a Japanese radio station.) Studio head Nate Blumberg told him of the "plans and expectations" for his career, but for almost five years he played mostly second leads and frequently character roles in heavy makeup. After a series of suspensions his contract was dissolved by mutual consent.

"They just didn't know what to do with me," reasons Coe in his still-heavy accent.

He returned to Broadway and auditioned along with Marlon Brando for the lead in *The Greatest of Ease.* Coe got the part, but the play closed during out-of-town tryouts.

He has played Jewish Freedom Fighters, Egyptians, Indians (both East and American), and all European nationalities. Until plans to film the life story of Bela Lugosi were canceled, Coe was the prime contender to portray the Hungarian actor.

Parts he tested for but did not get were the title role in *Demetrius and the Gladiators* and the role Richard Conte played in *Call Northside 777.*

Among his screen credits are: *Follow the Boys* (1944); *Rocky Mountain* (1950) with Errol Flynn and Sheb Wooley;* *Road to Bali* (1952); *Passion* (1954); *Sabaka* (1955) with Boris Karloff; *The Ten Commandments* (1956); *Hell Ship Mutiny* (1957) with Jon Hall;[8] *Snow White and the Three Stooges* (1961) with Carol Heiss;* *The Secret Invasion* (1964) with Henry Silva;* and *Tobruk* (1967) with Rock Hudson.

In recent years he has done mostly bit parts, some on television. He told one interviewer that he was nominated for an Emmy for his portrayal of Ira Hayes, the American Indian who was one of those who raised the U.S. flag on Iwo Jima. The files of the Academy of Tele-vision Arts and Sciences do not bear this out.

The highlight of Peter Coe's career was probably his chilling performance of the Nazi officer in *Men in Shadow* (1943). Until very recently it seemed he would finally have another chance at such a role in a movie. He had seemed set for the title role in *Klaus Barbie, the Butcher of Lyon,* but the production has been shelved because of legal considerations.

Wayne Parks

Peter Coe in 1986 with one of his three sons, Peter Knego, artist and record promoter. The actor lives in Pasadena.

For Richard —
Just remember I'm
not retired —
I've had a lovely
afternoon —

Nancy Coleman had been singled out for her performances in Kings Row *and* The Gay Sisters. *She believed Warner Brothers was grooming her for stardom, but in 1946, shortly after this publicity still was taken, her contract with that studio was terminated.*

Nancy Coleman

The actress, whose movie career was aborted because of her marriage, was born on December 30, in Everett, Washington.

She appeared in school plays and gave recitations. Her mother, who was the first female and the youngest person ever admitted to the local musicians' union, permitted her to have elocution lessons and was supportive of her goal. Nancy Coleman cannot recall a time when she didn't want to act. Her training came after she moved to San Francisco where she played on the popular radio shows *Death Valley Days* and *Hawthorne House*.

In January, 1938, Nancy spent $500, exactly half her life's savings, for a first-class passage aboard a luxury liner to New York City.

She modeled and appeared on such radio programs as *Grand Central Station* and *Young Dr. Malone* before replacing Nancy Kelly in *Susan and God* on Broadway. She remained with the play for its national tour, again in support of its star Gertrude Lawrence. During their Los Angeles engagement she made a screen test for the role of "Scarlett O'Hara." When the company reached Chicago she was wired by David O. Selznick to return to Hollywood to make another test, again for the lead in *Gone With the Wind*. Having no understudy, Nancy declined, feeling that to do otherwise would be unprofessional.

She was still on the road with *Susan and God* when she was offered a role in the play *My Dear Children* opposite John Barrymore. Again she had to decline, but shortly after her tour ended Nancy Coleman got the title role in *Liberty Jones* (1941), opposite John Beal.[8] A few days after reading for this Philip Barry play with music she had auditioned for *Claudia*. By the time she was told that the part was hers she had to decline. She heard later that Dorothy McGuire,* who became a star as "Claudia," had also tried out for *Liberty Jones*.

Her notices as "Liberty Jones" brought Nancy contract offers from David O. Selznick and Warner Brothers. She chose the latter and was cast in *Kings Row* (1942), the role for which she is best known.

She played opposite John Garfield in *Dangerously They Live* (1941) and with Errol Flynn in *Desperate Journey* (1942) and *Edge of Darkness* (1943). Barbara Stanwyck was the star of *The Gay Sisters* (1942) and Geraldine Fitzgerald had the meatier part, but Nancy still came off very well. She was very believable as the repressed patrician in *In Our Time* (1944) and more than held her own with Ida Lupino and Olivia de Havilland in *Devotion* (1946) in which they played the Brontë sisters.

During the four years she spent on the Warner lot she had two minor disappointments. She was tested for the part in *They Died with Their Boots On* that went to Olivia de Havilland. She was told she had the lead in

The Constant Nymph, only to read in the newspaper several days later that Joan Fontaine would play it on the screen.

"Neither loss broke my heart," said Ms. Coleman in 1985. "I was the first choice for *The Constant Nymph,* but Charles Boyer had casting approval and insisted that he play opposite someone with a bigger name. My consolation was the knowledge that my studio still had big plans for me. I was being 'built.' I was to be a star."

Her casual dates with Charlie Chaplin were duly reported in the press and smiled upon by the studio. But when Nancy and Whitney Boulton, who headed the Warner publicity department, announced their engagement, they were immediately made aware of the disapproval of the front office. How, her fiancé was asked, could he be effective as the press agent for his own wife? Marriage to a publicist, a profession that rates even lower in the Hollywood pecking order than an agent, was not what her studio had in mind for her.

Nancy became Mrs. Whitney Boulton and her husband resigned and took a similar job at Columbia Pictures, but it was immediately obvious that the "big plans" she had been told of had been canceled. When she became pregnant she was placed on suspension. After bearing identical twin daughters she was returned to the Warner Brothers payroll, but not to favor. Instead of roles carefully tailored to suit her she was relegated to uninteresting small parts. Calls to her agent, Lew Wasserman, were not returned. She asked for and was granted a release from her contracts with Warner Brothers and her representatives, MCA.

The only work her new agents were able to get her was opposite Michael O'Shea[8] in *Violence* (1947), a Monogram cheapie, and in *Mourning Becomes Electra* (1947). The latter, based on the Eugene O'Neill play, was considered prestigious but fared poorly with critics and at the box office. Her salaries for both pic-

Phil Boroff

Nancy Coleman beside an early portrait of herself. The door of her apartment in Manhattan Plaza bears an anti-nuclear proliferation poster.

tures were one-third of what she had been making at Warner Brothers.

In 1948 the Boultons moved to New York City. He returned to journalism and she acted on live television shows such as *Kraft Television Theatre* and *The U.S. Steel Hour.* In 1952 Nancy replaced Martha Scott in the Broadway production of *The Male Animal.* She played on the television soap *Valiant Lady* for two years, leaving it to do *The Desperate Hours* (1953) on Broadway. Since then she has toured South America and the Middle East in the State Department–sponsored tours of *The Glass Menagerie* with Helen Hayes and as Helen Keller's mother in *The Miracle Worker.*

Both of her daughters were already married when her husband died in 1969. Nancy Coleman and her Siamese cat, "Lady Tiang," now share an apartment in New York City. She often auditions for plays and television shows.

"I do not wish to be thought of as retired," she said in 1985. "I'm just not working at present. My mother and her family lived into their nineties. It may take some time, but I'll be back in one medium or another."

Peggy Cummins was described in the Los Angeles Times *as "cuddly and lethal" in its review of* Gun Crazy *(1949). The unrelenting pace of the picture and the intensity of the performances, especially hers, have brought it cult status. It has also been released under the title* Deadly Is the Female.

Peggy Cummins

The actress who almost starred in *Forever Amber* was born Margaret Diane Augusta Cummins in Prestatyn, North Wales, on December 18. She grew up outside of Dublin where her father was a music scholar and journalist. Her brother is the landscape painter Harry Cummins. The family attended the Unitarian Church. Her mother, who had a great love of the theatre, encouraged Peggy to pursue a career and instilled in her "that whatever hap-

pens, it's your life, so get on with it!"

Peggy was seven years old when she was picked from her dance class in the Abbey School of Ballet to play a part in *The Duchess of Malfi* at Dublin's Gate Theatre. She debuted in London on her thirteenth birthday in the title role of *Junior Miss.* The play was a major hit in the West End during World War II, and she performed it right through the Blitz for 1000 performances.

Peggy Cummins had made *Dr. O'Dowd* (1940), *Salute, John Citizen* (1942), and *Welcome, Mr. Washington* (1944) in England before Darryl F. Zanuck saw her in *Junior Miss* and signed her to a Twentieth Century–Fox contract. She arrived in Hollywood in October, 1945, amidst a burst of publicity. At first, the studio planned to cast her as a supporting player in *Cluny Brown,* but that plan was dropped after she was tested for and won the most sought after part of the forties, the title role in *Forever Amber.*

When Twentieth Century–Fox acquired the screen rights to the smash best seller *Forever Amber,* it was considered that studio's answer to *Gone With the Wind.* The historical novel by Kathleen Winsor was the most controversial of the time. No expense was to be spared on its filming, and the search for the actress to play its heroine promised to be as extensive and as highly publicized as had been the one for "Scarlett O'Hara." The inevitable comparisons were made to Vivien Leigh when it was announced that Peggy Cummins, a virtually unknown actress from English films, had been chosen as "Amber."

Almost forty years later, Peggy Cummins talked about what happened: "I was quite wrong for 'Amber'—at least the way the studio perceived her. They were determined that she should have a widow's peak, so I had to wear a small toupee. I looked absurd. The script was being rewritten as we were shooting. Then I became ill, and Fox decided to start over again with a different cast and director. Still, I was terribly disappointed because this was to have been such an important picture. When I saw it, of course, I just felt relieved.''

Forever Amber, which starred Linda Darnell, was released in 1947 to almost universally negative reviews and did very poor business.

Although she never became the star many had predicted, Peggy's memories of Hollywood are very happy ones. Her dates with millionaire dilettante Huntington Hartford and Cary Grant were ''great fun.'' She grew very fond of Ethel Barrymore when they made *Moss Rose* (1947) and thoroughly enjoyed the experience of filming *Green Grass of Wyoming* (1948) with Lon McCallister.* Her other pictures of that period are *The Late George Apley* (1947) and *Escape* (1948).

During her early years on the Dublin stage, Ms. Cummins often played boys. After returning to England, she put the experience to good use in *Peter Pan* (1955), which was very well received.

Her screen appearances after leaving Hollywood have been in *English Without Tears* (1949), *Meet Mr. Lucifer* (1953), *Cash on Delivery* (1956), and *The Captain's Table* (1958). Her favorite among her English movies is *Who Goes There?* (1952) because it gave her a chance to play comedy. The last time she acted was in the picture *In the Doghouse* (1962).

Ironically, *Gun Crazy* (1949), the movie for which Peggy Cummins is best remembered, was made for very little money but with great care. While never ever verging on vulgarity, she exudes a sensuality that makes the seduction and corruption of her leading man, John Dall, totally believable. The sexual tension between them and her subtle-but-sure domination of Dall put *Gun Crazy* in a class with some of the highly esteemed European examples of *film noir.*

Curse of the Demon (1958), another low-budget film in which Peggy starred, has a

Richard Lamparski

Peggy Cummins named her Alsatian "Bo" for Bo Derek. She is one of the dogs that guard "Butler's Farm," the forty-acre estate in Sussex, England, owned by the Dunnetts.

strong cult following among horror-movie fans.

In 1950, she married Derek Dunnett, the scion of England's largest seed business.

Now that her son and daughter are adults and her husband has retired, Peggy Cummins feels she would like to act again. ''Stage, screen, TV—character part or starring role,'' she said in 1984. ''If I think I could do a good job with it, I'd do it, and I think I still have some very good work left in me.''

The Dunnetts' house in Sussex, England, which was built in the eighteenth century, has on its grounds upward of fifty head of sheep and a swimming pool. Aside from the large oil painting of Peggy in her prime by Vasko Lazzolo, there is no evidence of her career on display in the home.

Lil Dagover was brought to Hollywood by Warner Brothers amidst a blaze of publicity. Press releases claimed the actress wore only white and had a $300,000 insurance policy on her famous back and shoulders. After her one U.S. film, The Woman from Monte Carlo *(1931), failed at the box office, she returned to Europe where she remained a major star for many years.*

Lil Dagover

The first lady of the German cinema was born in Madiun, Java, on September 30, 1897. Shortly after the death of her father, a German forestry expert, her mother brought her to Germany. Originally, her name was Marta Maria Liletts.

As a schoolgirl she frequently saw plays and began to entertain thoughts of being an actress, but her ambition was strongly discouraged by her mother. At an early age, she married the actor-playwright Fritz Daghofer, but he too was against a career.

It was director Robert Wiene, struck by her beauty and poise, who believed she would be effective in films. When his judgment was seconded by Fritz Lang, she was given a contract with UFA, in 1918 the most important studio in Europe.

She was widowed just about the time *The Cabinet of Dr. Caligari* (1919) went into release. The picture, which was directed by Robert Wiene, was a major success worldwide and is now considered a cinema classic.

After *The Spiders* (1919) and *The Three Lights* (1921), in which Fritz Lang directed her, Lil Dagover was as popular as any star on the Continent, a position she sustained throughout the twenties. She was also in *Dr. Mabuse,* perhaps Lang's masterpiece, which was made years before it was seen in the United States in 1927. Under the direction of F. W. Murnau, she starred in *Tartuffe* (1925), another silent that is held in high regard by most scholars.

Her pictures were released in English-speaking countries as: *Between the Worlds* (1924), *Beyond the Wall* (1927), *Love Makes Us Blind* (1927), *Discord* (1928), *Hungarian Rhapsody* (1929), and *Hungarian Nights* (1930).

The Woman From Monte Carlo (1931), the only film she ever made in the United States, was disappointing. She always referred to it as "my Hollywood adventure" and held no bitterness toward the experience. Forty-five years after she left, Lil Dagover told writer John

Kobal how she remembered the time spent making the movie at Warner Brothers: "From the moment I arrived I sensed a jealousy, antipathy toward me. I knew I would have to fight the hostility, and I am not the type to fight."

Dagover was a sophisticate, a thoroughly modern European woman and a rather unlikely candidate for stardom in Hollywood films. She came at a time when U.S. audiences seemed to have tired of heavily accented foreign stars. In the film colony, her vegetarianism was thought to be "crackpot" and her bookishness was considered "highbrow." She loved solitude, the actress said, shortly after her arrival. It was a wish her American colleagues granted her in the extreme. "I was all alone in Hollywood," she said in the interview with Kobal. "Totally alone."

Her following in Europe hardly noticed *The Woman From Monte Carlo*. She had filmed *Das Alte Lied* (1930), the previous year, which was a great hit. *Elizabeth of Austria* came out in 1931 and was followed by *Congress Dances* (1932). Both were enormously popular in her homeland, and the second was acclaimed everywhere.

Some of the pictures she made after she returned to Germany were: *Eine Frau die Weiss Was sie Will* (1936), *Schlussakkord* (1936) under Douglas Sirk's direction, *The Kreutzer Sonata* (1937), *Dreikland: Triad* (1938), *Fridericus* (1939), *Bismarck* (1940), *Kleine Residenz* (1942), *Es Kommt ein Tag* (1950), *Das Geheimnis* (1952), *Confessions of Felix Krull* (1958), and *Die Buddenbrooks* (1959).

Lil Dagover went into virtual retirement after the death of her husband, George Witt, in 1973. Until then she remained a box office draw in Germany and Austria, whether she appeared on the screen or in a play. She did comedy as skillfully as drama and played with nearly all the great German comedians of the time. Although she took character roles in the later years, the artist always received the atten-

Jon Virzi

During the last years of her life, Lil Dagover lived in a cottage on the movie lot in Munich that had once been UFA, the studio where she made the silent classic, The Cabinet of Dr. Caligari *(1919).*

tion and billing afforded a star.

Maximilian Schell, who had admired her work since he was a boy, persuaded her to appear under his direction in *The Pedestrian*, which was nominated for an Oscar as the Best Foreign Film of the year in 1973, and again in *Tales from the Vienna Woods* (1978).

The vitality, chic, and glamour she maintained throughout her life earned her the unofficial title "The Lynn Fontanne of Germany."

Lil Dagover died on January 23, 1980.

Alex D'Arcy's latter period in films is notable for his role in How to Marry a Millionaire *(1953) in which he was pursued by the gold-digging Marilyn Monroe.*

Alex D'Arcy

The suave actor of screen and stage was born in Cairo, Egypt, on August 10. Professionally, he has always used the family name of his French mother. His father was a Turkish pasha who owned vast cotton fields in Egypt. Alexander's surname is Efflatoun.

Alex was a teenager summering at his family villa on the Riviera when he met Rex Ingram. The American director was very taken with Alex's dark good looks and suggested that he try acting. That profession was unacceptable to his father, but Ingram gave the boy a small part in the silent *The Garden of Allah* (1927), which he made in the south of France.

Alex and his father reached an agreement whereby he was to have six months of financial assistance while he tried to establish himself in the British film industry. Within sixty days of his arrival in London, he was signed to play the lead in the early talkie *Paradise* (1929).

In *Paradise*, Alex's Continental accent and suave manner worked very well for him. The nominal star of the picture was Betty Balfour, who was considered "Britain's Mary Pickford," but it was D'Arcy who was singled out in most notices. One hailed him as the "new Valentino."

Alex D'Arcy made over a dozen English and French movies before he was brought to Hollywood by Warner Brothers.

Who's Who in Hollyood calls him "the perfect gigolo." In *The Awful Truth* (1937) he causes the break-up of Irene Dunne's marriage to Cary Grant. In *Topper Takes a Trip* (1938), a dematerialized Constance Bennett character removes his trunks in the beach scene. The dog, which was an important part of the happenings, was the same one that appeared in *The Awful Truth*. Production was held up when it nipped D'Arcy on the forehead after he had been "depanted."

If his career had kept pace with his social life in Hollywood, Alex D'Arcy would have been a star. His credentials were such that social climbing was unnecessary. Once the Countess De Frasso, who was at her zenith as a filmdom hostess, let everyone know he was "the real thing," he was sought out by the people thought to be "top drawer." The American millionairess had known him in Europe during her marriage to a titled Italian.

He renewed acquaintances with Simone Simon.* He had made a picture with her in her native France. Through her he had immediate entrée to the younger set. Tennis, which happened to be D'Arcy's game, was "in." He was seen around town with Rita Cansino who was to become Rita Hayworth.

D'Arcy had been dating Arleen Whelan* for a few months when, after an evening of bowling with gossip columnist—broadcaster Jimmy Fidler, they decided to elope. The 1940 marriage alienated both from Louella Parsons because she had been scooped. Alex's wife, a favorite of Fidler's rival up until then, was known as the "Cinderella Girl" because she had been "discovered" while working as a manicurist. Alex's friend Howard Hughes provided the couple with air transport to Nevada. Three years later they were divorced.

His other screen credits include: *Stolen Holiday* (1937); *She Married an Artist* (1938); *Good Girls Go to Paris* (1939); *Fifth Avenue Girl* (1939) with Verree Teasdale;* *City of Chance* (1940) with Donald Woods[9] and Lynn Bari;[8] *Marriage is a Private Affair* (1944) with the late James Craig; *The St. Valentine's Day Massacre* (1967); *Seven Minutes* (1971); *The Blood of Dracula's Castle* (1967) with Paula Raymond; and *Dead Pigeon on Beethoven Street* (1972).

On Broadway he appeared in *Keep Off the Grass* (1940) with Jimmy Durante and *Yours Is My Heart* (1946) with Richard Tauber. *Heads or Tails,* a Mary Boland vehicle of the mid-forties, closed while on the road. He was the master of ceremonies of two Parisian revues that played Manhattan's Latin Quarter.

The first of two chances for stardom came when he made extensive tests with Greta Garbo for a film that was never made.

The second opportunity was as the lead opposite Joan Fontaine in *Frenchman's Creek*. Days after he was told he had the role D'Arcy was drafted.

He has lived in Europe for many years and for a long period had a very successful restaurant in Berlin with his second wife, who is German. They are now divorced.

It was Alex D'Arcy who introduced his close friend Darryl F. Zanuck to Bella Darvi, thus beginning what was the producer's most costly and destructive affair.

He had a daughter by his second marriage. To be near her D'Arcy spends several months each year in Hollywood where she is beginning an acting career under the name Susanna D'Arcy. On one of his recent visits he had dinner with an old friend and former date, Mary Carlisle,* and her husband.

Richard Lamparski

Alex D'Arcy spends several months each year in Hollywood visiting his daughter, but his residence is Cannes, France.

"Fifty-Million Frenchmen can't be wrong!" was the theme of the publicity campaign to launch Danielle Darrieux in her first Hollywood movie, Rage of Paris (1938). When she came to the United States to make that film she was already the most popular screen star in France and most likely would have had much success in the United States. But litigation and World War II intervened. When she returned to the film capital it was to play Jane Powell's mother in Rich, Young and Pretty (1951).

Danielle Darrieux

The international star of French cinema was born in Bordeaux on May 1, 1917. Her father, a physician, took his family to Paris in 1919; he died five years later.

Danielle was studying the cello when a family friend brought her to the attention of the director of *Le Bal* (1932). She played what she was, a very young girl. Both she and the picture received much acclaim. After a few smaller parts Robert Siodmak directed her in the musical *La Crise est Finie* (1935). Her career almost from the beginning had been under the guidance of writer-director Henri Decoin, whom she married in 1935. He was to direct many of her films and advise Danielle even after their divorce at the beginning of World War II.

The world first became aware of Darrieux when Charles Boyer insisted on her as his co-star in *Mayerling* (1936), a highly romanticized version of the deaths of the Crown Prince of Austria-Hungary and his cousin-mistress. Dubbed in English, it did good business and was chosen by the New York Film Critics as the year's Best Foreign Film. Years later, again paired with Boyer, she made *The Earrings of Madame de . . .* (1953), another huge commercial and critical success everywhere.

In 1942 she married Porfirio Rubirosa who at one point was arrested by the Germans despite having diplomatic status. It was supposedly through her influence with the high-ranking military that he was released. After their 1948 divorce he became world-famous for his marriages to and divorces from Doris Duke and Barbara Hutton. There was also a tempestuous affair with Zsa Zsa Gabor that made headlines everywhere in the fifties.

Perhaps the most remarkable thing about the career of Danielle Darrieux is the hold she has had on the French public. She starred in three films made after the Germans marched into Paris, including *Premier Rendezvous* (1941) with Louis Jourdan, the first movie to be made under the Occupation. After France's liberation the Maquis placed her name on the execution list. But the sentence was revoked and she was never imprisoned. Furthermore, there was almost no interruption of her career

44

and she seems to have lost few fans.

In the book *The Great Movie Stars, The International Years,* David Shipman wrote of her: "For forty years she has represented to many the ideal French woman." He also stated that "No actress—not even Myrna Loy—was as adept at light sarcasm."

She refuses to single out any one of her pictures as her favorite, maintaining "the public decides which is the best. And how could I judge when I've not seen all of my films?" Among the outstanding ones are: *Ruy Blas* (1948), *La Ronde* (1954), *Le Plaisir* (1954), *Five Fingers* (1952), *Adorable Creatures* (1956), *Rouge et Noir* (1958), and *Loss of Innocence* (1961).

Her name has shared movie marquees and posters with such stars as Jean Gabin, Fernandel, the Polish tenor Jan Kiepura, Richard Todd,* Gerard Philipe, Vittorio De Sica, Daniel Gelin, Sacha Guitry, and James Mason. She has played the mother of Richard Burton in *Alexander the Great* (1956), of Alain Delon in *The Devil and the Ten Commandments* (1963), a prostitute, and one of Bluebeard's wives.

She had sung in some of her movies and on the stage, but had never been on Broadway before taking over the lead in the musical *Coco* from Katharine Hepburn in 1970. When they met for the first time backstage the star asked Hepburn, one of her favorite actresses, to autograph her program. She was equally pleased to meet "Coco" Chanel for the first time and secure permission to play the legendary couturière. It did not, however, revive her screen career. "So many people came back after the show to say nice things," she says with a shrug. "But no one offered me a part in anything."

Since 1948 Danielle has been the wife of writer-producer Georges Mitsinkides. They live in a suburb of Paris and are the parents of a son.

Madame Darrieux insists that her life is proof of destiny. "Nothing else makes sense," she said in September, 1985. "I was not a girl who hoped and prayed and planned. Everything just happened to me and I accepted it. It's been good. I'm happy, but I don't believe I brought any of it about. It was just *supposed* to be."

Maree Breyer

In the mid-eighties she had a long run in Gigi on stage in Paris. Danielle Darrieux received star billing in the role that was taken by Hermione Gingold in the 1958 film musical. She has never seen the screen version.

Rosemary De Camp made over three dozen movies, but is best known for playing the sister of Bob Cummings[9] on his TV show from 1955 to 1959 and the mother of Marlo Thomas on That Girl *from 1966 to 1970. Perhaps her greatest exposure on television was as spokesperson for Borax products for twenty-five years.*

Rosemary De Camp

The character actress was born in Prescott, Arizona, on November 14, 1910. Her father was a mining engineer.

At Mills College, Rosemary majored in speech and psychology while dating a law student named John A. Shidler. By the time she received a master's degree, they had decided to go their separate ways. It was 1941 before they became reacquainted and were married. By then, he had become the youngest judge in the state of California.

In the early 1930s, after a two-week stint on *One Man's Family,* a radio program done from the West Coast, she joined a tour of *The Drunkard* that ended in New York City. There,

she got a small part in the Broadway play *Merrily We Roll Along* (1934) through Sam H. Harris. Producer Harris, along with the Marx Brothers, owned the mine that Rosemary's father ran.

Although the actress almost never listened to radio, she began acting frequently in the medium. Goodman Ace used her regularly on his comedy program *Easy Aces.* Until the first rehearsal of the show, Rosemary thought it was about the game of bridge.

It was Martha Scott who got Rosemary her first screen part, a fact that Ms. De Camp frequently mentions. When she was signed to play the title role in *Cheers for Miss Bishop* (1941), Ms. Scott strongly recommended her to play an immigrant girl. The two had worked together on radio, and Rosemary's ability to master dialects had especially impressed her. As the star of the picture, Martha Scott was able to insist that Rosemary be lighted and photographed with equal care. Because her debut had been so effective, she was cast in *Hold Back the Dawn* (1951) as a pregnant woman determined to have her child in the United States.

In those two pictures, Rosemary De Camp, who was past thirty, played a teenager and a very young woman. From then on, however, she played older women, frequently much older than she was. In *Yankee Doodle Dandy* (1942), she portrayed the mother of James Cagney, although she is more than ten years younger than the star.

She was Sabu's mother in *The Jungle Book* (1942) and the matriarch of a show-business family in the musicals *The Merry Monahans* (1944) and its sequel *Bowery to Broadway* (1944). Rosemary played Robert Alda's mother in *Rhapsody in Blue* (1945) and Ginger Rogers's French maid in *Weekend at the Waldorf* (1945). Wanda Hendrix[8] was her daughter in *Nora Prentiss,* as was Doris Day in *On Moonlight Bay* (1951) and again in its sequel

By the Light of the Silvery Moon (1953).

Some of the other Rosemary De Camp screen credits are: *Blood on the Sun* (1945); *Pride of the Marines* (1945); *Night Unto Night* (1949) with Ronald Reagan and Osa Massen; * *The Story of Seabiscuit* (1949) with Lon McCallister; * *Look For the Silver Lining* (1949) in which she played June Haver's mother; *Night into Morning* (1951) with Nancy Davis; *Scandal Sheet* (1952); *The Treasure of Lost Canyon* (1952) with Charles Drake; * *So This is Love* (1953) with Jeff Donnell; * *Many Rivers to Cross* (1955) with Josephine Hutchinson; *Strategic Air Command* (1955); *13 Ghosts* (1960); *Tora! Tora! Tora!* (1969); and *Saturday the 14th* (1981).

In the movie *The Life of Riley* (1949), Rosemary played the long-suffering wife "Peg" to William Bendix's "Riley." In the early TV series of the same title, she played "Peg Riley" opposite Jackie Gleason.

Rosemary De Camp originated the role of "Judy Price," nurse-confidante to the kindly physician, on the *Dr. Christian* radio series in November, 1937. The title role was played by Jean Hersholt. During most of her seventeen years in the role, the cast was required to do two live shows before a studio audience three hours apart. The earlier broadcast was heard on the East Coast. Unlike most programs then, there was no summer hiatus, which meant a rehearsal and two shows weekly, fifty-two weeks a year.

When asked why she is so seldom seen now on television, Rosemary explains the difficulty the schedule of a series imposes on the life of a family. "Because I live at the beach, I have to get up at 4 A.M. when I work," she said in 1986. "Why should I get up at that ungodly hour? I did a minuscule part on *Hotel* last year just to let people know I'm still alive."

The Shidlers are active members of the Democratic Party and frequent travelers. Recent trips have been to the People's Republic

Richard Lamparski

Rosemary De Camp, her poodle "Star," and husband, retired Superior Court Justice John A. Shidler, live near the Pacific Ocean in Redondo Beach, California.

of China and New Zealand.

She has remained on good terms with all of the stars she has supported, but found two particularly trying. One, she believes, "really dislikes all women although his image is just the opposite." The other, "considers anyone on her set, maybe in the world, to be a threat."

In the home of her parents acting and show business were not considered serious interests. Throughout their marriage, Judge Shidler and Rosemary have not socialized with people she has worked with and do not discuss her career.

"I've been very lucky," she once said. "I put everything I had into any role I played, but I never did anything to get any work. And yet for years, I was kept very busy. I even missed a few things while I was having four daughters of my own. The fact that some people remember me flatters me more than I can express."

The book she wrote about her Irish setter, *Dear Duke,* was published in 1962. She is presently working on her autobiography, *A Light Heart.*

Speaking about the partial loss of hearing she has recently experienced, she said: "Like most people, I only half-listened to people before this happened to me. But I've taught myself to pay strict attention to the other person, and I get along fine. Not so incidentally, I'm a better person because of it."

While they were making the film **Mad Love** *(1935), Peter Lorre used to sneak up behind Frances Drake and whisper into her ear, "It's only me, your little Peter."*

Frances Drake

The cultured screen menace was born Frances Morgan Dean on October 22, 1913, in New York City. Her education, which included finishing school, was acquired in Canada and England.

Frances was living in London with her aunt and grandmother when her father, who was in the mining business, was wiped out by the 1929 Wall Street crash. Had family finances not forced her she would not have gone into show business or any other profession.

She loved ballroom dancing and formed a team with a handsome young man with a similar social background. They played smart clubs such as Ciro's and The Barclay and appeared in the English production of the Broadway hit *Potash and Perlmutter* at the Gaiety.

She played in *Little Earthquake* (1933) in the West End and then entered movies for the reason "They paid even better than the stage."

After *The Jewel* (1933) with Jack Hawkins and *Two Hearts in Waltz Time (1934)* opposite the Danish star Carl Brisson she had two Hollywood offers. Frances chose to sign with Paramount rather than Fox or Universal because, "They offered the most money."

Lest she be confused with Frances Dee,[8] the studio changed her name and claimed in her publicity that the actress was actually related to the legendary pirate.

When Renee Adoree died, Frances was cast in the part that had been written for the silent star in *Bolero* (1934). She liked the picture's star George Raft,[8] but commented on his co-star Carole Lombard: "Her language was every bit as foul as you've heard. But I don't remember anyone being amused by it and the technical people on the sets were very put off by her curses and vulgarities."

M-G-M was so intent on having her as the other woman in *Forsaking All Others* (1934) that scenarist Joseph L. Mankiewicz rewrote a key scene to please her.

Joan Crawford, the star of *Forsaking All Others,* and Loretta Young,[8] who Frances supported in *Love Under Fire* (1937), are remembered as, "Both quite horrid to me, each in her own hateful way. But filmmaking is so terribly boring that I found their antics not only stimulating, but very instructive. I learned a lot about the politics on a movie set. I picked up so much from Crawford I thanked her at the end of the picture. You should have seen her face. She was always very sweet to me after that. Women like that are so very easily threatened because their careers are *everything*. They have no identity beyond their billing."

In another loan-out she made the horror film *The Invisible Ray* (1936). She liked both its stars, Bela Lugosi and Boris Karloff. However, when Karloff first spoke to her Frances burst out laughing. She had never been to one of his movies and was startled by his famous lisp.

She was very emotionally involved with the late Louis Hayward and would have married him had he asked her one more time: "I was hopelessly mad about him, but he was so good-looking and charming I couldn't see how I could possibly hold him. Louis, like everyone else, thought I was terribly sophisticated. Well, I was a virgin—that's how much I'd seen of life. Had he proposed a fourth time I'm sure I'd have said 'yes.'"

Shortly afterward a handsome young aristocrat who had seen her in *Ladies Should Listen* (1934) asked a former Eton classmate to introduce them. In 1939 she married the second son of the earl of Suffolk and Berkshire.

Her late husband, the Honorable Cecil Howard, disapproved of her being in pictures and did not get on well with most of her Hollywood acquaintances. He insulted her agent publicly. According to Frances, she continued only as long as she did because he had not yet come into his inheritance. *Affairs of Martha* (1942) was her swan song.

Some of her other motion pictures were: *Les Miserables* (1935); *The Preview Murder Case* (1936); *Midnight Taxi* (1936) with Brian Donlevy;* *You Can't Have Everything* (1937); *Lone Wolf in Paris* (1938) with Francis Lederer;[8] and *It's a Wonderful World* (1939) with Claudette Colbert and James Stewart.

About Randolph Scott,[8] her leading man in *And Sudden Death* (1936), she says: "He seemed to think acting was memorizing lines and remembering when to repeat them." She thought Hedy Lamarr,* the female star of *I Take This Woman* (1940), to be, "As utterly

stupid as she was beautiful."

"From beginning to end my career was because of money," she said recently. "Yet, I did miss it a bit for a while. I consoled myself that at least I'd not have to be anywhere near such coarse, crass people as Al Kauffman and Harry Cohn."

Kauffman, a Paramount executive, had demanded she sleep with him. Later, when she had a Columbia contract, Cohn did the same.

Ms. Drake says that Fredric March and John Boles were equally aggressive, if less verbal. "They just lunged without any warning."

Just before he died in spring 1985 Frances promised her husband that she would personally look after their aged cat, a stray that had come to them over a decade ago. For that reason she never travels.

Her friends are the former British star Joyce Howard* and Constance Moore,[8] who lives close by.

The private road that leads to Frances Drake's hilltop house in Beverly Hills is shared by the widow of director Fritz Lang and the cinematographer Laszlo Kovaks.

Richard Lamparski

49

John Justin and June Duprez, along with the late Sabu, were the stars of The Thief of Bagdad *(1940), the Alexander Korda production that won Oscars for Special Effects, Color Art Decoration, and Color Cinematography.*

June Duprez

The leading lady of the movies was born during an air raid in Teddington, England, on May 14, 1918.

Although her father was an American vaude-villian, her early acting ambitions were not taken seriously. June was allowed to join the Coventry Repertory Company because her parents believed the hard work required would soon discourage her.

She never developed a real ambition but enjoyed acting. Her first husband, a Harley Street physician, encouraged her to pursue a career. But after his wife became so well known through the success of *Four Feathers* (1939), he became jealous and possessive. Alexander Korda, the producer, moved the filming of *The Thief of Bagdad* (1940) to Hollywood and subsequently June and the doctor were divorced.

Her exotic beauty and slightly aloof manner were seen in *The Cardinal* (1936), *U-Boat 29* (1939) with Valerie Hobson,* *They Raid By Night* (1942), *And Then There Were None* (1945), *The Brighton Strangler* (1945), *That Brennan Girl* (1946) with James Dunn[8] and Mona Freeman,[8] *Calcutta* (1947) with Alan Ladd, *1 + 1* (1961), and *The Last Tycoon* (1976).

Hollywood, where she lingered throughout World War II, was not to her liking. Korda and her agent set her price at $50,000 per picture. The steep salary, coupled with her slightly exotic beauty and somewhat cool manner, brought her career to a standstill. At one point she was so impoverished she nibbled on dog biscuits, which she covered with marmalade.

"Whenever you see a 'Sherlock Holmes' movie, say a prayer for 'Dr. Watson,'" June has been quoted as saying. "Because if it hadn't been for the kindness of Nigel Bruce and his wife, I just don't know what I'd have done in Hollywood. They kept me circulating socially when I was stagnating professionally. And the times they gave me dinner! But the very worst part was the men out there. I spent a few minutes at a Barbara Hutton party talking with David O. Selznick. Later that same night, he appeared at my door, and when I wouldn't let him in, he broke my window. Another time, on a warm day, I had my apartment door opened and in walked Harry Cohn—right into my house. I'd never met him. I didn't know who he was, even when he told me. When I told my agent that I nearly had him arrested, he told me that such a thing would have ruined *me. Me!* I had been assured that I was the prime contender for the lead in *Sundown,* the part that was to be the making of Gene Tierney, but after that horrible scene with Selznick, it was never again mentioned. You may wonder how a film to be made at one studio could be affected by another. By the simple fact that my agent was Myron Selznick, David's brother. It seems I had made a member of his family look foolish. Do you wonder why it's called a 'jungle'?''

Even when Cary Grant and Clifford Odets, the director, wanted June for *None But the Lonely Heart* (1944), the front office at RKO strongly objected to the casting. She believed that the movie contains her best screen work.

According to author Charles Higham, June Duprez assisted the FBI during World War II in surveillance of Fascist sympathizers in Hollywood and activities of enemy agents in Mexico.

June left Hollywood at the first opportunity to move to New York—an offer to act with the company run by Margaret Webster and Eva Le Gallienne. Under their auspices, she appeared on Broadway in *What Every Woman Knows* and *Androcles and the Lion.* George S. Kaufman directed her in the Broadway production of *Town House* in 1948, the year in which she married a wealthy sportsman.

June has two daughters by that marriage. It ended in 1965. She lived in Rome for a number of years after the divorce.

In 1984 at the time of her last interview, she was living in a large garden apartment in the Knightsbridge area of London. She had a Siamese cat and a close relationship with a member of the English nobility. She was considering having some minor plastic surgery done and planned a trip to the United States to see her only grandchild, a boy.

She died in her sleep on August 17, 1984.

Richard Lamparski

This photograph of June Duprez was taken in her London flat on August 17, 1984, less than three months before her death. She was sixty-six years old.

Leif Erickson married Frances Farmer in spring, 1936, less than a year after he signed with Paramount Pictures. He and his wife, who also was a contractee at that studio, were costarred in Ride a Crooked Mile *(1938).*

Leif Erickson

The big, brawny leading man and character actor was born William Wyecliffe Anderson in Alameda, California, on October 27, 1911. His father was a sea captain. His mother worked as a journalist with the *San Francisco Chronicle* under her maiden name, Margaret Medbury.

After being taken to an opera when he was seven years old, he decided to sing professionally. He left Beverly Hills High School before graduating to take a $15-a-week job with a repertory company.

He sang and acted in road companies of *Moon Madness* and *Princess Ida* before becoming the vocalist with Ted Fio Rito's band. Then he played "Oberon, King of the Forest" in the Max Reinhardt production of *A Midsummer Night's Dream* that toured the United States in the early thirties. When that show closed he spent one and a half years with Olsen and Johnson in *Hellzapoppin',* singing and playing the trombone. In 1935, during the show's engagement in Peoria, Leif received a wire from Hollywood offering a contract with Paramount Pictures.

Erickson was with that studio for almost three years. He made his screen debut as a corpse in *Wanderer of the Wasteland* (1935) and went on to support Greta Garbo in *Conquest* (1937) and Johnny Downs* and Eleanore Whitney* in *Thrill of a Lifetime* (1937).

After his contract expired the 6-feet-4-inch blond moved to New York where he appeared in half a dozen Broadway shows, including *Margin for Error* (1939) and *Higher and Higher* (1940). He returned to Hollywood to support Hedy Lamarr* in *H. M. Pulham, Esq.* (1941) and Irene Hervey* and Bela Lugosi in *Night Monster* (1942) before joining the United States Navy.

"That war really messed up the momentum of my career," he once commented. "After spending three and a half years teaching photography in Pensacola, Florida, I rode a motorcycle to Hollywood where I found myself doing exactly the same thing at Cal-State for twenty dollars a day. The movie industry had the postwar blahs and there was very little work for anyone other than top stars."

Leif Erickson made appearances in *Sorry, Wrong Number* (1948), *The Snake Pit* (1948), *Joan of Arc* (1948), *Miss Tatlock's Millions*

(1948) with the late Wanda Hendrix[8] and John Lund,* *Love That Brute* (1950) with Jean Peters,[9] and *Show Boat* (1951).

In *Tea and Sympathy* (1953), his return to Broadway, he originated the role of the insensitive headmaster, a part he repeated in the 1956 screen version, again with John Kerr.* He was with Bette Davis in *The World of Carl Sandburg* (1960) on Broadway and with Helen Hayes in *The Skin of Our Teeth* and *The Glass Menagerie.* The latter two were productions sponsored by the United States State Department and toured Europe, South America, and the Middle East before being presented in New York City in 1961. Leif also headed the road tour of *Sunrise at Campobello,* playing Franklin Delano Roosevelt.

On the screen he was seen in *With a Song in My Heart* (1952), *Carbine Williams* (1952, *On the Waterfront* (1954), *The Fastest Gun Alive* (1959) with Russ Tamblyn,[9] *Istanbul* (1957) with Cornell Borchers,* *Kiss Them For Me* (1957) with Suzy Parker,* *Twilight For the Gods* (1958) with Arthur Kennedy,[9] *A Gathering of Eagles* (1963) with Mary Peach, *Roustabout* (1964) with Elvis Presley, and *The Carpetbaggers* (1964).

He supported Joan Crawford in *Strait-Jacket* (1964) and again in *I Saw What You Did* (1965), but was unable to support his family on acting alone. When he was cast as "Big John Cannon" in *The High Chaparral,* he was working as a broker of pleasure boats. The western television series, which ran from 1967 to 1971, was a comeback professionally and financially. Since then he had been in the films *Man and Boy* (1972), *Winterhawk* (1975), and *Twilight's Last Gleaming* (1977).

Erickson's second wife was the late Margaret Hayes. Their 1942 marriage ended in divorce after one month.

On Christmas Eve, 1945, he married a WAC he had met while serving in the United States Navy during World War II. Their two grand-

Richard Lamparski

The actor in his Malibu home beside a portrait that was done of him about the time he changed his name to Leif (pronounced "life") Erickson. Nine months after this photo was taken he died at age seventy-four.

children are by their daughter, who is a nurse. Leif's son, who had been a Green Beret, was killed in a 1971 automobile collision.

He did not cooperate with the authors of the books on Frances Farmer and had not seen the feature film *Frances* (1982). "Frances was always such a perfectionist," he had said of his first wife. "She absolutely tormented herself and everyone around her with that obsession. I guested on the TV program she hosted in Indianapolis near the end of her life and she was still driving herself toward the same utterly unobtainable goal. She was a dear person, but sad. So terribly sad."

Leif Erickson died after a long illness on January 29, 1986.

David Farrar's favorite photograph of himself, taken at London's Theatrical Garden Party in 1950. He likes it, "because it is one of the few times I looked cheerful!"

David Farrar

The heroic English star was born on August 21, 1908, in Essex.

Of his childhood he writes: "Apparently showed histrionic leanings from early age as I played Shakespearean roles at school."

After some time spent with a repertory school and then in touring companies, David became actor-manager of his own company in 1930. The same year he took over the lead in *The Wandering Jew* in the West End, bringing notices that immediately established him as one of the most promising young leading men in the West End.

He took over London's Grafton Theatre for a series of plays, as he puts it: "Of course, playing the leads. As George Arliss once said, 'Well, there's one advantage of having your own theatre—you can always choose the best parts.'"

He says he was "lured" into films in 1937 when he made his screen debut in *The Face Behind the Scar.* Until the war broke out his screen career consisted of "big parts in small pictures and small parts in big pictures," according to Farrar.

Shortly after a bomb hit his theatre he was called up by the Ministry of War and put to work making propaganda films. He is responsible for the feature *For Those in Peril* (1944), much of which was shot during actual maneuvers in the English Channel.

The Dark Tower (1943) with the late Ben Lyon and *They Met in the Dark* (1943) came out during the War. Immediately afterward he made *Lisbon Story* (1946), now a cult film because of the appearance in it of the legendary tenor Richard Tauber.

When David Farrar arrived in New York City in 1947, his film *Frieda,* which introduced Mai Zetterling* to the world and was a smash hit in Europe, was playing at one Broadway theatre and *Black Narcissus* at another.

Black Narcissus (1947), which costarred Deborah Kerr, was about sexual frustration and madness among a group of Anglican nuns. The Roman Catholic Church, through its Legion of Decency, deemed it a mortal sin for any member of the religion to view the film. It was rated "C" for "condemned" until a few minutes of footage were edited out. After the ban was lifted, it did very well at the box office in the United States and won two Oscars.

The Wild Heart (1950) with Jennifer Jones was nowhere near the success in the United States that it was in England under the title *Gone to Earth.*

He was offered the lead role of Edvard Grieg in the screen version of *The Song of Norway,* but the movie was to be shot in Hollywood and Farrar was committed in England. Once he was contractually free, there began years of commuting between Hollywood and London, starting with *The Golden Horde* (1951).

After that he appeared in *Night Without Stars* (1951) with Nadia Gray,* *Obsessed* (1951) with Geraldine Fitzgerald, *Duel in the Jungle* (1954) with George Coulouris,* *Lilacs in the Spring* (1954) with Anna Neagle, *Tears for Simon* (1957), *Solomon and Sheba* (1958), *John Paul Jones* (1959) with Bette Davis, *Middle of Nowhere* (1960), and *Wild for Kicks* (1962) with Shirley Anne Field.*

United States television viewers probably know him best for his portrayal of the strong, silent "Mr. Dean" in *Black Narcissus* and the "Black Duke" in *Son of Robin Hood* (1958).

Farrar believes there were two major "might have beens" in his career. He could have played the villain in the 1952 version of *Ivanhoe,* but declined because it was not the title role. As he now admits, "The part I had been offered, which was subsequently played by George Sanders, was the most colorful. In retrospect it was a bad mistake." He would have played the title role in *Ethan Frome,* but the film was never made. Bette Davis, who was to have been his costar, told him it was canceled when she became pregnant.

In 1962 he played Xerxes, which he considered to be a "wonderful, flamboyant part," in *The 300 Spartans,* and "then I quit while the going was good!"

David met his wife, Irene Elliot, in 1926 when he was playing the title role on stage in *David Copperfield.* He describes her as an "actress and beautiful pianist." After she died in

Adam Oliver Robertson

David Farrar, a widower, lives near his daughter on the Natal coast of the Republic of South Africa.

1976, he followed their only child to the Natal coast of the Republic of South Africa.

He admits to having made no effort to keep in touch with those he knew in England and has been rumored dead among his profession.

He lives with his dog, a few miles from his daughter. Farrar describes his activities as "a bit of writing and painting. I play the piano to myself and get in eighteen holes of golf three times a week. I read a lot and average fifteen crossword puzzles a week."

He sums up his career thusly: "Tough, frustrating, but with many wonderful moments and memories. I found being a star a lonely business. I have no friends. Ain't that sad?"

Alice Faye had a screen presence of warmth and softness, but she was never clinging. She threatened neither men nor women, making her the ideal mate, in-law, or big sister. As her fans delight in saying, "There's no one who doesn't like Alice Faye."

Alice Faye

The onetime queen of Twentieth Century–Fox was born in the "Hell's Kitchen" area of Manhattan on May 5, 1915. Her original name was Alice Jeanne Leppert.

After some training and chorus work under Chester Hale, she became a chorine at the Nils T. Granlund clubs.

It was Rudy Vallee* who first appreciated Alice's unique qualities. When they appeared in the *George White Scandals of 1931,* he tried to get her a featured spot but failed. Faye's first important exposure was as vocalist on Vallee's radio program in 1933. When Vallee's costar, Lilian Harvey,* walked off their picture, *George White's Scandals* (1934), he succeeded in having her replaced by Alice Faye. It led to a contract.

The look and personality that by 1938 had catapulted her to being one of the top-rated stars in the world emerged in the 1937 musicals *On the Avenue, Wake Up and Live, You Can't Have Everything,* and *You're a Sweetheart.*

Her other screen appearances were in: *Now I'll Tell* (1934), which starred Spencer Tracy and Helen Twelvetrees; *She Learned About Sailors* (1934); *365 Nights in Hollywood* (1934); *George White's 1935 Scandals* (1935); *Every Night at Eight* (1935); *Music Is Magic* (1935) with Thomas Beck;* *King of Burlesque* (1936); *Poor Little Rich Girl* (1936); *Sing, Baby, Sing* (1936); *Stowaway* (1936); *Sally, Irene, and Mary* (1938); *In Old Chicago* (1938); *Alexander's Ragtime Band* (1938); *Tail Spin* (1939); *Rose of Washington Square* (1939); *Hollywood Cavalcade* (1939); *Barricade* (1939); *Little Old New York* (1940); *Lillian Russell* (1940); *Tin Pan Alley* (1940); *That Night in Rio* (1941); *The Great American Broadcast* (1941); *Weekend in Havana* (1941); *The Gang's All Here* (1943); and *Four Jills in a Jeep* (1944).

"I Feel a Song Coming On," "You're a Sweetheart," and "You Turned the Tables on Me" are among the songs she introduced. Another, which she sang in *Hello, Frisco, Hello,* won the Oscar as the Best Song of 1943 and became one of the major hits of World War II in England. When Alice appeared at the Royal Variety Show before England's Queen Elizabeth II late in 1985, that was the song she sang—"You'll Never Know."

"Alexander's Ragtime Band" and "Hello, Frisco, Hello," which had been popular early in the century, were hits all over again after Alice Faye sang them in movies and, in the opinion of many, made them her own.

Alice enjoyed making films and wanted to continue, but desired to play more varied roles. She believed that playing a victimized spinster in *Fallen Angel* (1945) would establish her as a dramatic actress. She was so disappointed with the film that she went from its screening directly to her car, not even bothering to remove her personal effects from her dressing room. She returned to the Fox lot sixteen years later, settling her contractual commitment by appearing in *State Fair* (1962). About that, her penultimate movie, she says: "I don't know what happened to the picture business, and I'm sorry I went back to find out." Her last film, *The Magic of Lassie* (1978), starred James Stewart.

When she married Phil Harris [9] in 1941, many friends and fans predicted they would not stay together and that it would harm her career. From the outset, she stated that her husband's well-being and that of her eventual family took precedence over any professional consideration. As it turned out, the network radio show Alice and Harris did together from 1948 until 1954 sustained her popularity after she had ceased making movies.

The couple has two daughters, both married. As of 1986, they had four grandchildren.

Asked on a TV talk show whether she could define the reason her marriage has worked so long and, seemingly, so well, she replied: "Well, we both travel much of the time." (Long pause.) "Separately!"

Alice Faye fans around the world exchange bits of news and facts about their star: That she has poodles named "Chulla" and "Jessica," paints kittens and flowers in oil, enjoys Mexican and Japanese foods, does needlepoint, spends at least one month a year at a health spa, is friends with Ruby Keeler and Dolores Hope,

Frank Walshon

Alice Faye lives in Rancho Mirage, California, on the grounds of the Thunderbird Country Club. Her home faces the golf course and her neighbors include Arthur Lake,[8] "Dagwood Bumstead" of movies and radio, and silent star Billie Dove.

considers London her favorite city, the yellow rose her favorite flower, and caramel her favorite flavor. Patou's Joy is her scent.

Many of her pictures are among the most consistent box office draws at revival theatres, rating-getters on TV, and sales leaders in videocassettes. In the United Kingdom, she is even more popular than in the United States. Yet none of her good fortune seems to have inspired envy or jealousy.

In 1971 when Rex Reed interviewed Alice Faye, who had been his favorite throughout childhood, he wrote, "She's a rarity—a movie star who isn't at all disappointing to meet."

EMI/Angel Records

"A sort of contemporary Laurel and Hardy team on a cerebral level" is how the **Daily News** *described* At the Drop of a Hat *when the two-man show debuted on Broadway in 1959. Another review called Flanders and Swann "a pair of English elves."*

Flanders and Swann

The English musical duo, once described by American theatre critic Walter Kerr as "just two men alone on the stage completely surrounded by talent," met first as students. They collaborated on *Go at It,* a show of semiprofessionals that was so well received at the Westminster School that it was presented on the West End in 1940.

Donald Swann spent World War II in Greece with an ambulance unit. Michael Flanders, while serving with the Royal Navy, contracted polio. He was an invalid for the rest of his life.

In 1947 Swann was offered a chance to write for musical reviews to be produced in London. When he informed the producer that he could only write music he was told to "find a collaborator." He got in touch with Flanders and they revived a professional partnership that continued for over twenty-five years. Their greatest success was the West End show *Airs on a*

Shoestring. For nine years they wrote only for others.

In 1956 Flanders and Swann began performing their own material in an evening of wonderful nonsense they called *At the Drop of a Hat.*

What followed was a long run in London, two seasons on Broadway, a world tour, and five record albums, and the *Flanders and Swann Songbook.* Eventually there was a sequel, *At the Drop of Another Hat.* As in the original the bearded, bluff Flanders wrote all of the lyrics and did most of the singing. Nearly all of their music was by Swann.

Their combined efforts were described as being "like 'Falstaff' singing duets with 'Hamlet.'" Whether in Australia or at the Edinburgh Festival, their ditties such as "Mud, Glorious Mud," "I'm a Gnu," and "Madeira, M'Dear?" charmed and amused the audiences. Their sense of the ridiculous was appreciated on American television, where Ed Sullivan presented them on several of his shows.

Although Flanders's words at times had social or political bite, they were never vulgar and seemingly offended no one. Progressive fans in South Africa congratulated the pair when the government-controlled radio played one of their songs, which was about the marriage of a vine to a melon, without its being censored.

In the late sixties they paused while both considered the offers that had been made to them individually and as a combination.

"We might have done a musical or a film," says Swann. "We almost certainly would eventually have written all new material for the greatly changing times and performed it."

Then, in 1975, Michael died of heart failure. "It was such a shock—finding he was no longer there!" said Swann in 1986. "Since then I've been doing all the things I might have done had we not met or succeeded together. Nourishing and rewarding work, but I still miss his companionship."

Howard W. Hays

Donald Swann is the divorced father of two daughters. He and the eldest, a theatrical agent, share a terrace house in the Battersea section of London.

Donald Swann has composed cantatas, hymns, and a musical for children. Michael's widow, Claudia Flanders, has been widely recognized in the United Kingdom for her efforts to obtain proper accommodations for the disabled.

Recently divorced after twenty-five years, Swann is presently seriously considering migrating to the United States where he would totally involve himself with the peace movement among the Quakers. He is, however, not a member of their church.

"I love America," he said in 1986. "And I know the terrain, having pushed Michael's wheelchair up and down so many of its streets. I'd move there, metaphorically speaking, at the drop of a hat."

Sally Forrest was publicized as a discovery of Ida Lupino, who starred her in Not Wanted *(1949), the first movie she ever produced. Ms. Lupino directed and produced three other pictures with Sally.*

Sally Forrest

The star of movies and Broadway was born on May 28 in San Diego, California. Her mother was of German descent. Her father, a career boatswain's mate in the U.S. Navy, was born in Ireland. Her original name is Katherine Sally Feeney.

The Feeneys were amateur but accomplished ballroom dancers. When their daughter showed a keen interest in dance, she was enrolled in classes about the same time she entered first grade. In time her instructor taught her without charge in exchange for her services as an assistant.

Metro-Goldwyn-Mayer signed Sally to a contract as a chorine that began as soon as she graduated from high school. In August, 1945, she and her family moved to Hollywood. She worked on and in the dances seen in *Till the Clouds Roll By* (1946) and *The Kissing Bandit* (1948). After eighteen months, during a retrenchment program her option was dropped.

Sally was working with Anthony Dexter,* teaching him Spanish dances in preparation for his starring role in *Valentino,* when her entire life changed. As she left the studio one afternoon, she literally bumped into a young agent named Milo Frank. She felt attracted to him, but no names were exchanged. When he learned her name and address, he sent a telegram offering to represent her.

Sally became Frank's client and steady date. He convinced her to change her name and let him present her as an actress-dancer.

Ida Lupino had coscripted *Not Wanted* (1949) and was about to produce it herself when Frank sold Sally Forrest to her for the leading role. Both Sally and the picture were very well received by critics. The film made its cost of $115,000 in profits many times over.

The pert blonde with ice blue eyes was presented to the public as a Hollywood Cinderella story. No mention was made of *The Daring Miss Jones,* an extremely low-budget exploitation film she made sometime before *Not Wanted.* When the color feature was released in 1951, the distributors tried to exploit Sally Forrest's name and the brief scene she had in panties and brassiere. Betty White was also in it.

Sally and Keefe Brasselle were *The Young Lovers* (1949), an Ida Lupino production, which she also directed. Brasselle had been opposite her in *Not Wanted.* Ms. Lupino used them again as a team in *Never Fear* (1950). Their fourth appearance together was in *Ban-

nerline (1951), not one of Lupino's pictures.

When asked about *Keefe Brasselle's* unsavory reputation, Sally Forrest said: "I may have been the very first of the many who disliked him. We both had the same 'best side' and used to almost Indian wrestle to give the camera the angle we wanted."

In August, 1951, when Sally and Milo Frank were married, Ida Lupino was matron of honor. Not long afterward, Sally returned to M-G-M, the studio where she had started, as a well-established dramatic actress who was also an excellent dancer.

In 1951 Sally supported Boris Karloff in *The Strange Door* and Red Skelton in *Excuse My Dust.* The same year she made *The Strip,* notable as the film in which the song "A Kiss to Build a Dream On" was introduced.

When Milo Frank took an executive post with CBS Television, she moved with him to New York City. She worked in summer stock and took over the lead in *The Seven Year Itch* when Vanessa Brown left the Broadway show. The play's producer refused to let her out of the contract when Donald O'Connor asked for her to play opposite him in the screen version of *Call Me Madam.*

Sally returned to Hollywood to make *Code Two* (1953) with Elaine Stewart, and *Son of Sinbad* (1955) with Dale Robertson* and Lili St. Cyr.* Fritz Lang directed her and Ida Lupino in *While the City Sleeps* (1956). *Ride the High Iron* (1957) with Don Taylor* was her last feature.

Milo Frank is now a consultant to the international communications industry and some media figures. He and Sally make at least two annual visits to clients in the Orient and take frequent trips elsewhere. While she does not work directly with him, Mrs. Frank considers herself "very much a part of everything Milo does" and always accompanies him.

In 1960 Sally and George Chakiris headlined in an act at the Last Frontier in Las Vegas.

After an interval of twenty-four years, she was back on stage as the star of *No, No, Nanette* at San Diego's Starlight Theatre.

"I still miss it from time to time," she said in 1986. "I signed with an agent recently, so I'm available again, unless it interferes with being with my husband. But I know what competition there is for roles to be played by ladies my age. If I don't get a job, I won't be surprised or even disappointed. I think people considered me Mrs. Milo Frank, so I wasn't thought of when parts have come up over the years. But he happens to be a fascinating person to be married to. It's not as though I've led a boring life."

Sally and her husband, Milo Frank, live in the Beverly Hills mansion built in the twenties for director George Fitzmaurice. The childless couple have a Lhasa Apso and three cats.

In 1938 Ann Gillis played "Becky Thatcher" in David O. Selznick's production of The Adventures of Tom Sawyer *and the title role in* Little Orphan Annie.

Ann Gillis

The child star was born Alma Mabel Conner in Little Rock, Arkansas, on February 12, 1927. Her parents moved about a great deal in South America during her early childhood until her father died while they were in Chile.

Ann describes her mother as "the definitive Southern belle. Very pretty and with all the charm those women are known for." Shortly after being widowed she remarried and they settled for a while in New Rochelle, New York. But that husband, the fourth of her eventual seven, failed to give her the glamorous life she was determined to lead. It was the time of the child star and after Ann got some attention appearing in a local little theatre presentation and then guested on stage with Rudy Vallee, her mother decided to take her to Hollywood. Ann's stepfather agreed that they could have six months to give her a chance in the movies. On the train she caught the attention of movie columnist–broadcaster Jimmy Fidler. He gave her some publicity that was both encouraging and effective.

Mother and daughter arrived in the film capital on August 5, 1935. By the following January Ann had played a small part in *The Great Ziegfeld* (1936) and a featured role in *The Singing Cowboy* (1936).

"That was the beginning of my screen career and the end of my mother's marriage," recalls Ms. Gillis. "We were atypical of most of the mother-daughter teams in Hollywood, because with us it wasn't the money. Mother always married men who were quite capable of supporting us. Putting me in pictures was her way of lording it over her own family. But at the same time I was supposed to remember that while I acted in movies I was 'no movie actress.' You see, she looked down on picture people. In her mind we were Southern gentry gone slumming. So, of course, I was not allowed to socialize with any of the other kids."

Ann Gillis made thirty-seven feature films including *Off to the Races* (1937) with the late Shirley Deane, *Peck's Bad Boy at the Circus* (1938) with Tommy Kelly,* *Beau Geste* (1939), *Little Men* (1940) with Jimmy Lydon,[8] *Mr. Dynamite* (1941) with Irene Hervey,* and *Meet the Stewarts* (1942) with Francess Dee.[8] Ann was in *Janie* (1944) with Joyce Reynolds* and one of its sequels, *Janie Gets Married* (1946), with Joan Leslie[8] and Robert Hutton.[9] She supported Abbott and Costello in *In Society* (1944) and *The Time of Their Lives* (1946). She was with Deanna Durbin in *Nice*

Girl (1941) and was slated for another with the star, but, says Ann, "Deanna nixed me. When we worked together she gave me the silent treatment. Not a word did she say to me except in our scenes together. Who knows why? I guess she, like the rest of us, had her problems."

When given the right material Ann was a very fine actress. Her hysterics when she is lost in a cave in *The Adventures of Tom Sawyer* (1938) were considered too realistic by the parents of some of the children who identified and panicked in the theatres. Although it was a low-budget picture, *Big Town After Dark* (1947) gave her the meatiest role of her career as a heavy. It was her last Hollywood film.

"I always did exactly what I was told to do, whether it was my mother, a director, or a teacher," said Ann recently. "Then I became an adult, at least officially, and I called a halt to a life I'd not chosen and didn't enjoy." She says the part of growing up that she liked best was school. "I was a darn good student," she says. "In a classroom I excelled and was really getting high marks, which was quite different from 'Ann Gillis getting a big part or a good review.'"

She moved to New York City, married actor Richard Fraser and was seen on several live television shows. After they moved to London she did some television shows, including two episodes of *The Saint*. Her acting swan song was playing Gary Lockwood's mother in *2001: A Space Odyssey* (1968).

Ann divorced Richard Fraser in 1970, two years before he died. She is the mother of three sons.

The life she leads today, which she has described as "very quiet and selfish," includes an occasional exhibit of her oil paintings, bridge, reading, knitting, crocheting, and some writing.

She has no contact with anyone from her acting days and shows little interest in her films. She did, however, consent to appear when two of them were screened recently in the small Belgian community where she lives. "Afterwards they asked me to tell them all about Hollywood," she said in a 1984 interview. "Can you imagine trying to make anyone who hasn't gone through it understand what the Hollywood experience is like in your native tongue? Well, go try it in Flemish!"

Richard Lamparski

Ann Gillis in the apartment she shares with a Belgian man in Kontich, a suburb of Antwerp, Belgium.

Years before Marius Goring became known to U.S. moviegoers for such roles as the composer in The Red Shoes *(1948) and the sensitive German general in* So Little Time *(1953), he played romantic leads in West End plays. Emlyn Williams seriously considered him for the role of the young miner in the original production of* The Corn Is Green.

Marius Goring

The English character actor was born on the Isle of Wight. His birth date is May 23, 1912. Marius is the son of Charles Goring, the doctor and statistician who in his 1913 book, *The English Convict,* dispelled the widely held belief that there was a "criminal type." His work within English prisons had been dramatized in the late sixties on BBC-TV in the series *The Expert,* which starred his son. Marius was six years old when his father died.

Before he was old enough to go to school Mrs. Goring introduced her son to the theatre. She was a professional pianist and never discouraged the boy when he claimed he wanted to be an actor. "But," adds Goring, "she was adamant that I get a decent education, first. That only strengthened my resolve, because I never seriously considered another profession for an instant." After being paid his first salary, $1 a week, for appearing in a play at Christmastime, he considered himself professional. He was then fifteen years old.

While at Cambridge Goring acted in plays, as he did while studying at two German universities and at the Sorbonne. He returned to England as an apprentice at the Old Vic. When the actor scheduled to play "Macbeth" broke his ankle and the understudy, who was Alastair Sim, lost his voice, Marius acted the leading role for three performances at age twenty.

He was seen in *Rembrandt* (1936), *The Spy in Black* (1939), and *Pastor Hall* (1940) with Nova Pilbeam* before making his reputation with English movie audiences in *The Case of the Frightened Lady* (1940), which had been a hit for him on stage.

Despite the success he had achieved at a relatively early age and the high expectations his colleagues had for him, Marius Goring was devastated when impresario Binky Beaumont replaced him during tryouts of a play that starred Diana Wynyard. "I got the sack while we were playing in Manchester," he remembers. "I came very close to jumping out of my hotel window. When I got back to London Larry Olivier asked if I'd like to take over for him in a part he was tiring of. Like an idiot, I refused, thinking my career was over. To a serious young actor, one's career *is* one's life."

His proficiency in "high German" was put to good use as a member of British Intelligence during World War II. At the same time, he was playing Adolf Hitler on a popular radio series heard throughout the British Isles.

Even after the international acclaim he received for his work in the picture *The Red Shoes* (1948), Goring has continued to consider himself essentially a stage actor. The exceptionally versatile actor has since then appeared in *Take My Life* (1947) with Greta Gynt,* *Mr. Perrin and Mr. Traill* (1948) with David Farrar, *Pandora and the Flying Dutchman* (1951), *The Magic Box* (1951), *The Barefoot Contessa* (1954), *Son of Robin Hood* (1958) with Jack Lambert, *The Treasure of San Teresa* (1959) with Dawn Addams,* *Exodus* (1960), *First Love* (1970), *Holocaust* (1977), and *La Petite Fille en Velours Bleu* (1978).

In 1941 he married Lucie Mannheim, the German-born actress who was seen in *The Thirty-Nine Steps* (1935), *So Little Time* (1953), and *Bunny Lake Is Missing* (1965). Marius considers their appearances on stage together, playing in both English and German, to be the high points of his career. She died in 1976.

Goring met his present wife, producer Prudence FitzGerald, when she chose him from his photo in a casting directory for a part on a television show. They share a seventeenth-century house in London's Hampton Court that looks out onto a royal park.

He is seen freqently on British television and works almost constantly on the stage in England. *The Winslow Boy,* starring Marius Goring, was very well received throughout the tour of the United Kingdom in 1984. But his recent work is almost unknown in the United States, where he never became the name that he is in the United Kingdom. He played Germans so frequently and convincingly, many American moviegoers were confused as to his nationality. Since he has made only a few Broadway appearances and has never made a picture in Hollywood, he has not had the personal publicity a foreign character actor of his standing would receive in the American press.

Marius Goring was for a time a vice-president of British Equity and is still one of the union's trustees. He is also a member of London's venerable Garrick Club where this photograph was taken by the author.

Richard Lamparski

After leaving Rowan & Martin's Laugh-In, Teresa Graves made the movies Black Eye (1973) and Vampira (1974). In the latter she played the part of David Niven's wife.

Teresa Graves

The television star was born in Houston, Texas. She does not disclose either the day or year of her birth, lest she be the subject of an astrological chart. Her family moved to Los Angeles just before she entered first grade.

Teresa appeared in school plays and intended to take speech and drama in college. But just as she was graduating from high school, Mr. Graves, who worked as a security guard at a rehearsal hall, arranged an audition with the Young Americans.

She toured for one year as a Young American and then spent the next five with another musical group, The Doodletown Pipers.

"Everything came on a platter to me," Teresa said in 1986. "George Schlatter and I had met when I was singing with the Pipers and thought of me when he started to produce *Laugh-In.*"

Throughout 1969 and 1970, she was seen weekly on what was then the most popular TV show in North America.

From *Laugh-In,* Teresa went to Vietnam to entertain U.S. troops as part of Bob Hope's show. When she returned, Buddy Hackett used her as his opening act at appearances in Las Vegas and Lake Tahoe. At one of the engagements she drank a glass of water, as was her habit every night just before going on stage. A few minutes into her act, she collapsed and was rushed to a hospital. It was obvious that poison had been deliberately placed in her glass, but neither the motive nor the culprit was ever known.

In 1971, Teresa Graves and John Amos played a married couple on the comedy-variety show *The Funny Side,* which lasted from September through December, 1971, on NBC-TV.

Teresa became "Detective Christie Love," the starring role in *Get Christie Love!* after Cicely Tyson refused it. Ms. Tyson decided against doing the series when it conflicted with the opportunity to play the part in *A Woman Called Moses.*

It was six months from the time Teresa made the pilot as "Christie Love," hip supercop, to when it was sold to ABC-TV. During that time, she had begun a program of Bible study with her cousin, a Jehovah's Witness. In January, 1974, she was baptized in the faith. In September, the series began on the network.

David Wolper, who produced the first thirteen segments, agreed to her requirements. No smoking or swearing was allowed on the *Get Christie Love!* set. The L.A.P.D. policewoman she portrayed on that show was considerably different from the character in the pilot. She was an undercover officer who often bent the rules but never lied. She carried a gun but never killed anyone. Nothing the star considered to be excessively violent was ever shown, and the subject of spiritualism could not be part of any plot.

The producers who took over for the final thirteen episodes were less accommodating. Ms. Graves says they wanted "Christie" to be what she describes as "more ethnic" and become romantically involved with men. She argued that the Italian male supercop "Columbo," as played by macho Peter Falk, carried no gun, never raised his voice, and was never shown in private life.

"My average all through school was A," said Teresa. "I thought 'Christie' came over cool because she was intelligent. After a year, we agreed to disagree. I realized they had a job to do, and they saw that I had certain principles that I could not compromise."

She has since turned down a role in *Roots* because the character appeared in bed with a minister. Cicely Tyson played Gary Coleman's mother in a made-for-TV movie Teresa refused. Perhaps the most lucrative offer she has received was a print-advertising campaign for a cigarette, which she would not even consider doing.

Eleven years after her career came to a virtual standstill, Teresa Graves said: "I loved performing and still miss it sometimes. But we almost never go to a movie theatre and often have to turn off the TV because it is so vulgar, even violent. It is very, very rare I see any that I would want to be part of."

Since *Get Christie Love!* went off the air in mid-1975, its star has been spending a minimum of ninety hours every month canvassing

Michael Knowles

Teresa Graves and her husband, a bus driver, are members of the congregation of the Kingdom Hall of the Jehovah's Christian Witnesses in Inglewood, California.

Los Angeles residences to sell subscriptions to *Watch Tower* and *Awake,* publications of the Jehovah's Christian Witnesses and seeking conversions to her faith. Frequently, she finds herself talking with former fans who open their front door with the greeting, "Hey, aren't you that 'Christie Love'?"

In 1977, after nine months of chaperoned courtship, she married a fellow Witness. Adhering to their beliefs, the childless couple do not vote and will not salute the flag.

Her husband remembers having seen *Get Christie Love!* several times and thinking the character needed a "real straightening out."

Teresa Graves Reddick, the name she now uses, insists she and her husband are in total agreement about her role in their home: "I am completely submissive to my husband in any and all matters," says the actress whose image was that of the "in-charge" woman.

In a recent interview she said: "Now a smoking ban is considered safer and healthier for everyone. And a refusal to do open-mouth kissing is frequently written into contracts. It seems that what was so old-fashioned then is now just good sense. It has always been to my advantage practically, as well as spiritually, to adhere to the laws of the Lord, Jehovah."

Monte Hale and Adrian Booth were paired in six of the nineteen westerns he starred in for Republic Pictures. Their first, Home on the Range *(1946), was the first color western ever made at that studio and featured Robert Blake, who was then billed as "Bobby."*

Monte Hale

The screen's singing cowboy was born in San Angelo, Texas, on June 8, 1921. His original name was Monte Ely. He was still in grammar school when his parents separated and he was sent to live in rural Kansas with his uncle, a bootlegger.

His heroes as a boy were the cowboy stars Ken Maynard and Bob Steele[9] whose pictures he saw whenever he had the dime admission. It took Monte over a year to save $8.50, the price of his first guitar.

After an old man showed Monte the guitar's basic chords, he was playing and singing in a Galveston vaudeville theatre. Hale's break came when he was picked by Phil Isley, a local theatre owner, to be the opening act at the war bond rallies he was producing. Isley, the father of Jennifer Jones, was so impressed with audience reaction to Monte that he wired Herbert J. Yates, recommending that Hale be screen-tested.

Yates, the president of Republic Pictures, took him to the set of *The Big Bonanza* (1944) and ordered its director to film Monte singing "The Old Chisholm Trail." The song was used in the film and Hale was placed under contract.

Yates first used him in small parts in the serial *The Purple Monster Strikes* (1944) and several westerns. The studio had just lost Gene Autry,[8] its biggest star, and Monte was being groomed to replace him. Yakima Canutt, the early western star and well-known stunt coordinator, was charged with teaching Hale some techniques of horseback riding and how to fake a fistfight for the screen.

Monte Hale's first eight starring vehicles were in either the Magnacolor or Trucolor processes. The pictures had guest appearances by Roy Rogers, Dale Evans, Allan "Rocky" Lane, and the late Don "Red" Barry, but when they did not do as well as expected at the box office the filming was done in black and white. The late Don Miller stated in his book *Hollywood Corral* that the last eleven Monte Hale starrers were "better than the color ones, not so pretentious and helped by better scripting. Hale's moderately pleasing vocal efforts were similarly downplayed, and then dispensed with."

His screen image was that of an easy-going cowpoke. Perhaps too easygoing for Republic Pictures, whose westerns were usually full of fight scenes. "I never could quite get it across that I was really dangerous," Monte said recently.

He left Republic after *The Missourians* (1950) and toured for a while with rodeos and carnivals. He played Rock Hudson's lawyer in *Giant* (1956) and the town drunk in *The Chase* (1965). He has appeared on television's *Gunsmoke, Honey West,* and *Wells Fargo,* but insists he is now completely retired from acting.

Monte's early marriage to Peggy De Castro of the De Castro Sisters was very brief. He has been married since 1977 to his present wife, Joanne, a successful businesswoman. The man who claims his boyhood goal was "not much beyond plowing" is the co-owner of five residences throughout Southern California.

In his heyday Monte was thought to resemble both Ben Johnson and Johnny Mack Brown. Sloan Nibley, former Republic sce-

narist and husband of Linda Stirling, one of that studio's leading ladies, saw him recently and described his old friend as looking like "the Super Chief—coming right at you."

He has all nineteen of his films on 16mm film and videocassettes in his condominium across from the Santa Barbara Biltmore Hotel, but never watches them. "Cowboy stars are supposed to be brave, but I just don't have that kind of courage anymore," explains Monte.

Monte Hale with the saddle his close friend Gene Autry used in many of his westerns. The saddle and Monte's collection of police badges, believed to be the largest in the world, will be among the many memorabilia at the Gene Autry Western Museum. Under present plans it will be built in Griffith Park and will be open to the public by 1987.

Adrian Booth and her husband, actor David Brian, live in Sherman Oaks, California.

Margaret Hamilton never considered her portrayal of the "Wicked Witch of the West" to be among the best of her over seventy screen parts and she did not wish to be remembered for that role in The Wizard of Oz *(1939). She did enjoy playing the witch, however, and refused several lucrative offers to do witches on TV commercials, believing it would cheapen her original characterization.*

Margaret Hamilton

The character actress was born in Cleveland, Ohio, on December 9, 1902. Her father, an attorney, and her mother, a musician, were sympathetic to her early theatrical ambitions, but insisted she first learn to support herself in another profession.

Margaret very much liked teaching children and planned a career in education. After earning a degree she spent several years with a Cleveland kindergarten and the Rye Country Day School. She appeared on stage at the Cleveland Playhouse while running her own nursery school but would have continued to teach had she not won a part in a Broadway-bound play during summer vacation.

The play was *Another Language,* a critical and box office hit of 1932. Margaret was singled out for praise as an acerbic but loving wife. She was in the 1933 movie, also, but always felt the best work of her career was done in the stage version.

Again, in 1934, she played on Broadway in *The Farmer Takes a Wife* and then repeated her performance in the 1935 motion picture. Throughout her movie career Ms. Hamilton continued to appear in plays. Over a dozen of them were Broadway productions such as *Outrageous Fortune* (1943), *Goldilocks* (1958), *Utbu* (1966), *The Devil's Disciple* (1970), and *Come Summer* (1969). In the mid-seventies she toured for fifty-one weeks in *A Little Night Music* and in 1978 the Cleveland Playhouse opened its season with Margaret Hamilton in the thriller *Night Must Fall.*

She made frequent appearances on radio dramatizations and had running parts on the television soap operas *Secret Storm* and *As the World Turns.* She was a regular on the prime time series *Ethel and Albert* and *The Egg and I.*

Her film credits include: *Chatterbox* (1936) with Anne Shirley; *Mountain Justice* (1937) with Josephine Hutchinson; *Nothing Sacred* (1937); *The Adventures of Tom Sawyer* (1938); *A Slight Case of Murder* (1938) with

Jane Bryan;[8] *Mother Carey's Chickens* (1938) with Ruby Keeler;[8] *Breaking the Ice* (1938) with Bobby Breen* and Irene Dare; *Babes in Arms* (1939); *Play Girl* (1941) with James Ellison;[8] *Johnny Come Lately* (1943) with Marjorie Lord;* *Guest in the House* (1945); *Janie Gets Married* (1946) with Robert Hutton[9] and Joan Leslie; *Dishonored Lady* (1947) with Hedy Lamarr;* *The Sun Comes Up* (1949) with Claude Jarman, Jr.;[8] *Riding High* (1950) with Nancy Olson;* *Wabash Avenue* (1950); *Mad Wednesday* (1950); *Thirteen Ghosts* (1960) with Donald Woods;[9] *Rosie!* (1968) with the late Brian Aherne;[8] *Brewster McCloud* (1970); and *The Anderson Tapes* (1971).

Hers was the voice of a character in a long-running Tip-Top bread television commercial, and for Maxwell House Coffee she appeared as "Cora," a New England storekeeper.

In the later years of her life Margaret recorded books for the blind and worked with physically and emotionally disabled veterans interested in theatre and broadcasting. She was a registered Republican and a member of Friends of Animals.

Aside from her dual role of the schoolteacher "Miss Gulch" and "The Wicked Witch of the West" in *The Wizard of Oz* (1939), probably her best-known part was in *My Little Chickadee* (1940) as the priggish gossip.

Her only marriage was to a landscape architect. It ended in a 1938 divorce after seven years. When she died on May 16, 1985, she was survived by her son, a newspaper publisher, and three grandchildren.

Ms. Hamilton never lost her interest in and concern for children. She founded a kindergarten in the Presbyterian church she attended and served as president of the Beverly Hills Board of Education for several years. She was frequently recognized by children, some of whom were threatened by their memories of her as the green-skinned, cackling witch. She

Alan Hefner

Margaret Hamilton was being honored by the Philadelphia chapter of the Sons of the Desert, the Laurel & Hardy fan club, when this photograph was taken shortly before she died on May 16, 1985.

did not believe that those under seven years old should be exposed to *The Wizard of Oz* or any other film likely to frighten them. Although she enjoyed the children she acted with, Margaret advised anyone who asked her opinion not to allow youngsters to perform professionally.

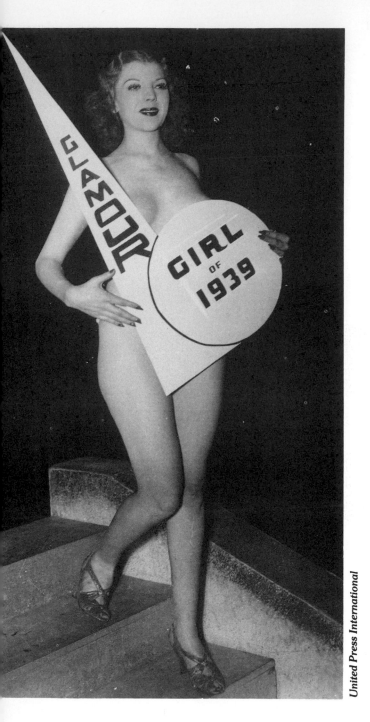

Burlesque queen Margie Hart holding the trylon and perisphere, symbols of the World's Fair of 1939. About the same time, Danny Kaye was performing a song with lyrics that referred to farmers who "used to utterly utter when Margie Hart churned her butter."

Margie Hart

"The poor man's Garbo" was the title her press agent gave her four decades ago. The burlesque queen of the thirties and forties, like the movie star, managed to get publicity for herself without disclosing her background and private life. On stage, however, Margie Hart was *too* revealing—even for burlesque.

Her contemporary Sherry Britton* claims Margie's revelations closed down all burlesque in New York City in 1941 and again the following year.

As Sherry remembers her: "There was a New York City detective absolutely crazy about Margie. Eventually, he left his wife and three kids because of her. Whenever headquarters was about to send plainclothesmen to check out the show he'd know about it and tip her off. He was very jealous and they had had a fight when the second bust came. Margie Hart is really responsible for closing down burlesque in New York. She wasn't a real beauty, but Margie always had gorgeous clothes and a real star presence which in burlesque is not easy to bring off. She was also much brighter than anyone of the rest of us, excepting Gypsy Rose Lee. When we were both at Minsky's our billing was equal and we alternated as the closing act. But she made a huge salary, while I was paid $75 a week. I can't remember what we fought about, but she called me a 'dirty Kike.' Then after she'd left the business I heard she owned a dress shop called *Shmatta*, which I thought was a Hell of a nerve. Margie Hart was

72

one who brought elegance to the business. I didn't like her then, but that was then. I understand she has married into the kind of life she always wanted and I'm very happy to hear it."

Ann Corio, another of the great strip-tease artists of the period, has called her "the most daring stripper of them all." In her book *This Was Burlesque* she wrote of Ms. Hart's paneled gown, which seemed to cover everything until, by her unique artistry, the panels parted. According to the author, "Margie didn't wear a G-string, most of the time."

For a brief time it seemed that Margie Hart might become much more than a star of the runway. She appeared in the title role of the Monogram film *Lure of the Islands* (1942). Bruno of Hollywood and George Hurrell both photographed her. Columnist Leonard Lyons claimed, probably accurately, that she made more annually than the combined salaries of Hedy Lamarr* and Rita Hayworth.* But a screen career never developed.

The major disappointment of her career was *Wine, Women and Song,* a box office and critical disaster of the 1942 Broadway season. It starred pixyish comedian Jimmy Savo and was declared "indecent" and closed down by judicial order. The publicity made Margie Hart's name even more of a draw on the burlesque wheels.

She was married to and divorced from television comedy writer Seaman Jacobs. Their son, who is studying at MIT, was the swimming champion of Beverly Hills High School and an honor student. The actress Morgan Hart is her daughter by a subsequent marriage to the owner of a chain of poker parlors.

Since 1982 Margie has been Mrs. John Ferraro, wife of the Los Angeles City Councilman. Ferraro, who was an All-American in 1944 and 1947, is a member of the National Football Hall of Fame. Still shy of interviews, the former stripper kept in the background during his 1985 run for the mayoralty.

Lee Salem

Margie Hart with her husband, Los Angeles City Councilman John Ferraro, during his unsuccessful campaign in 1985 to unseat Tom Bradley as mayor of Los Angeles.

A bust of the "Incomparable Hildegarde," along with her trademarks, a pair of opera gloves and a silk rose, are on permanent display at the Smithsonian Institution. Included in the exhibit, which is between Jimmy Durante's hat and Frank Sinatra's tie, is the sheet music for some of the songs closely associated with her: "Darling, Je Vous Aime Beaucoup," "The Last Time I Saw Paris," and "I'll be Seeing You."

Hildegarde

The American chanteuse was born Hildegard Loretta Sell on February 2, 1906, in Adell, Wisconsin. Both of her German immigrant parents were musical and encouraged her interests. But the plans for a career, which were entirely hers, began as she daydreamed about a glamorous life while writing her first name over and over. It seemed to her hopelessly ordinary until the "e" at the end evolved. The first of her fantasies came to realization a few years later when her family moved to Milwaukee.

While clerking in the notions department of Gimbels in downtown Milwaukee, she studied classical composition. However, once she saw Gerry and Her Baby Grands on stage, Hildegarde decided to play popular music and joined the act.

The vaudevillian and show-business historian Joe Laurie, Jr., heard her demonstrating songs in Irving Berlin's office and brought her to the attention of Gus Edwards. It was impresario Edwards who changed her billing to simply "Hildegarde" when he cast her in *Stars on Parade*. She toured in the revue playing in a skit opposite Eddie Garr, father of Teri Garr.

It was in Europe that Hildegarde developed the style and following that made her an international star. It was also where she came under the auspices of Anna Sosenko,* a personal manager of legendary reputation within the theatrical profession. "Anna Sosenko Presents . . ." preceded her billing "The Incomparable Hildegarde" for the many years they were together. Ms. Sosenko saw to it that her client was slickly packaged, well publicized, and highly priced. She also wrote "Darling, Je Vous Aime Beaucoup," the singer's signature song and her biggest hit.

Her return to the United States in 1939 was preceded by stories in the press about the American who had been accepted abroad by such Continental luminaries as Noel Coward and Sweden's Gustavus V. The cover story in *Life* magazine coincided with a weekly featured spot on the network radio show *Ninety-Nine Men and a Girl*. She guested on all the top variety programs and soon had her own series, *The Raleigh Room*. Her sponsor, Raleigh Cigarettes, promoted its product and star in a long-running billboard and print advertising campaign that made her upswept frizzed hairdo and long gloves famous.

She became even more widely known because of the Hildegarde jokes that were part of the routines of many comedians of the time. Her clothes got her named as one of the country's "Best Dressed" three times. Milliners twice chose her as "Best Hatted." She was sculpted in bronze by Gwen Lux, painted by William Gropper, caricatured by Xavier Cugat,* and photographed by Karsh.

Sosenko always presented her client to the press and public as an American who had made good abroad. Her famous billing "The Dear Who Made Milwaukee Famous," which was given to her by Seaman Jacobs, emphasized to audiences that, despite the chic gowns and the French lyrics, she was one of them. The Middle American, then referred to in the nitery business as the "Butter and Egg Man," was made comfortable by her jokes about her Midwest background. Their wives were taken by her chic and the romanticism of her songs. For many Americans, Hildegarde was their first experience in a nightclub. To their astonished delight, she never talked down to them. It made them feel sophisticated, too.

She frequently fluttered the silk-and-lace handkerchief with which she held a microphone. Her other prop was a bouquet of long-stemmed roses, which she distributed to women in the audience. Hildegarde still holds the record for the longest running engagements at the famed Persian Room of New York's Plaza Hotel.

A well-remembered feature of her act during World War II, whether she was performing in a nightclub or at a military installation, was to ask the officers present to stand and salute the enlisted men in the audience.

Her admirer Eleanor Roosevelt once read a proclamation declaring Hildegarde "The First Lady of the Supper Clubs." Her place at the top of the profession was sustained until the mid-sixties when the famous rooms where she headlined either closed or underwent a drastic change in policy.

Jerry Siegan

"The Dear Who Made Milwaukee Famous" in her East Side Manhattan apartment just before her eightieth birthday.

Hildegarde's recordings, some of which are still in print, prove that her legend was built on more than effervescence, high style, and hype. Her musicianship is rated very highly among professionals. Her precise reading of song lyrics has won her many admirers among songwriters, including Stephen Sondheim and Marvin Hamlisch. She introduced "All of a Sudden My Heart Sings" and "The Last Time I Saw Paris." Her poignant rendition of the latter is, for many, the definitive version.

Throughout her seventies, Hildegarde continued to write, lecture, and perform. Her health and vitality she attributes to natural foods and vitamins, a regimen she took up years ago when she stopped smoking (her brands were Spuds or Kools—not Raleighs). She celebrated her eightieth birthday by giving a concert at Carnegie Hall.

Rose Hobart was frequently considered for the same screen roles as Gale Sondergaard. Both of the striking, gifted character actresses were blacklisted.

Rose Hobart

The actress, whose career was ended by the blacklist, was born on May 1, 1906, in New York City. Her father was Paul Kéfer, a well-known cellist of the time. Her mother sang in opera under the name of Marguerite Hobart. Although both parents attempted to interest her in a musical career, Rose decided to act.

She was fourteen when she debuted with a stock company and by the following year she was playing the lead in *Liliom* opposite Joseph Schildkraut. Broadway audiences first saw her in *Lullaby* (1923).

Rose Hobart had a reputation and a follow-ing on Broadway when she first came to Hollywood in 1930. She had originated the leading female role in *Death Takes a Holiday* (1929) but left the hit play to accept an offer from Fox Films to do *Liliom* (1931) on the screen. It was a big-budget picture and would most likely have made her a star. But its central character was played by Charles Farrell, whose performance was so poor it spoiled the film and ruined his chance for remaining the star in talkies that he had been in silents.

Her other important film role at this time was as Fredric March's fiancée in *Dr. Jekyll and Mr. Hyde* (1932). She became a friend of March and his wife Florence Eldridge then and remained close until his death.

Rose was signed by Universal Pictures. Although she was cast opposite Conrad Nagel, Douglas Fairbanks, Jr., and Ben Lyon, [8] well-established stars in movies, she thought the films she was making were of poor quality. When she was cast in *East of Borneo* (1931) her disillusionment was complete. She deliberately caused delays in the filming and made complaints to the front office until her contract was dissolved. Had she remained with that studio Rose would probably have done *Back Street*. James Whale, its director, wanted her. Instead, Irene Dunne [8] made the picture, which was one of her early hits.

Rose returned to Broadway where she played in *I Loved You Wednesday* (1932), *Girls in Uniform* (1933), *With All My Heart* (1936), and *Siege* (1939). Although she was well received in all of her stage efforts, none of the plays were successful enough to make her a star.

"I had no trouble finding roles in the theatre," she now admits, "but the ones that would have put me over all seemed to be going to actresses who had become marquee names through movies. Had I stuck it out just a while longer I think I would have been one of them."

After Rose returned to the film capital in

1939 she free-lanced, mostly as a character actress. She did have the second lead opposite John Loder in *The Brighton Strangler* (1945), but the only other occasions when she was top-billed were in B pictures such as *I'll Sell My Life* (1941) and *Prison Girls* (1940).

She supported Joan Crawford in *Susan and God* (1941), and Humphrey Bogart and Charles Drake* in *Conflict* (1945), Bob Hope in *Nothing But the Truth* (1940), and Eleanor Powell in *Lady Be Good* (1941). Some of her other credits during this period were *Ziegfeld Girl* (1941), *Dr. Gillespie's New Assistant* (1942), *Swingshift Maisie* (1943), *Claudia and David* (1946), *The Farmer's Daughter* (1947), *Song of the Open Road* (1944), and *Cass Timberlane* (1948).

She was particularly effective as a heavy and is philosophical about the fact that most fans know her for the menacing characters she played in *The Soul of a Monster* (1944), *Bride of Vengeance* (1949) with John Lund,* *The Cat Creeps* (1946) with Lois Collier, and *Singapore Woman* (1941). In the serial *Adventures of Smilin' Jack* (1943), she was Nazi agent "Fraülein Von Teufel" who killed people with poison needles that she shot from a fountain pen.

When she first came to Hollywood Rose Hobart participated in the formation of the Screen Actors Guild. She was a member of the Actor's Lab troupe that entertained United States troops in the Aleutian Islands during World War II. That early union activity and association with a group that by the early fifties had been cited as subversive got her name on the blacklist. She described her testimony before the House Committee on Un-American Activities as "not very cooperative."

The part of a maid on the television series *Peyton Place* and two appearances on *Cannon* are the only acting she has done since 1949, the year of her last motion picture.

Recently, she talked about her experience: "Fortunately I had been a patient of David Seabury* for a number of years before the blacklisting. What I learned about myself during our sessions was of great help. Then when it happened I was in the throes of motherhood. At age forty-two I had my first and only child. The baby and my marriage took up much of my time. It was awful, of course—losing a career and having so many people turn against you. But for many others it was much, much worse."

Rose's husband, architect Barton H. Bosworth, is now deceased. She edits and writes for *The Haven News,* the in-house organ of the Motion Picture Country House and Hospital where she has resided since 1982.

According to Rose Hobart being blacklisted had and continues to have ramifications: "I was not allowed to serve on the board of the PTA when my son was in grammar school. And just the other day someone here took me aside as I left the dining room to tell me that it made no difference to her that I had been on the blacklist. It had never occurred to me that it had until she mentioned it."

Rose Hobart is a Science of Mind practitioner. She lives at the Motion Picture and Television Country House in Woodland Hills, California.

Bobby Downey

Eddie Hodges was thirteen years old when he starred on his own sixty-minute television special, The Secret World of Eddie Hodges *in 1960. He had become so popular in his home state that the governor of Mississippi proclaimed an "Eddie Hodges Day."*

Eddie Hodges

The child star of the sixties was born on March 5, 1947, in Hattiesburg, Mississippi.

Eddie Hodges is disinclined to discuss his early years or his career. Recently he summed up the latter as a "negative experience."

According to his early publicity he made his debut singing "Jesus Loves Me" on a local radio program when he was less than two years old. His father, who was his manager, told the press he had brought his son to New York City after so many people had insisted Eddie was an exceptional child.

The red-haired boy was first seen on Jackie Gleason's TV show doing an imitation of Johnnie Ray. He was not yet in grammar school.

When he was eight years old Eddie was pitted against Patty Duke on the TV quiz show *Name That Tune*. He and his partner, Marine Corps Major John Glenn, shared $32,000 in prize money.

In December, 1957, *The Music Man* opened on Broadway with Eddie in a featured role. "Gary, Indiana," one of the musical's most popular songs, was his big number. By the time the award-winning show was made into a motion picture he had outgrown the part.

His movie debut was in *A Hole In the Head* (1959) in which he had a duet with Frank Sinatra. The song they introduced, "High Hopes," won the Academy Award as the Best Song of 1959.

Of his single recordings the only one to really qualify as a hit was "Girls, Girls, Girls (Are Made to Love)," which was released in 1962. "I'm Gonna Knock on Your Door" was on the *Billboard* magazine's "Hot 100 Chart" in 1961 and "If I Cried (Would You Come Back to Me?)" received a lot of air-play on West Coast radio.

He supported Henry Fonda in *Critic's Choice* (1960) on Broadway and played his son in the motion picture *Advise and Consent* (1962).

With his wholesome, middle-American looks

and image he seemed perfectly cast in the title role of *The Adventures of Huckleberry Finn* (1960). He had a prominent part in *Summer Magic* (1963) and *The Happiest Millionaire* (1967), both big-budget productions of the Disney studios.

His next film, *C'mon, Let's Live a Little* (1967), starred Bobby Vee* and was aimed for the youth market. Hodges appeared to be making a smooth transition from young boy roles. It was his last time on the screen.

Eddie Hodges had been having problems with drugs and alcohol for some time when he realized he could no longer perform. Looking back, he says that Elvis Presley had every reason to have him fired when they made *Live a Little, Love a Little* (1968) together. His recollection is that he was "totally stoned every day on that set."

In a rare interview he stated: "Since I was a very little kid I had wanted to be a movie star. At least, that's what I was always told. Then about 1961 I began to feel confused. Boys in their mid-teens have enough pressure from the identity crisis they go through, but as an actor, I had two images to worry about. My career had changed life in our home and our family began to come apart."

In 1969 Hodges was drafted, but in less than a year he was discharged. He says he was in agreement with his commanding officers, that he was "unable to adjust to life in the U.S. Army."

He has lived in Mississippi since 1974 when he entered a drug rehabilitation program. While recovering from his years of chemical abuse he earned an M.A. degree from the University of Southern Mississippi.

Eddie has been married three times and divorced twice. He is the father of twins, a boy and a girl, by his second wife. He and the present Mrs. Hodges live with her three sons by a previous marriage in Long Beach, Mississippi.

He plays the guitar and sings, but only for his

Elaine Hill

In 1985 Eddie Hodges came to Hollywood for the first time in over fifteen years to be part of a tribute to Iggie Wolfington. They were both in the original Broadway cast of **The Music Man** *in 1957.*

family. He describes his voice today as being "a whole lot different."

The former star works in Gulfport, Mississippi, at the C.P.C. Sand Hill Hospital. He is the program coordinator of drug treatment for adolescents.

Of his life today he says: "I'm challenged by what I do and it is very rewarding at times. I know where these kids are coming from, because I'm just an older version of them. I'm a junkie and a drunk, too, but I'm arrested. And with the grace of God, tomorrow too, I will be sober and drug free. Just like them, I go a day at a time."

79

The late Mrs. Holt and her son, David, in 1934, two years after they came to Hollywood from Florida. David says that when Freddie Bartholomew replaced him in the title role of **David Copperfield**, *it "pretty near broke my mother's heart, but it didn't mean shit to me."*

David Holt

The boy who almost became the screen's "David Copperfield" was born on August 14, 1927, in Jacksonville, Florida. When she was a girl his mother had longed for an acting career, but her parents strongly disapproved of the theatre as being "sinful." Thwarted, she vowed to make her son a star.

David was raised with the story that from the time he was two years old he went into a dance whenever music was played on the radio. But in an early interview Mrs. Holt told how her boy "from the day he was weaned" was made to understand that "his career was priority number one and that not a moment was to be wasted on other things." When he was three she took him to a local dancing teacher who

was instructed to "get him ready to go on the stage."

David took to dancing, especially tap, and developed quite a reputation in his hometown. One of his most enthusiastic fans was a local bookie who was acquainted with Will Rogers. When the actor-humorist, who was at the time one of the most popular men in the United States, came to town David danced for him. Rogers praised him highly and told the Holts that if they would bring their son to Hollywood he, personally, would see to it that he got a screen test.

"It was the worst part of the Depression," David said in 1985. "And my dad had a really good job with Ford Motor Company. But he quit and we came to California in a trailer and headed right for the Fox studios. That's where Will Rogers was. But he wouldn't even see us. Didn't seem to remember anything about us. Well, as my dad used to say, 'If I ever run into Will Rogers again he won't ever be able to say he never met a man he didn't like.'"

Mr. Holt managed to work off and on for $4 a day on a WPA project. Between jobs the family had to seek handouts at Aimee Semple McPherson's church.

Harold Lloyd saw David in a play and gave him a part in his movie *The Cat's Paw* (1934) with Una Merkel, but the Holts were four months behind in rent when Dick Moore became ill and their son got the part in *You Belong to Me* (1934) and a contract with Paramount Pictures.

Among his screen credits are: *Age of Indiscretion* (1935) as the son of Paul Lukas and Helen Vinson;[9] *The Last Days of Pompeii* (1935); *Military Academy* (1940) with Tommy Kelly;* *The Pride of the Yankees* (1942); *The Human Comedy* (1943) with Butch Jenkins;* *The Cheaters* (1945); and *The Courage of Lassie* (1946) with Elizabeth Taylor. In both *What's Cookin'?* (1942) and *Top Man* (1943), Universal low-budget musicals, David was one of the singing group "Jivin' Jacks and Jills."

The picture that was thought would really bring him to prominence was *David Copperfield* and his studio loaned him to David O. Selznick to play the title role. But the producer had originally wanted Freddie Bartholomew* for the role. When he became available, even though David had been on the film with W. C. Fields for two weeks, he was replaced.

He liked all the children he worked with except Jackie Searl.* "The obnoxious brat he played was exactly the kid he was," David insists. "A real pain in the ass."

Of the girls he liked Edith Fellows[8] and Sybil Jason[8] as friends. His big crush was Ann Gillis who was his date in 1944 when their car was struck by another, throwing Ann through the windshield. His recollection in 1985 was that Ann Gillis was "the prettiest girl in Hollywood in those days and with a pair of tits that wouldn't quit."

Jane Powell was the girl he came very close to marrying. Told that she now shares a house with Dickie Moore, Holt said: "He's just getting even with me for *You Belong to Me.*"

He says that from the first day in public school, "My life was hell. My mother made me wear short pants—white short pants. Every boy in that school wanted to punch out the 'movie star,' 'cry-baby,' 'sissy,' and most of them tried. Fortunately, I had been scheduled to do a picture with Max Baer that was canceled when he lost the championship. But we'd gotten friendly and he taught me to box— really box. I whipped more asses at that school!"

When he was not required on the set Holt spent every free moment with songwriters. He began composing when he was fourteen. With Bob Wells he wrote material Doris Day recorded. Sammy Cahn was his partner on a song that Dean Martin performed. His biggest success was "Mobile," written with Wells. In the early days of rock and roll he put out sev-

Bobby Downey

David Holt is divorced. He shares a condominium in Orange County, California, with a cairn terrier. The picture in the background is one of several that he painted.

eral records as "Davy Holt and the Hub Caps."

Since 1962 he has been in the real estate business. In early 1985 he sold his interest in a housing development and retired to do "whatever I pleased for the rest of my life."

One of the first things he did was to get back into jazz. He has just recorded an album to be entitled *The Jack Montrose—Pete Jolly Quartette Play David Holt.*

In late 1985 Holt spoke of what had happened: "Because I could dance my folks went through hell so I could be in movies. But I didn't dance in pictures. I cried! At one point I had polio, which I believe was a result of the stress I felt in the studios. My parents broke up. My father resented that I was paid so much more than he was. When it was all over there was no money. At least they never gave me a penny of it. Then it was my turn to be resentful. Right before he died I told my dad I wished we'd stayed in Florida and remained normal people. He agreed."

81

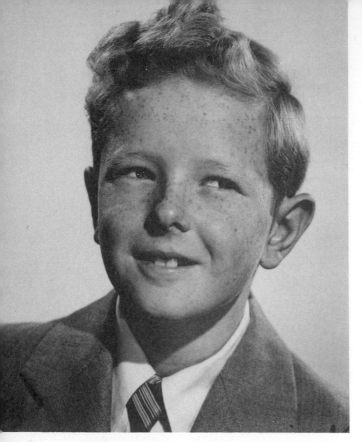

Jimmy Hunt is best remembered for his role in Invaders from Mars *(1953), his last movie until he played a small part in the 1986 remake.*

Jimmy Hunt

The child actor of movies was born on December 4, 1939, in Los Angeles. His full name is James Walter Hunt.

Jimmy and his younger sister were brought up in Culver City near the M-G-M studios. His parents, however, had never considered an acting career for either child. When their son came home from school and told them he had been picked from his first grade class to test for a movie role they were dumbfounded. A talent scout had chosen Jimmy because of his freckles and grin to portray Van Johnson as a boy in *High Barbaree* (1947).

"Dad was a tool and die maker," says Jimmy. "We were strictly lower middle class people. Actually, that's the way we stayed. As long as they were satisfied that I was getting a good education the acting was all right. My sister and I are still very close, so there was no problem with jealousy."

Placed under contract, the six-year-old attended M-G-M's "Little Red Schoolhouse" along with Roddy McDowall and Elizabeth Taylor, who used to hold him in her lap. Child actors seemed to Jimmy "just like other kids." He enjoyed going to the movies with Margaret O'Brien,* but his first real crush was on Gigi Perreau.*

He supported such stars as Claudette Colbert, Barbara Stanwyck, Ronald Reagan, Bing Crosby, and Bob Hope. Jimmy liked all of them, but his special favorites were Joel McCrea,[8] Fred MacMurray, and Glenn Ford—in that order.

Jimmy Hunt appeared in *The Mating of Millie* (1948) with Willard Parker,* *The Sainted Sisters* (1948) with Veronica Lake[8] and Joan Caulfield,* *Sorry, Wrong Number* (1948) with Leif Erickson, *Pitfall* (1948) with Ann Doran[8] and Lizabeth Scott,* *Rock Island Trail* (1950) with Adele Mara,* *The Capture* (1950) with Duncan Renaldo,[8] *Shadow on the Hill* (1950) with Barbara Billingsley,[8] *Saddle Tramp* (1950) with Wanda Hendrix,[8] *Cheaper by the Dozen* (1950) with Robert Arthur,* *Katie Did It* (1951) with Mark Stevens, *Belles on Their Toes* (1952) with Debra Paget,* and *Lone Hand* (1953) with Charles Drake.*

The only time Hunt has encountered anyone from his acting days is when he accidentally met his onetime stand-in, a midget. He is never the first to mention his movie career, but is pleased when people know him from his pictures. As the sales manager for an industrial tools and supplies firm he finds the recognition often helpful in making conversation with clients.

He is pleased to hear from fans, who usually want to know about his experiences when making the cult film *Invaders from Mars* (1953).

"It's interesting that that film, probably the lowest-budget feature I ever made, is the one that still attracts people. It's also the one that made me conclude that I didn't want to continue acting. As a little kid all acting seemed to be was memorizing lines. The older I got the more serious I became about getting a scene right on the first take. Adult actors all made jokes when they blew their lines. Kids just feel dumb when it was their fault. So acting became harder for me all the time. *Invaders from Mars* was real work. I told my folks I wanted to quit. It was the only time we ever quarreled. They wanted to make sure I realized the financial consequences. Once they saw how strongly I felt they accepted it and we never looked back."

The money his parents saved for him was used to bring his bride back from Germany, where they met during his stint in the United States Army, and for the down payment on their first home.

The Hunts converted to Mormonism several years ago. Jim is in the bishopric of his local congregation and the eldest of their two sons is doing missionary work in Korea. A Jimmy Hunt film festival was held at his church as a fund-raiser.

Jim Hunt says his worst experience as a child actor was when he broke his arm while making *Weekend with Father* (1952). After the limb was set it was taped to his side and he continued on the film. "No one made me finish the picture that way," he said recently. "I wanted to. I considered myself a professional. In other words, I never had any really bad times as a boy actor. But I wanted to excel in sports, and auditions and shooting schedules interfered constantly. Unlike the other boys, I'd show up for an interview without any photo composite or list of credits. I think I got several parts just because I came over as what I always remained—just a kid."

There were offers of screen parts throughout his teen years but he turned all of them down. The only time he had even a tinge of regret was when he didn't have the money to buy the Corvette he wanted so much—"But not enough to go back into pictures," he quickly adds.

Jim Hunt feels he was very lucky in his early years because he does not feel scarred in any way and is glad he made the movies he did. He would not, however, allow his children to act until they were out of college.

Jim Hunt's last two films were both entitled *Invaders from Mars*. Over twenty years after he made the original he played the local sheriff in the remake that was released in 1986.

Morgan Neiman

Jim Hunt in his Simi Valley, California, home with his stepdaughter, Courtney.

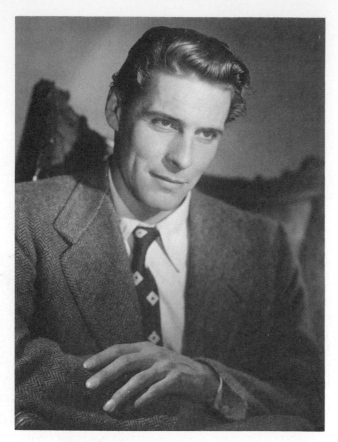

Breaking the Sound Barrier *(1952) is the film for which John Justin is usually recognized. In his other big picture,* **The Thief of Bagdad** *(1940), he was in costume.*

John Justin

The British leading man was born in London on November 24, 1917, of an English mother and an Argentinian father. His original name was Juan Ledesma.

He lived in the Argentine until he was taken back to England in 1927 and placed in a public school. He made his decision to act after appearing in his first school play. At age sixteen

John joined the Liverpool Repertory Company, where he received his basic training.

"Then," recalls the actor, "there loomed very large in my young life a somewhat older woman. There had been several such ladies but this one, unfortunately, was married. There was a great scene in which her husband played a prominent role. The upshot was that I left immediately for Argentina. It's called 'getting out of town.' I wanted to go to America but couldn't get a visa, so I worked for a while on my family's ranch and sang for a time in a Buenos Aires nightclub. When I returned to England I managed to get a scholarship to the Royal Academy of Dramatic Art from which I fled after two terms, both of which were quite awful. Then I was with John Gielgud for a season of Shakespeare, which did me a great deal of good."

After Justin made his West End debut in *Dear Octopus* (1938), he was asked by several studios to make still and screen tests. "Somehow," he insists, "there always was a request to remove my shirt. Even when being tested as a possible leading man to Judy Garland and then to Deanna Durbin they wanted me stripped to the waist. Then, for once, the disrobing made some sense. The other fellow, Sabu, didn't have a shirt on either."

The picture with Sabu was *The Thief of Bagdad.* It has played continually around the world since it was made in 1940. Its producer, Alexander Korda, pacted the actor.

In *The Gentle Sex* (1943), he was directed by Leslie Howard. He supported Edward G. Robinson in *Journey Together* (1945). Among his other screen appearances were: *The Angel with a Trumpet* (1949) with Wilfred Hyde-White; * *Hot Ice* (1953); *Melba* (1953) with Patrice Munsel; * *Crest of the Wave* (1954) with Jeff Richards; *The Man Who Loved Redheads* (1955) with Moira Shearer; * and *Safari* (1956) with Victor Mature. *

He was costarred in *Call of the Blood*

(1947), *The Techman Mystery* (1955), *The Spider's Web* (1960), and *The Village* (1953).

Justin's agreement with Korda expired in 1949, but even during the years he was under contract he appeared in plays. The stage was and is his prime interest, but in a 1984 interview he admitted to having lost much of the enthusiasm he once had for acting. He was at the Old Vic for their season of 1959–60. He played "Captain Hook" to Margaret Lockwood's* "Peter Pan" in 1949–50 and repeated the role opposite the late Sarah Churchill during the 1958–59 season, again in the West End.

Signed to a one-film-per-year contract with Twentieth Century–Fox, John lived in Hollywood only while making *King of the Khyber Rifles* (1953), *Untamed* (1955), and *Island in the Sun* (1957). "It was not my sort of place" is his only comment.

He played characters in *Savage Messiah* (1972), *Lisztomania* (1975), *Valentino* (1977), and *The Big Sleep* (1979), he insists, "for the money alone."

He spent part of World War II as a test pilot and flight instructor in the Royal Air Force.

John was in *The Mousetrap* early in its record-breaking West End run. During the year he spent playing the role he and a colleague developed a new system of setting women's hair. They spent a great deal of time and effort in an attempt to market the process. There was commercial interest in it and he received publicity pertaining to it, but the idea never came to fruition.

He is pleased by the continuing popularity of *The Thief of Bagdad,* which he describes as "very good for what it is." He feels *Breaking the Sound Barrier* (1952) and *The Village* (1954) were his best movies. The former was a box office and critical hit worldwide. The latter was an intelligent and moving film that was made in Switzerland. In the United States it played only in art houses.

Explaining his career of late, he said: "I'm simply not interested in doing not-very-good things, or not-very-well-done things. If I'm offered something that I think is first-rate I take it, but really good things just don't come around that frequently. Any actor will tell you that if he's honest. I did a French play a few years ago at the Edinburgh Festival. It was the last thing that I could consider nearly really good. I act on radio because I enjoy the freedom of the medium. The films, I confess, for a long, long time are few and far between and then only for the money."

Adam Oliver Robertson

John Justin shares a flat in the Swiss Cottage area of London with his fourth wife, one of his three daughters, and his dog.

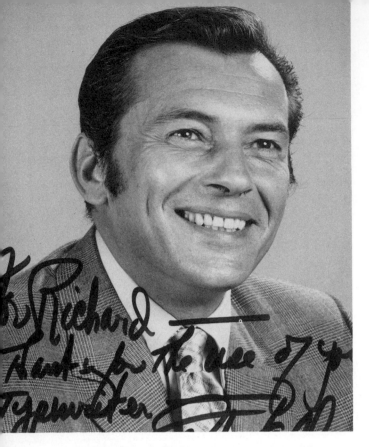

The general public recognizes Jack Kelly for his role on Maverick, *the western TV series that ran on ABC from 1957 to 1962. And his appearances in science-fiction features have made him known to enthusiasts of both genres.*

Jack Kelly

The costar of *Maverick* was born in Astoria, Long Island, New York, on September 16, 1927. His father was a ticket broker and his mother was a leading model with the John Robert Powers agency.

Jack Kelly began his career by posing as an Ivory Soap baby when he was two weeks old. Throughout his boyhood he worked as a model, appeared on radio programs, and acted in plays.

His Broadway debut was in *The Street Singer* (1929). When he giggled with another boy during Ethel Barrymore's soliloquy she had him fired from the cast of *The Ghost of Yankee Doodle* (1937) and barred from auditioning for her next play. He played in *The School House on the Lot* (1938), a play about children who act in movies, before moving with his family to Hollywood.

The Kellys went west after his older sister, Nancy Kelly,* had made a strong impression on Broadway in *Susan and God*. She was brought to the film capital to play Tyrone Power's wife in *Jesse James* (1939). Jack made brief appearances in *Young Mr. Lincoln* (1939) and *The Story of Alexander Graham Bell* (1939), and was enrolled in public school.

After serving as a weather observer in the United States Air Force during World War II he briefly attended UCLA. "Somewhere along the line," Kelly says, "the ambition I thought I had to become an attorney ran adrift."

He hitched a ride back to New York City, determined to earn a living as an actor, but vowing not to accept any help from his sister. The day he arrived Jack got a job flipping the announcement cards on Fred Waring's television show.

Agent Henry Wilson arranged for the young actor to return to Hollywood to test for *Saturday's Hero,* a part that was played by John Derek. Instead he became one of the Universal contract players the fanzines used to refer to as "young hopefuls." Rock Hudson, Hugh O'Brian, and Tony Curtis were some of the others in that group.

In 1955 he played in *Kings Row,* a television show adapted from the 1941 feature film. Kelly had the part that Bob Cummings[9] played in the original. He was seen often in television plays opposite such stars as Loretta Young[8] and Jane Wyman.

Jack erroneously believes he is remembered solely for the part of James Garner's younger brother on *Maverick,* the show that ran on ABC-TV during the late fifties and early sixties. The series was a huge success in North America and parts of Europe, but a few of his movies are also well known.

The Night Holds Terror (1955) is considered an exceptionally fine low-budget film. *Forbidden Planet* (1956) introduced "Robby the Robot," a cinematic device that made subsequent screen appearances and developed a following of its own. *Cult of the Cobra* (1955) with Faith Domergue* and *She-Devil* (1957) with the late Mari Blanchard are held in high esteem by fans of low-camp.

Some of his other screen credits are: *Where Danger Lives* (1951); *The Redhead from Wyoming* (1953); *Black Tuesday* (1954) with Jean Parker;* *To Hell and Back* (1955) with Gregg Palmer,* Charles Drake,* and Susan Kohner;* *Julie* (1956) with Doris Day; *FBI Code 98* (1964); and *Love and Kisses* (1965) with Rick and David Nelson.*

Early in his adult career he was married to May Wynn, a former Copa girl who became a screen actress.

In 1969 he married a nonprofessional who moved with him to New York City where they lived for the three years he hosted the daytime NBC-TV game show *The Sale of the Century.* When it left the air the couple settled in Huntington Beach, California.

He played a police captain in *Get Christie Love!,* the 1974–75 television series that starred Teresa Graves.

Jack was a volunteer in the presidential campaigns of Adlai Stevenson and John F. Kennedy. After working in a few local campaigns he ran for city councilman and won the first of two four-year terms in 1980. Since then Mrs. Kelly has managed their real estate investments in the area.

He is still in touch by phone with Jim Garner and Rory Calhoun. Although they are on good terms, he has not seen his sister in some time.

He considers himself a Roman Catholic, but a "fallen-away" one. His teenage daughter, Nicole, has never been baptized.

In late 1985 he summed up his attitude toward his career: "Within my limitations I was fine, but at my age I just cannot be a journeyman actor. I did ten *Hardy Boys* episodes, but I am not about to even consider anything short of a running part. I simply cannot afford to. Not only do my tenants not go on hiatus, they never refer to my ratings or middle-age spread."

Ron Alexander

When Jack Kelly's second four-year term as city councilman of Huntington Beach expires in 1988 he is barred by law from running again. The position pays $176.00 a month.

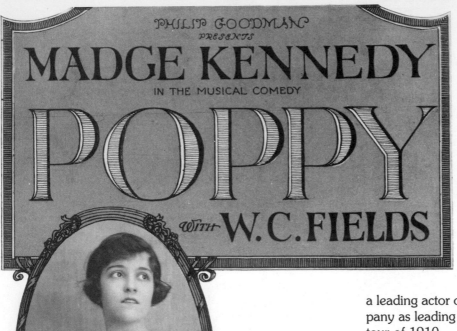

PHILIP GOODMAN
PRESENTS

MADGE KENNEDY
IN THE MUSICAL COMEDY
POPPY
WITH W.C.FIELDS

Madge Kennedy remembers W. C. Fields, an established artist of pantomime and juggling, as being very insecure in his first real acting role in Poppy. The Fields personality first emerged in that Broadway production of 1923. When the comedian made the movie version in 1936, his part was considerably larger and he was starred.

Madge Kennedy

The star of Broadway and silent films was born in Chicago, Illinois, on April 19, 1891. In 1892, her family moved to Cucamonga, California, and eventually to Riverside, California.

She drew and painted from a very early age and in 1906 went to New York City for courses at the Art Students League. Madge had intended to become an illustrator until she appeared in a student musical.

The first stage appearance led to an amateur play in which she impressed Henry Woodruff,

a leading actor of the day. She joined his company as leading lady on its U.S. and Canadian tour of 1910.

By 1912, Madge Kennedy was a Broadway star in *Little Miss Brown.* Having made her reputation in that bedroom farce, in 1914 she originated the leading role in another, *Twin Beds.* The play was considered at the time "about as far as you can go" and some communities banned the road company.

Madge was firmly established as what she calls the "Queen of the Negligee Operas." Her innocent air, refined manner, and the chic of her gowns kept her material in the realm of the respectable, if risqué.

In 1915, she headed the cast of another hit, *Fair and Warmer.* Since Madge was already a star, Samuel Goldwyn, who was then still known as Goldfish, had to pay her a star's salary when she signed with him in 1917. She made $2,500, plus a liberal allowance for clothes. Under his auspices, Madge starred in twenty-one features, all very much the same as her plays.

In the first of her starrers, *Baby Mine* (1917), Frank Morgan was with her. The late May McAvoy,[8] later a star, supported Madge in *A Perfect Lady* (1918). John Bowers,* whose suicide became the model for "Norman

Maine" in *A Star Is Born,* was her leading man in four of her vehicles.

After she left Goldwyn, Harold Bolster, whom she had married during World War I, produced *The Purple Highway* (1923) and *Three Miles Out* (1924) under their own banner. Had they acquired the necessary financing, *Dorothy Vernon of Haddon Hall* would have starred Mrs. Bolster. Failing to do so, the couple sold it to Mary Pickford, who made it into a great success.

After four more silent pictures, she was absent from the screen until she played a judge in *The Marrying Kind* (1952). After her first husband died in 1927, Ms. Kennedy had a great success on the stage in *Paris Bound* (1928).

In 1934, Madge married William Hanley, a director-producer of network radio. She appeared in a few plays, but her widowed mother was in frail health and most of her time was taken up as wife and daughter in Los Angeles. Asked if she missed acting during her long hiatus, she said: "No, I loved acting, but then I've enjoyed everything I've done. Looking after people you love is very happy work."

Madge got excellent notices in *The Marrying Kind* and became a close friend of its director, George Cukor. She had been recommended for the part by the late Ruth Gordon, who remembered the high quality of her stage work. Cukor used her again in *Let's Make Love* (1960), and she would have been seen in his never-completed Marilyn Monroe vehicle *Something's Got to Give* (1962).

She was also in *The Rains of Ranchipur* (1955), *Lust for Life* (1956), *The Plunderers of Painted Flats* (1959) with Skip Homeier,* *The Baby Maker* (1970), and *Marathon Man* (1976). Critics singled out her performance in *They Shoot Horses, Don't They?* (1969), and cultists revere her for an appearance in *The Day of the Locust* (1975).

In 1984, she told Tony Slide that the sole regret of her life was that she had never been cast as a villainess. "I wanted to play 'Lady Macbeth,'" she told the film historian. "I thought she was kind of a charmer, and it should be played rather arch."

But in 1986, she modified the remark: "'Regret' is too strong a word. My life has been so filled with wonderful things and people I wouldn't *dare* regret anything. Noel Coward, 'The Master' as they rightly called him, liked my high comedy so much he offered me *Fallen Angels,* but I wasn't free to do it. So when he and Gertie Lawrence left *Private Lives* in 1931, Otto Kruger and I took over for them. Now that was a *great* compliment. Both of my marriages were long love affairs. I'm in my nineties, and I *still* enjoy watching *M*A*S*H* and having a glass of pink champagne now and then. My dear friend Lon McCallister* calls me almost every day to see how I am. I've been a very fortunate person all my life."

Madge Kennedy sums up her philosophy thusly, "Every day is a new beginning."

Jim Janisch

Widowed since 1959, Madge Kennedy lives in an apartment near Bullocks Wilshire in Los Angeles. The nonagenarian is looked after by a live-in companion, a young woman recently immigrated from El Salvador.

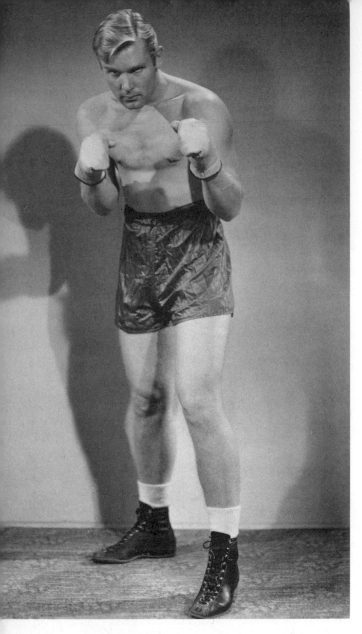

Joe Kirkwood, Jr., was, for most fans of the comic strip character, "Joe Palooka" come to life on the screen. He played the fictional prizefighter in eleven feature films and was the star and coproducer of the TV series.

Joe Kirkwood, Jr.

The champion golfer who became "Joe Palooka" of movies and TV was born on May 30, 1920, in Melbourne, Australia. Although he was brought to the United States at the age of six and has never returned, he is an Australian citizen.

Joe Kirkwood, Sr., was considered to be one of golf's great trick-shot artists and, during the twenties and thirties, won the British, Australian, New Zealand, and Canadian Opens. During the latter part of his career, he was often partnered with U.S. champion golfers Gene Sarazen and Walter Hagen. He was also Dwight Eisenhower's golfing instructor.

Although father and son were very close, Joe, junior did not begin playing golf seriously until he was about sixteen years old. Under Joe senior's tutelage, he won almost $25,000 in prize money before he turned twenty-one.

Kirkwood's movie career came about when he was noticed during a golf tournament by Michael Curtiz and David Butler. He cannot remember whether Sam Snead or Ben Hogan won that day, but at the end of the game he was approached by the directors and asked whether he would consider being screen-tested.

"I thought they were two faggots," says Kirkwood. "My golf buddy, Herb Tobias, laughed like hell when I told him that. Herb was a very big agent and the next day he called me with the Warner Brothers contract he had negotiated and that I signed." At Warner's, he had a brief-but-intense affair with Eleanor Parker, a fellow contractee at the studio.

After playing small roles in several features, his services were sold to the producer Hal E. Chester, who starred him in the title role in a series of pictures as "Joe Palooka," the hero of the comic strip of the same name.

The character was first portrayed on the screen by Stuart Erwin in the feature *Palooka* (1934). Jimmy Durante played his manager-trainer "Knobby Walsh" in that adaptation.

Ham Fisher, the cartoonist who created "Joe Palooka," was so pleased with Kirkwood as "Palooka" he eventually assigned him the TV rights to the property.

Leon Errol was the "Knobby Walsh" of the early Kirkwood "Palooka" features. Upon Errol's death in 1951, James Gleason took over. On the TV program, William Frawley had the role of his ringside adviser.

"Palooka's" girlfriend "Ann Howe" was played by Elyse Knox* in most of the movies. On the TV show that was syndicated in the mid-fifties, Cathy Downs had the part. She was also Kirkwood's wife in real life until their 1955 divorce. They had been out of touch for years, when Joe learned she was in reduced circumstances. He was setting up a trust fund for her when, in 1976, he learned she had died.

Over thirty years ago, Joe Kirkwood, Jr., acquired several acres of land on Ventura Boulevard in the San Fernando Valley. Intending to film a TV sitcom about a professional golfer, he built a golf course there. The series never got on the air, but the property is the basis for his considerable fortune. It now houses a sports center, bar, and restaurant.

Of his religious background Joe says, "I was a Catholic, but I gave it up for Lent." He believes much of his creed of fair play and consideration for others was derived from golf. "It is a game," he explains, "where if you cheat, you are only cheating yourself. What better rule to live by?"

Since the forties, when Joe learned to fly, he has owned and piloted a series of airplanes. The actor Robert Francis was piloting one of Kirkwood's aircraft when he was killed in a crash in 1955.

Joe Kirkwood, Jr., and his wife, Joyce, have been together since 1958 and were married in 1980. They have homes in Sherman Oaks, California, and Hawaii.

Kirkwood is personally building a home, golf range, and landing strip on the mile of beachfront he owns on the Hawaiian island of Kauai. He allows no one else to drive his D-9 Caterpillar bulldozer, the largest model made.

In his first interview in many years, Kirkwood spoke about his life: "Movies were fun and golf still is. But the most gratifying accomplishment has been the sports center. It supports many families and gives people much-needed exercise. I feel good, but I've had radiation therapy. I have no children, and it would be nice to be remembered for this place. So, it really burns the hell out of me that the lease holders changed its name. But most people still call it 'Joe Kirkwood's place.' It's like Graumann's Chinese."

Richard Lamparski

Joe Kirkwood, Jr., still plays golf regularly and frequently appears at senior citizen tournaments. Among golf professionals he is always called "Palooka."

Patric Knowles supported Errol Flynn in **The Charge of the Light Brigade** *(1936),* **The Adventures of Robin Hood** *(1938), and* **Four's a Crowd** *(1938).*

Patric Knowles

The "threat to Errol Flynn" was born Reginald Laurence Knowles on November 11, 1911, in Leeds, England.

His first job in the theatre was driving a van transporting scenery for a Shakespearean troupe. After appearing in bit parts during their tour of Ireland, Knowles went on to act with a series of repertory companies. His first movie was *Irish Hearts* (1934), which was followed by *Men of Tomorrow* (1933) with Robert Donat, and *Abdul the Damned* (1935).

In March, 1935, he went under contract to Warner Brothers. In their London studios he made *Honours Easy* (1935) with Greta Nissen,* *Two's Company* (1939) with Mary Brian, [8] and *Irish for Luck* (1936) with Margaret Lockwood.*

When he was told that he was being sent to Hollywood he immediately proposed to his girlfriend, Enid Percival. She retired from acting when they were married in October, 1935.

Jack Warner brought the actor to the United States ostensibly to play a supporting role in *The Charge of the Light Brigade* (1936), but the word around the studio was that he was meant to keep the picture's star, Errol Flynn, in line. Flynn's obstreperous nature was considered a serious problem at Warner Brothers. But instead of becoming rivals Patric and Flynn became such close friends that the star acted as godfather to Knowles's son, Michael.

Knowles stayed with Warner Brothers for three years. Subsequently he was under contract to RKO, Republic, and Paramount. The latter was his favorite studio, but he readily admits that he is best known for the movies he made as a Universal contractee: *The Wolf Man* (1941), *Frankenstein Meets the Wolf Man* (1943), and *Who Done It?* (1942) with Abbott and Costello.

The picture he is proudest of is *How Green Was My Valley* (1941), which he made while on leave from the United States Army.

While at Warner Brothers Knowles had learned to fly under the tutelage of George Brent. Patric, Brent, and Patric's closest friend, Edward Norris,* spent World War II as flight instructors in the U.S. Army Air Corps. They spent most of their free time together as well during that period in spite of the fact that both Brent and Norris had been married and divorced from Ann Sheridan. "A thing like that is merely a coincidence, and would never be an obstacle to gentlemen," explained Knowles recently.

The only time he was suspended happened when he was at Universal. The studio refused to allow him to accept an offer to star in a play on Broadway. When he did return to the lot he was cast in *Always a Bridesmaid* (1943) with the Andrews Sisters, a part that he feels was a punishment for his rebellion.

Along with bearing a resemblance to Errol Flynn Patric shared his fondness for alcohol and wild times. Louella O. Parsons described him as "one of Hollywood's naughty boys" when the columnist reported several of the fracases Knowles was involved in at nightclubs. He spent the night of St. Patrick's Day, 1947, in jail after what one news account described as a "brawl in an alley."

Among his Hollywood credits are: *It's Love I'm After* (1937) with Bette Davis; *The Honeymoon's Over* (1939) with Marjorie Reynolds; *Another Thin Man* (1939); *Married and in Love* (1940) with Helen Vinson;[9] *Mystery of Marie Roget* (1942); *Lady in a Jam* (1942) with Irene Dunne,[8] *This Is the Life* (1944) with Susanna Foster;[8] *Kitty* (1946) with Paulette Goddard;* *The Bride Wore Boots* (1946) with Barbara Stanwyck; *O.S.S.* (1946); *Monsieur Beaucaire* (1946); *Ivy* (1947) with Joan Fontaine; *Calcutta* (1947) with June Duprez; *Dream Girl* (1948); *The Big Steal* (1949) with Jane Greer;* *Quebec* (1951) with Corinne Calvert;* *Band of Angels* (1957); *Auntie Mame* (1958); *The Way West* (1967); and *The Devil's Brigade* (1968).

Knowles was seriously considered for *My Fair Lady* before Rex Harrison was cast, but has no regrets because "I just dreaded the singing part of the role."

He played opposite Claudette Colbert on a television pilot and believes they would have had a long run had it gone on the air. But when the star was told that she was required to do the commercials she withdrew.

The film he most enjoyed making was *Chisum* (1970) in support of his friend John Wayne. It was one of Patric's last movies.

His novel *Even Steven* was published in 1960.

Knowles and his wife have a son, a daughter, and four grandchildren. They have considerable holdings in commercial and residential real estate. He drives a classic Cadillac that is the envy of Edward Norris, a car collector and the only friend Patric has from his years in films. He spends several days each week teaching ceramics and woodcarving to residents of the Motion Picture and Television House and Hospital near his town house in Woodland Hills, California.

Brian Ough

Patric Knowles collects memorabilia from his screen career. The frame on his left contains a miniature of the large bronze star bearing his name on the Hollwood Boulevard Walk of Fame.

Charles Korvin made films and was the star of his own TV series, Interpol Calling, *but has received his greatest exposure as the dance instructor who teaches "Alice Kramden" to dance the mambo on a segment of* The Honeymooners.

Charles Korvin

The Continental leading man was born Géza Kaiser in Pöstyen, which was then in Hungary. His birth date is November 21, 1912.

As he describes his background: "My father's family were vintners, probably from Austria or Germany originally. When my father married a Jewish girl the family became very distant. But when his brother married the Jewish girl's sister there was a complete break."

When Korvin left Hungary in 1929 with the intention of migrating to the United States, he was denied a visa. He spent several years in London earning his living as a stevedore, watchman, and tango dancer. He had had experience as a photographer in Hungary and after moving to Paris he was able to get some work as a cameraman. His opportunity came when he acted as a cinematographer for a documentary that was made on the Spanish civil war. He realized about that time that his real interest was acting. The director of that film arranged for Charles to come to America.

During his eventful voyage to the United States Korvin, who was in third-class quarters, became acquainted with the novelist James Hilton. He had known the author of *Lost Horizon* slightly in London, but this meeting began a lifelong friendship.

He found work in New York radio and spent several seasons with the Barter Theatre in Virginia. He appeared with Dolly Haas in *Winter Soldier* (1942) and in *Dark Eyes* the following year. In both he was billed as Géza Korvin. The day after *Dark Eyes* opened he had offers from Paramount, David O. Selznick, and Universal. On the advice of his agent, the renowned Charles Feldman, he signed with Universal.

His debut was as the suave French detective in *Enter Arsene Lupin* (1944). Despite low production values Charles Korvin projected definite screen presence. He suspects he made a major mistake in not accepting *White Tie and Tales,* in which his studio wanted to costar him with Ella Raines.[9] On his agent's advice he turned it down. "My real forte is comedy," he said recently. "Had I done it my career might have been a very different kettle of fish."

Charles remembers Hollywood as a "very phony atmosphere. If my latest picture was doing well I'd get a good table, but . . . well, even when I was young that foolishness bored me."

He found Merle Oberon "quite charming" in social situations but a very difficult costar. They played opposite each other in *This Love of Ours* (1945), *Temptation* (1946), and *Berlin Express* (1948). Korvin remembers her as "infuriating" during all three filmings.

In his own estimation his best screen work was done in *The Killer That Stalked New York* (1951). Then he did *Lydia Bailey* (1952) and *Sangaree* (1953).

He has always preferred stage work and live television to film. He was seen frequently on television dramas during the fifties and played one of the title roles in *The King and I* for three seasons throughout the United States.

He has been living abroad "more or less" since he remarried in 1957. His filmed television series *Interpol Calling* was a success in the United States and Europe. It was made in London in 1959.

The Broadway role that he thinks would have reestablished him as a romantic star was in *Ondine*. He lost out to Mel Ferrer, who became the husband of Audrey Hepburn, the star of the play.

He was first married to the late actress Helena Fredericks, a union that he describes as "utterly miserable." They were divorced in 1955 after what Korvin describes as "a few years of total agony followed by a few years of separation."

Charles Korvin readily admits that he misses acting and would "love to act again." But, he says, "I know the business—out-of-sight, out-of-mind." He lives mostly in the south of France in a two-story home he built on the residuals from Lufthansa commercials. For seven years his voice was heard on radio and television as that of "The Red Baron." Carl Reiner is one of his neighbors.

Richard Lamparski

Charles Korvin lives mostly on the French Riviera, but spends winter months skiing in Switzerland where he owns an apartment.

Charles and his present wife, the widow of a wealthy movie producer, are both United States citizens. They keep an apartment in Klosters, Switzerland, where they go to ski during the winter months, taking with them their two dachshunds.

Korvin believes he probably is the last person ever to dance with Greta Garbo. "It was just once around the floor after dinner," he says. "But she swore to me she hadn't danced in a long time and never would again. It's a nice distinction."

Billy Lee's most important role came when he replaced an ailing Baby Sandy in the Biscuit Eater. *Although not an A picture, it was one of Paramount's biggest grossers of 1940. Thirty-two years later Walt Disney remade the film with Johnny Whitaker[9] in the role Billy had originated.*

Billy Lee

The boy actor of the screen was born on a farm near Terre Haute, Indiana, on March 12, 1929. His full name is Billy Lee Schlensker. His father, because of his asthma, moved his wife and children to Los Angeles when Billy was very young.

Billy does not know how he got his training or when he began performing professionally. He has been told that he sang and danced in vaudeville even before the Schlenskers arrived in Hollywood. He is the only member of his family to ever work in show business.

When he was discovered his publicity called him a former member of the Meglin Kiddies, a popular troupe of young children who were presented in musical reviews at presentation houses throughout California in the thirties. Billy's father, who managed his career, permitted this as a way of thanking Ethel Meglin, the troupe's director, after she recommended Billy for *Wagon Wheels* (1934).

His only screen appearance before then had been in *The Little Broadcast* (1933). That one-reel short served as an impressive movie debut for the boy. Even though he had no dialogue, Billy's tap dance stood out.

From *Wagon Wheels* (1934) he got a contract with Paramount Pictures. Their publicity department put out a press release claiming he could play most of the instruments in an orchestra, do tap dancing and ballet, sing, ride a horse, and yodel. He also proved to be capable of giving a more than competent performance when given the opportunity.

His biggest role came when Baby Leroy, who had the lead in *The Biscuit Eater,* fell into a creek while on location and got a severe cold. Billy replaced him in what became a "sleeper" when it was released in 1940.

Among his other motion pictures were: *Rose Bowl* (1936) with Tom Brown* and Eleanore Whitney;* *Too Many Parents* (1936) with Frances Farmer; *Wild Money* (1937) with Edward Everett Horton; *Make a Wish* (1937) with Bobby Breen;* and *Jeepers Creepers* (1939) with the Weaver Brothers* and Elviry.

At Paramount Billy attended school with Bonita Granville[9] and Billy Barty and became mascot of the studio's baseball team. He enjoyed making pictures, but always considered what he was doing as "work." "I was in a business," he has said. "Even as a little kid I knew that. People were all nice to me and you could have fun, but we were there to make a movie and I was expected to hold up my end of it. I was at least eight years old before I realized that not all kids were movie actors."

In early 1943 without a word of explanation Mr. Schlensker took his family back to the farm in Indiana. His father continued to book him into vaudeville shows where he sang and danced until the age of seventeen. Billy announced that he was leaving show business.

"By then I was already living on my own," he said recently. "Dad didn't like me quitting, but there really wasn't anything he could do about it."

He enlisted in the U.S. Army for two and a half years. Shortly after his discharge he was drafted because of the Korean War. Billy formed musical combos that played NCO and officers' clubs during both tours of duty.

Billy Lee played guitar evenings in a club for ten years while he established a business of renting construction equipment. Several years ago he sold his firm and now considers himself retired. He and his wife have their home on an acre and a half of property near Palm Springs.

Billy was married for several years before he told his wife anything about his childhood. He uses his original name and never tells people about his boyhood.

He is not in touch with anyone he ever worked with. One he would like to see again is Donald O'Connor. He and Billy became close friends when they appeared together in two Charlie Ruggles—Mary Boland starrers. "Just can't bring myself to call him," he admitted recently. "He might think I needed a handout or wanted a job."

In autumn, 1984, he talked about how he feels now: "There are so many things I don't know about my career. Like how it began or why we left Hollywood. Dad never told me

Gawain Bierne-Keyt

Billy Lee Schlensker lives with his wife on the one and a half acres of land he owns near Palm Springs, California.

anything except what he expected of me. All I wanted to do was please him. I don't know how much money I was paid or what happened to it. I do know he never worked again after I went under contract, nor did he do anything after we returned to Indiana. I have three daughters and a son. I often think that I raised my parents' family and then a family of my own."

Mr. Schlensker never allowed his son to see the films he appeared in. Billy now collects them.

He responds to all fan mail personally and welcomes correspondence at: P. O. Box 3217, Beaumont, CA. 92223.

"Sonny Boy," the song Al Jolson sang to Davey Lee in **The Singing Fool** *(1928), was as popular as the movie. After supporting Jolson in another film,* **Say It with Songs** *(1929), Davey Lee was starred in the feature* **Sonny Boy** *(1929).*

Davey Lee

The first child star to emerge from talkies was born David Lee in Hollywood on December 29, 1924. His father worked in the print shop at Paramount Pictures.

Davey's older brother, Frankie Lee, acted occasionally in movies. When their mother was unable to get someone to baby-sit with her younger son she took both boys on a casting call at Warner Brothers. *The Jazz Singer* (1927), an Al Jolson starrer released the year before, had ushered in the sound era and was Warner Brothers' biggest grosser. The studio was now looking for an unknown boy to play opposite Jolson in his second talkie, *The Singing Fool.*

While his mother waited in the casting office with Frankie, Davey was left on his own to play. When Mrs. Lee and his brother found him, the boy was playing piggyback with Jolson. At the star's insistence the boy was signed.

The highlight of *The Singing Fool* (1928) is the scene in which Jolson sings "Sonny Boy" to a dying Davey. The picture and the song were such hits that Jolson and Davey were immediately cast in *Say It with Songs* (1929), another sentimental feature with songs. Jolson enjoyed working with the boy on the scenes they had together and played with him on and off the set. Adoption was mentioned at one point, but firmly rejected by Davey's parents.

Other of his films are: *Frozen River* (1929) with Rin-Tin-Tin; *Skin Deep* (1929) with John Bowers; and *The Squealer* (1930) with Dorothy Revier. * His personal favorite is *Sonny Boy* (1929) in which he starred with Edward Everett Horton.

Davey Lee made a tour of the Keith-Orpheum vaudeville circuit. In one city he was so mobbed by fans his mother tried to remove him from the crowd. But Davey was elated and struggled free by striking her so hard with his fist her nose bled.

"I felt terrible when I realized what I'd

done," he admitted recently. "But she was trying to take a little boy away from what he wanted most in the world—attention from lots and lots of people!"

That incident put an end to his career for many years. His parents placed him in public school and kept him away from any performing.

The late Frankie Lee was sent to medical school with money his younger brother had earned. The understanding in the family was that Davey would be repaid, but Frankie flunked out. "He hated me all his life," admits Lee. "I can't even blame him. I was the one who got all the attention." He has never learned where the rest of his monies were used because his parents' estate was minuscule.

After graduating from Hollywood High School Davey served as a combat medic during the Allied invasion at Normandy and later with Patton's Third Army. He has been divorced three times from what he describes as "aggressive women who aspired to be entertainers. They had to take the initiative because I've always been terrified of females."

He spent twenty years playing cocktail piano in New York City. Originally he had moved east in hopes of breaking into Broadway shows, a goal he never achieved.

Davey attended the Al Jolson Centennial held in New York City in spring, 1985, and said of the experience: "It was just about the best time I had had since leaving pictures. All these people not only knew who I was, they treated me just like I used to be treated. It was like being a star again, if only for a few days."

Lee supports himself with a job in an aircraft parts firm near Sun Valley, California, where he lives. His condominium is shared with a nameless cat and is decorated in western memorabilia.

He would very much like to act again and regularly sends his résumés and composites to casting directors.

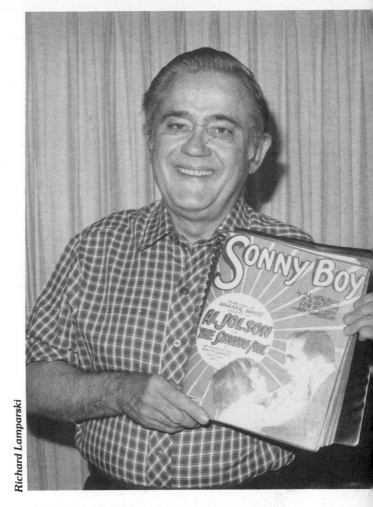

Richard Lamparski

"I sing Jolson songs but never attempt to imitate him," says Lee of the act he performs frequently for senior citizens. "'Sonny Boy,' my finale, really goes over well because everyone remembers it and they know I'm that little boy he sang it to."

He has regular sessions with a psychologist to relieve his frustration. Says Lee, "I'm deeply resentful that I'm not a star. Even my signature is the same as it was when I was a boy. A large part of me is still 'Sonny Boy.' After all, that was the happiest time of my life."

Mark Lester first came to real prominence in Our Mother's House *(1967). In it he played a stuttering orphan, one of seven children who try to keep their mother's death a secret. It was that part that won him the title role in the screen musical* Oliver!, *the winner of the Best Picture Academy Award of 1968.*

Mark Lester

The child star of the late sixties was born on July 11, 1958, in Oxford, England. He was still a baby when his parents moved to the Richmond area of London.

When Mark was two and a half years old, his father learned that a child about that age was required for a TV commercial. Michael Lester, a model and bit actor, suggested his son, and he was hired.

"He was an exceptionally pretty child," his father once said, in explaining why Mark had caught on so quickly among commercial producers. By the time he was cast in a small role in *Sanctuary* (1961), his first feature, the boy's face had become familiar throughout the United Kingdom. He was a student at the Corona Stage School, the alma mater of many English stars.

Mark was in six more movies before being cast in *Our Mother's House* (1967). That role brought him a great deal of attention and the admiration of Jack Clayton, who told his colleague, Sir Carol Reed, how easily the boy took his direction. After a screen test, Reed signed him for the stellar part in *Oliver!,* the most important male child role of the decade.

The *1968 Film Daily Yearbook* named Mark, along with Jack Wild, also of the *Oliver!* cast, and Leonard Whiting,* another English boy and the star of *Romeo and Juliet,* as three of the Filmdom's Favorite Five for that year.

For several years after *Oliver!* Mark was publicized as being the world's highest paid boy actor. His father, who wanted to produce, formed a corporation in which he and his son were partnered.

One of those who directed Mark during the period after *Oliver!,* when he was reportedly the highest paid boy actor in the world, recently recalled the father-son team: "Mark's dad really wanted what he felt was best for the boy. But if we needed him to work longer than the child labor laws permitted, or if he was required when he should have been with the tutor, Michael Lester did everything he could to make his son available. That's what he thought was best for him."

Michael Lester managed his son's career, earnings, and publicity. He repeatedly told the press that Mark received no special treatment whether he was on a movie set or at home with his family. At the peak of his career, his annual income was reported to be a quarter of a million dollars, but he was given a weekly allowance of sixty cents. "One thing he *won't* be is spoiled."

Mr. Lester, who always insisted that he disliked stage parents and was not one, answered most of the questions from the press. To those inquiring about the psychological effects of starring in movies on a little boy: "He has nothing remotely resembling a star psyche," he insisted to Gabe Essoe in 1970.

When the remark was repeated to Curtis Harrington, who directed the fourteen-year-old in *Who Slew Auntie Roo?* (1972), he said: "You can add to that, he had no instincts for nor interest in acting. I found that if I showed Mark exactly what I wanted him to do right before a take, he could do it. But his attention span and memory were very short. He tried hard and wanted to please everyone, but he wished he was off playing. He just wanted to be what he was, a very young boy."

On the rare occasion when the child star spoke for himself, he seemed to confirm what the public had been told about him. He told Hearst feature writer Dorothy Manners that when his sister Davina did a walk-on in one of his pictures, she received more attention than he did.

After accepting a silver medal at the Moscow International Film Festival, where both *Our Mother's House* and *Oliver!* received awards, he was asked about the Soviet Union. "I hated it. It was horrible," was his reply.

Whenever asked if his son might be missing things most boys of his age require, Mr. Lester agreed that there most probably were. The *Los Angeles Times* quoted him in 1970 as saying, "This insane business could destroy him by the time he's eighteen. We realize that and try to adjust for it by making Mark's life as normal as possible." At another time he volunteered that their son had told him and his wife that he did not wish to act when he became an adult.

His films include: *Allez France!* (1964); *Spaceflight IC-1* (1965) with Bill Williams; *Fahrenheit 451* (1966); *Run Wild, Run Free* (1969); *Sudden Terror* (1970), a remake of *The Boy Who Cried Wolf; To Love Somebody*

(1971) with Jack Wild; *Black Beauty* (1971); *Scalawag* (1973), made with Kirk Douglas in Yugoslavia; *Graduation* (1974); and *Dance Under the Elms* (1975), made in Italy.

One of his London acquaintances insists that it was Lester's notices for *Crossed Swords* (1977), a remake of *The Prince and the Pauper,* that brought his career to a virtual standstill. Critics complained that his speech could not be understood. Mark's confidence was undermined, and he sought solace in travel and drugs. According to his own account, the 200,000 pounds his parents turned over to him were spent in a two-year binge.

By 1981, there were reports in English newspapers of a check for $7,000 that Mark had given to a writer who had agreed to ghost his autobiography. It was returned by his bank for insufficient funds.

During the summer of 1985, he went on tour with the play *Romantic Comedy,* but was replaced after a few weeks.

In October, 1985, he took a job tending bar in a Knightsbridge pub.

"Pint Puller: Mark Lester" was the caption on this picture that ran in late 1985 in London's **Daily Mail.** *The former child star was working as a bartender at the Britannia, a pub near Harrod's and a favorite of tourists from the United States.*

Boris Karloff once told a reporter for the Saturday Evening Post *that the role of "The Monster" in* Frankenstein *(1931) was the one he liked best and that his favorite scene in it was with "Little Maria." He strongly objected, however, to throwing her into the water. That part, which was not in the original feature, has been added to the recently released color version on video cassette.*

"Little Maria" Marilyn Wood

The actress known to horror fans as "Little Maria" was born in Los Angeles on July 17, 1924, and named Marilyn.

Placed in an orphanage by her natural parents, she was taken by a woman who had asked to see "the most beautiful baby you have." Within a week, Marilyn, who was not yet one month old, was playing a baby in a "Rin-Tin-Tin" movie.

She doubled for Sonny McKeen, star of the "Snookums" comedies, and played his leading lady in forty of the two-reelers.

The part that meant the most to her was in *A Wicked Woman* (1934), because Bonita Granville[9] had also tested for it. "Bonita," Marilyn recalls, "was always so competitive. The rest of us were just nervous wrecks. But she and Jane Withers were like the parents. They had that steely determination."

Her most vivid recollection of movie making was her screen test for *Over the Hill* (1931). Her mother had slapped her face so hard just before the scene was filmed that a woman's handprint showed clearly across her cheek.

She got the part, supporting Sally Eilers[8] and James Dunn.[8]

Marilyn got the part in *Frankenstein* (1931) because James Whale, who was directing the horror film, remembered her in a swimming scene in *The Big Trail* (1930).

What she most vividly recalls is a scene that was not in the movie when it was released in 1931. "The Monster" threw her into the water, expecting her to float like the daisies that she and the creature had been picking. When it was filmed, she had hurt her back, but a second take was required and the director, James Whale, promised her "anything" if she would do it over. Marilyn agreed and was given what she had asked for—a dozen hard-boiled eggs.

"Actually, he gave me two dozen," she said over fifty years later. "My mother was furious I hadn't asked for something like a bicycle. I loved hard-boiled eggs and at home I was only allowed one. She always had me on a diet."

Like "Little Maria," Marilyn was not at all put off by Boris Karloff in his makeup as "The Monster" and rode with him from his dressing room to the shore of the man-made lake on the Universal lot where the famous scene was shot. "He had such warmth and gentleness about him," she remembers. "There was little of either quality in the home I grew up in. I was very strongly drawn to him."

Some of her other screen roles were in *Two Gun Man* (1926), *The Case of Lena Smith* (1928) with Esther Ralston,[8] *Phantom in the House* (1929), *Let Us Be Gay* (1930), *Wild Girl* (1932), *Tugboat Annie* (1933), *Symphony of Life* (1935), *These Three* (1936), and *Rose of the Rancho* (1936). Marilyn had her first big crush while making *The Road Back* (1937). It was on the picture's star, John King. *

She worked less frequently as a teenager, and the roles were usually smaller, In 1943, when one of her pictures played the Marcal Theatre on Hollywood Boulevard, the marquee read:

JIMMY LYDON AND MARILYN WOOD
HENRY ALDRICH GETS GLAMOUR
MARILYN WOOD IS OUR CASHIER

In 1944 when Marilyn married an executive with a clothing chain, she severed all contact with her former profession. Neither her son nor her grandchildren ever expressed any interest in her career.

She believes her mother never forgave her for leaving acting. For over ten years after her marriage, Marilyn and Mrs. Wood did not communicate. Eventually, they were reconciled but, as she says, "I did not love her. I just couldn't."

In 1986 at the conclusion of the only interview Marilyn Wood has ever given, she said: "If she had encouraged and guided me, I really believe I would have become a very fine actress. I liked picture making. It was the threats and beatings that spoiled it all for me. Because she had warned me about nail biting and then caught me doing it, I had my hand held over a hot gas range. My father, who usually kept out of it, stopped her from severely burning me. I don't frequently look back on those years because when I do, those are the things that come to mind."

Marilyn Wood was a widow when she married a longtime family friend, a retired insurance underwriter, in 1982. The couple lives in San Gabriel, California.

Donald Watkins

In Good News *(1930), one of her early talkie musicals, Bessie Love was paired with Cliff Edwards, the vaudeville headliner known as "Ukelele Ike." He subsequently dubbed the voice of the animated "Jiminy Cricket" in* Pinocchio *and introduced "When You Wish Upon a Star," the song that won the 1940 Oscar. After he died in 1971, penniless and alone, Walt Disney Studios paid for his gravestone.*

Bessie Love

The star of silent pictures was born in Midland, Texas, on September 10, 1898. Her original name is Juanita Horton.

She was still a child when the Hortons moved to Los Angeles. Her father went into practice there as a chiropractor.

She was still in high school in 1915 when she got a job at a movie studio at $2 a day. Her name was changed immediately, "Because people can't pronounce Juanita and, besides, we want everyone to love you," she was told.

She came under the influence of D. W. Griffith who cast her as the "Bride of Cona" in his silent classic *Intolerance* (1916). According to her close friend, the historian of the silent cinema, Kevin Brownlow, when her services were lent to western star William S. Hart for *The Aryan* (1916), Griffith hailed her as "the most promising actress he had ever directed." She seemed the epitome of the child-woman, a character in which Griffith specialized. Her wistful quality was successfully exploited in the pictures he supervised.

By 1920 Bessie Love was starring in features produced by her own company. But, after all three of those films failed at the box office, her position in the movie industry was very precarious. The positive side of free-lancing, as the actress did for the next eight years, was that she was able to play a wide variety of roles. No star under contract to a studio would have been allowed to appear as the young, drug-addicted, nursing mother in the shocker *Human Wreckage* (1923) or the mother of an illegitimate child in *A Woman on the Jury* (1923). Because she needed the money to help support the lifestyle she and her parents had become accustomed to, Bessie played in westerns and shorts and appeared as a Chinese woman in the Poverty Row production *Purple Dawn* (1921). She was also able to act in plays and found that she liked the theatre just as well as movies.

She was the heroine of the prehistoric *Lost World* (1925), a South Sea Islander in *Soul Fire* (1925), a duchess in exile in *Young April* (1926), a thief in *Going Crooked* (1926), an actress in *Matinee Idol* (1928), a chorus girl in

Sally of the Scandals (1928), and a French girl in *Has Anybody Here Seen Kelly?* (1929).

Bessie's belief that a now-common effect was used for the first time in her film *Forget-Me-Not* (1922) has not been challenged. In it a drop of castor oil, representing a tear, was allowed to trickle slowly down the camera lens, resulting on the screen in a watery distortion of her face.

In *The King on Main Street* (1925) she introduced the Charleston, the dance craze of the twenties, to the screen. It was she who taught Noel Coward to Charleston.

Bessie and her costar Eddie Foy, Jr., did some dating while they made the talkie two-reeler *The Swell Head* (1929). When former boyfriend Irving Thalberg saw it he cast her in *Broadway Melody* and signed her to an M-G-M contract. It was that studio's first musical and was voted the Oscar for the Best Picture of 1928–29. She was nominated as Best Actress.

When she married the businessman brother of director Howard Hawks it was a social highlight of 1929 in filmdom. Cecil Beaton, visiting from London, recorded in his diary his excitement over the wedding party, which included Norma Shearer, Carmel Myers, Mary Astor, Bebe Daniels, and Bessie's closest friend, Blanche Sweet. [8]

She was in the all-star *Hollywood Revue* (1929) and three other sound films during 1930. During this period Flo Ziegfeld wanted to star her on Broadway in *Showgirl,* but the part went to Lupe Velez when Metro refused the loan-out. Not long after, the studio failed to pick up her option.

Her very uneven career in Hollywood ended with *Morals for Women* (1931), a B picture.

After filing for divorce in the mid-thirties Bessie and her three-year-old daughter, Patricia, settled in England.

Without ever losing her identity as an American actress she worked continually on stage, radio, television, and in pictures in the United Kingdom. She was in the West End versions of *Born Yesterday* and *Death of a Salesman*. She was "Aunt Pitty-Pat" in the musical *Gone With the Wind* at the Drury Lane in 1972 and had roles in the miniseries *Jenny* and *Jersey Lilly*. Reviewers, some unaware of her background, singled Bessie out for praise as Vanessa Redgrave's mother in *Isadora* (1969) and the nosy telephone operator in *Sunday, Bloody Sunday* (1971).

Her last public appearance was when she accompanied her old friend Lillian Gish to the reissue of *The Wind* (1928) in London in 1984.

The motion picture pioneer died on April 26, 1986.

Hannah Pepper

Photographed in 1986 by her granddaughter at Denville Hall, the retirement home for those in the acting profession, in Middlesex, England. She was a British subject and a student of Christian Science.

During their years together Ida Lupino and Howard Duff were teamed effectively in movies such as Jennifer *(1953),* Private Hell 36 *(1955), and* Women's Prison *(1955). Their TV series,* Mr. Adams and Eve *was made in the fifties, but continued for years in syndication.*

Ida Lupino

The star-director of movies and television was born in London on February 4, 1918. Her father's family had emigrated to England from Italy in the seventeenth century and was well established in the British theatre. Stanley Lupino, her father, starred in West End shows, some of which he authored, and films. Her second cousin, Lupino Lane, was a major name in English music halls. Ida's mother, Connie Emerald, was also from a theatrical family.

When Ida accompanied her mother on an audition she was noticed by Allan Dwan, a Hollywood director who was making *Her First Affair* (1933) in England. The teenager made her screen debut as a platinum blonde and was billed as "the English Jean Harlow." After five more features she was brought to the United States by Paramount Pictures, where she was to play the title role in their all-star *Alice in Wonderland.*

Her studio soon realized she was completely wrong to play "Alice." In spite of her youth her manner and voice were very adult. The actress herself once said she sounded like "a fat man who had been drinking a lot." Instead she was cast in such programmers as *The Search for Beauty* (1934) with Toby Wing[8] and *Smart Girl* (1935) with Pinky Tomlin.[8] Her role in *Peter Ibbetson* (1935) was small, but the *New York Times* reviewer singled her out as "excellent."

Her break came as a Cockney guttersnipe in *The Light That Failed* (1940). More than one reviewer compared her performance favorably to that of Bette Davis in *Of Human Bondage.* Warner Brothers signed her, many thinking as a "threat" to Davis, the star who was then the queen of the Burbank lot.

Her work in *They Drive By Night* (1940), *High Sierra* (1941), and *The Hard Way* (1942) not only stands the test of time but is all the more remarkable when it is realized that she was in her early twenties when the films were made.

In *Ladies in Retirement* (1941), a picture that has grown in reputation over the years, Ida was completely convincing as a woman a full generation older than she was. In it with her was the late Louis Hayward, whom she had married in 1938.

Her other notable pictures during the forties are: *The Sea Wolf* (1941); *Moontide* (1942); *Devotion* (1946), in which she played Emily Brontë; *The Man I Love* (1947); *Deep Valley* (1947); *Road House* (1948); and *Lust for Gold* (1949).

Ida Lupino once composed a complete score for one of her father's shows. She has written popular music and symphonies. The Los Angeles Philharmonic has performed her *Aladdin Suite*.

She scripted and produced features and, for a time, was the only woman in Hollywood active as a director. Although her films were not well distributed, they had originality, introduced new faces such as Sally Forrest and usually made money. The best was *The Hitch-Hiker* (1953), which starred the late Edmond O'Brien. [9]

After Lupino and Hayward were divorced in 1945 Ida married the dapper scenarist-actor Collier Young. They collaborated on scripts and coproduced her films. Their business association continued after their 1951 divorce, an act which she now calls "the biggest mistake of my life."

She says that when she confronted Young on his affair with Joan Fontaine he accused her of being unfaithful with Howard Duff. Both agreed to give up their lovers, but then Ida found that she was carrying Duff's baby. Subsequent to the divorce, Collier Young and Joan Fontaine were married, as were Ida Lupino and Howard Duff. To this day Ida blames Bridget, the daughter by Duff, with "ruining my life."

The private lives of Mr. and Mrs. Howard Duff were often made public because of their frequent noisy and boozy quarrels at parties and in restaurants. In the area where they once lived in a house that Lon Chaney, Jr., built, former neighbors still talk of their "knock-down, drag-out" fights. The present owner of the home has been assured that pieces of dinnerware and glass thrown by them at each other abound on his property.

In 1984 her affairs were turned over to a conservator by a Los Angeles court, a decision the star approved. Her legal guardian, a young woman, oversaw her divorce from Duff after a

Ida Lupino at a stables near her home in Van Nuys, California.

separation of twelve years and moved her from a garbage-strewn Brentwood estate into a smaller ranch house in Van Nuys. She has a cat, but after her sheepdog bit her lawyer he was given away. Her attorney, like her physician and psychiatrist, come to her home. When she does venture out it is for functions of the savings and loan company in which she owns stock.

Her housekeeper, like almost everyone else around her, is young and male. Two exceptions are her conservator and "discovery" Mala Powers. * Ms. Lupino is not in touch with any of her contemporaries, does not hear from any of her relations, and is not on speaking terms with her daughter, Bridget.

She sponsors two foster children and contributes to a shelter for battered women. She is Roman Catholic and has a strong devotion to Saint Jude, but usually insists that she is Anglican. At other times Ida claims to be Jewish.

Ida says she gave up directing after *The Trouble with Angels* (1966) because it simply did not pay as well as acting. The last time she acted was on a *Charlie's Angels* segment in 1977. She is, however, willing to appear again before the camera provided the part is one she considers a challenge. Or, as she says, "it pays one hell of a lot of money."

One of Siobhan McKenna's infrequent appearances in movies was in the all-star spectacle King of Kings *(1961) in which she played Mary, mother of Jesus.*

Siobhan McKenna

The first lady of the Irish theatre was born in Belfast on May 24, 1923. Her father, a professor of mathematics, set high intellectual standards for his children and hoped that she would take up his profession. Language was another of Mr. McKenna's keen interests and the family spoke only in Gaelic when at home.

She was strongly encouraged to take part in class plays by the Dominican nuns who taught her. In one production, which she also directed, she played a Chinese man and so entertained the bishop that he awarded her school a three-day holiday.

Siobhan had had strong leanings toward a religious vocation since childhood. When some of her writings were published in magazines, another career possibility opened to her.

In college she won honors in English literature, Irish literature, and French. She intended to work for a degree, but on the recommendation of her French professor, was auditioned and taken on by the Abbey Theatre.

By the late forties her reputation at home had spread to London, where she appeared in such plays as *The White Steed, Berkeley Square,* and *Fading Mansions.*

The first of many screen roles that she has rejected went to Deborah Kerr in *I See a Dark Stranger.* The head of the Abbey Theatre counseled her, "Take it and you'll be a star overnight. Stay with us and you'll be a *real* actress."

"Mind you," she adds, "he didn't say 'great' actress!"

That her name is pronounced "Shi-vaun" was well known to United States television audiences by the mid-fifties. Her appearances on *Hallmark Hall of Fame* specials were treated almost as events in themselves. The starring roles in *The Letter, What Every Woman Knows,* and *Cradle Song* brought her enormous prestige.

Among her few motion pictures are *Daughter of Darkness* (1948), *The Playboy of the Western World* (1962), *Of Human Bondage* (1964), and *Dr. Zhivago* (1965).

Broadway, as well as much of the Western world, saw her in the title role of *Saint Joan* during the fifties. Her biggest successes in the New York theatre were *The Chalk Garden* (1955) and *The Rope Dancers* (1957).

She enjoys watching movies, "especially

with those glamorous ladies, like Myrna Loy and the Bennett sisters,'' but has no regrets that she did not make more of them. She said in a recent interview: "Living in Hollywood, from what little I know of it, would not at all appeal to me. On film, they tell me, a performance lasts forever. But I'm a Catholic and we have a different concept of eternity. To me, someone telling me they vividly recall something I did on stage years ago—now, to have one's work *remembered,* that is truly a great compliment.''

She has acted on television recently, but in plays not seen in the United States. In late 1985 Ms. McKenna was preparing to play an elderly murderess in the Abbey Theatre's production of *Arsenic and Old Lace.*

What has been described as "a stentorian, polyphonic voice which she so artfully controls'' is a familiar one on radio plays heard throughout the United Kingdom and Ireland. She would be pleased to be best remembered for the acting she has done in that medium and on recorded dramatizations.

All five of the film offers she received after her screen debut in *Hungry Hill* (1947) were turned down. Over the years she had had many opportunities to appear on United States television and on Broadway, which she has rejected because of a commitment to her family. Some of the roles, she admits, were ones she wanted. A few, such as the play *The Loves of Cass McGuire,* were parts she wanted very much.

Recently she explained: "There was a period during my son's adolescence when I thought he needed his mother close by. Then my husband was ill for a long, long time. I was happy to stay with both of them. I consider myself very fortunate to have loved ones to look after.''

After her husband died in 1979 Siobhan was offered the lead in a Broadway play, which she passed on because her beloved Norwegian wolfhound had been given a prognosis of six to nine more months to live and required constant care.

"My agent told me he didn't think the producer would understand,'' she says. "I told him that 'Roary' needed me and that I *wanted* to be with him and that I wouldn't be interested in working for any man who could not understand!''

Richard Lamparski

Siobhan McKenna and her companions live in a two-story house with a large garden in the Rathgar area of Dublin. Her recently married son is a professional poker player and a licensed bookmaker.

Irene Manning played Gene Autry's cowgirl and Humphrey Bogart's gun moll, but is best known for appearing in the film musicals **Yankee Doodle Dandy** *(1942),* **The Desert Song** *(1943), and* **Shine On Harvest Moon** *(1944).*

Irene Manning

The "almost star" of screen and stage was born Inez Harvuot in Cincinnati, Ohio, on July 12. Her mother insisted that she sang "The Blue Ridge Mountains of Virginia" when she was eighteen months old.

At the age of thirteen she was part of a quartet that sang for the World Sunday School Convention before an audience of 7,000 at the Los Angeles Shrine Auditorium.

Even before graduation from the Eastman School of Music she had a contract with Republic Pictures. As Hope Manning she made the Gene Autry western *The Old Corral* (1936) and *Two Wise Maids* (1937), which starred Allison Skipworth and Polly Moran.

Still billed as Hope Manning she appeared on Broadway in *Susanna, Don't You Cry* (1939) and *All in Fun* (1940).

She was on tour opposite John Charles Thomas in *The Gypsy Baron* when she signed with Warner Brothers. The studio changed her first name to Irene, fearing the public might be reminded of another blonde singing personality, Hope Hampton, whose film career was a disaster.

Her first for the Burbank lot was *Yankee Doodle Dandy* (1942) in which she played vaudeville headliner Fay Templeton. Then she had straight acting roles in *Spy Ship,* a remake of *Fog Over Frisco,* and *The Big Shot.* In both of these 1942 programmers she had the lead, but was killed in the last reel.

The lead opposite Dennis Morgan[8] in *The Desert Song,* it was thought, would catapult her to stardom. She photographed beautifully in Technicolor, but in her opinion, her singing and that of her costar were poorly recorded. Because of world politics at the time, the picture's release was delayed until December, 1943, almost a year after it was made.

The late filmologist Don Miller was in agreement with Ms. Manning, that Warner Brothers never decided what to do with her. He added, however: "She was lovely to look at and listen to, and she could act. But she did possess that blonde chilliness that seems so often to go with thrushes—Lucille Norman, Florence George, Mary Ellis, etc.''

Screen work was never the enjoyable experience for her that the theatre always has been. But the only Hollywood personality she really disliked was Jack L. Warner. She remembers him as ''rather uncouth'' and says he once telephoned her to complain that she was holding up shooting by going too frequently to the toilet.

Quite recently Irene Manning was given an air-check of a broadcast she did from London on Thanksgiving Day, 1944, singing ''Begin the Beguine'' in German. She was in England with her own USO unit and was accompanied on the radio show by Glenn Miller and his orchestra, just before their ill-fated flight.

Subsequently she became quite well known in England. She played in the West End musicals *The DuBarry* and *Serenade,* toured the music halls, and for a while had her own BBC-TV show, *An American in England.* She played opposite Jack Buchanan, one of the country's most popular stars, in *Castle in the Air,* which ran in the West End for two seasons.

Since her last motion picture, *A Yank in London* (1946), she has toured in plays opposite Franchot Tone and Don Ameche, played the female lead to Steve Lawrence's ''Pal Joey'' and ''Anna'' to Fernando Lamas's Oriental potentate in *The King and I.* In 1961 she played the title role in the off-Broadway musical *The Tatooed Countess.*

Her other screen credits were: *Make Your Own Bed, The Doughgirls,* and *Hollywood Canteen,* all 1944 releases; and *Escape in the Desert* (1945), an up-dated version of *The Petrified Forest.*

On television she was ''Mrs. Dodsworth'' on the *Schlitz Playhouse* presentation of *Dodsworth* and supported Cyril Ritchard and Joan Greenwood* in the NBC-TV special *The King*

John Russell

Irene with Cameron Russell, one of her students. Ms. Manning gives private lessons in voice and acting technique for stage and camera in the San Francisco Bay area.

and Mrs. Candle in 1955.

On stage her near-miss with stardom came when she played the lead in Lerner and Loewe's *The Day Before Spring.* The musical reached Broadway in 1945, but soon closed.

Her first husband, from whom she was divorced, was screenwriter Het Manheim. Since 1964 she has been the wife of Maxwell W. Hunter, director of Strategic Affairs of the Lockheed Missile and Space Company. Their home in San Carlos, California, has sixteen-foot ceilings and a panoramic view of Palo Alto. She is step-mother to his five children.

Donald Vail Allen's critique, which ran in the Los Angeles Times *in May, 1966, began: "When the history of the folk-song craze that swept across mid-twentieth century America is finally written, I wouldn't be at all surprised if it opened with: 'In the beginning there was Marais and Miranda.'"*

Marais and Miranda

The international balladeers first met when Josef Marais (pronounced "Mar-ay") hired a Mrs. de Miranda as a translator during World War II. Marais oversaw all broadcasts to the Union of South Africa from the Office of War Information in New York City.

Roosje Lili Odette Baruch de la Pardo was a recent immigrant from the Netherlands. She had been born in Amsterdam on January 9, 1912, and was the mother of two children, but was separated from her husband, whose surname was de Miranda.

Josef Marais was born on November 17, 1905, in Sir Lowry's Pass, South Africa. He was not yet twenty years old when he went on a world tour as a violinist with the Cape Town Symphony Orchestra. When he met the woman who was to become his life partner, he had his own program, *African Trek,* on NBC radio in addition to the duties of his government job. He was also married.

As Miranda remembers it, "We sparked each other creatively from the very first time. But it was a while before either of us realized that we had, also, fallen very much in love."

By 1945, they had developed a repertoire, but she had never performed publicly, and the only time he had faced an audience was as a member of a large orchestra. Yet, their debut at the Village Vanguard, which has since become known as the "Cradle of Folk," was an immediate success. Their scheduled engagement of two weeks was extended to five and a half months.

From the club in Greenwich Village, the duo played a sold-out concert at Town Hall, which brought bookings across the United States. Eventually, they toured Western Europe, South Africa, and Israel. They filled in at the famed Turnabout Theatre in Los Angeles when Elsa Lanchester was unable to appear and performed one of their best-known numbers, "Zulu Warrior," in the movie *Rope of Sand* (1949).

The songs they sang, whether they were Celtic, Flemish, Afrikaner, or Stephen Foster, were introduced with bits of information about their roots. They sang the first few lines in the original language and would then segue into lyrics that Marais had written. As Miranda says, "We never tried for authenticity, but would retain the thoughts and sentiments. Like minstrels of the Middle Ages, we retold what we had heard or read."

His was a sonorous baritone and hers a lyrical soprano. His sober style provided a perfect contrast to her whimsical, flirtatious manner. Claudia Cassidy, dean of Midwest critics and one of their greatest enthusiasts, called their union, "a marriage planned in minstrel heaven." But it was Josef's first wife who gave the couple their greatest compliment. Shortly after he persuaded her to divorce him in 1947, she saw the couple perform for the first time. "Now I understand. You do belong together," was her comment.

When Marais and Miranda guested on TV with Doris Day, she joined them in singing one of their best-known songs, "Marching To Pretoria." They were presented on television by Red Skelton, also, but not by Ed Sullivan.

Miranda reasons that she and Marais were too subtle for the mass TV audience of the Sullivan variety show. Frequently, the biggest laughs at their concerts were delayed ones. Her tongue-in-cheek delivery and his drollery worked best with a live audience. Alluding to their artlessness and understatement of what they did, Claudia Cassidy once wrote, "They are not commonplace, these two."

Their recitals retained a freshness even for the many of their followers who attended year after year. They constantly added, eliminated, and shifted material. Their remarks to the audiences and exchanges with each other were never rehearsed or forced. Until the death of Josef Marais in 1978, the couple performed with the same enthusiasm for their art. The charm one held for the other was always apparent.

Of the two dozen albums they recorded, only *Souvenir of Marais and Miranda* is now in print. Miranda sells some of the others on cassette via the mail.

They were the vanguard of musicians performing folk ballads, but when the folk music craze hit its stride during the sixties, Marais and Miranda's bookings diminished. Josef's songs and stories about the African veld, where he grew up, ran throughout any evening with Marais and Miranda. Yet, their only statement was a plea for world fellowship and peace. Audiences, especially on or near campuses where heretofore they had been very popular, had come to expect more strident messages and earthier humor. The clarity of their diction and impeccable formal attire seemed out of context with the time.

Miranda, like Marais, has a Jewish background. She now is an adherent of the Huna religion, a metaphysical discipline of Polynesian origin, and considers herself a healer.

Miranda lives in one of the homes she owns in the Las Feliz area of Los Angeles. Her granddaughter lives next door with her mother, the divorced wife of Miranda's son by her first marriage. Her son is a musician and schoolteacher. Her daughter is a psychologist.

(She died on April 20, 1986.)

Miranda Marais with "Paullus," one of the pair of Polish roosters she kept on her property in Los Angeles. The widow also had sixteen hens, nineteen finches, and five cats.

Richard Lamparski

Jean Marais has been quoted as saying about his looks: "I believe that my physical appearance when I was young mysteriously answered the vague and fugitive taste of an era and fixed it, crystallized it for a time." In the late forties young men throughout Europe emulated his look.

Jean Marais

The once most popular male star of the French cinema was born on December 13, 1913, in Cherbourg, France. His parents separated shortly after his birth. Jean was raised in Paris by his mother.

He admits to having been "hopelessly spoiled and completely uninterested in school." Exasperated, his mother finally allowed him to enroll at the Théâtre de L'Atelier.

For four years he studied acting under Charles Dullin, the school's director, and Vladimir Sokoloff, who later had a Hollywood career as a character actor. Throughout the four years he was a student Jean appeared in movies such as *L'Epervier* (1933) and *Les Hommes Nouveaux* (1935).

The Jean Marais–Jean Cocteau collaboration began in 1937 when the beautiful young actor auditioned for the theatrical Jack-of-all-trades. Cocteau first cast him as "Sir Galahad" in a play he had written. Then, in 1938 he presented him on the Paris stage in *Les Parents Terribles*. Written by Cocteau, it was based on what Marais, who was by then his lover, had told him about his intense, neurotic relationship with his mother.

M. Marais believes that two people totally changed his life. His lengthy personal and professional liaison with Cocteau begat the films for which he is best known internationally and those for which he is likely to be remembered. The older man also gave him important career guidance and influenced his taste. The second pivotal personality was the French star Marugerite Jamois who, at the time he was being hailed as the most exciting young actor in France, predicted that his future would be a very limited one.

"To everyone else I was a great success," he said recently. "But to La Jamoise, who I held in high esteem, I would be seduced into being always what came easily to me. I *had* to prove her wrong. I have repeatedly taken parts totally unlike anything I've done before with her prophecy in mind. She meant to warn me and I am deeply grateful to her."

Marais, under Cocteau's auspices and at times with his scripts, had a string of successes on the Paris stage. But not until he played Don José in *Carmen* (1946) were United States audiences aware of him. In the title role was Viviane Romance* who was then number one at the French box office. Although not really convincing as a team, their individual sexualities and Bizet's music made the picture a hit, even in neighborhood theatres in North America.

Because of Marais, Cocteau, who had startled the world with his picture *Blood of the Poet* (1933), returned to the cinema. The first of their filmed collaborations seen in the United States, *Beauty and the Beast* (1947), perhaps the most successful, was the actor's idea. Then they made *Ruy Blas* (1948), *The Eternal Return* (1948), *Eagle with Two Heads* (1948), *The Storm Within* (1950), which was the screen version of *Les Parents Terribles, Orpheus* (1950) and its sequel *Testament of Orpheus* (1962).

Many predicted that the sensitive young man would be corrupted by Cocteau's life-style, which was seen as decadent. Instead, Marais is credited by those who knew the couple as being responsible for his mentor's giving up hard drugs. Long after they ceased being lovers, they worked together on screen and stage.

Throughout the fifties he was one of the Continent's leading heartthrobs. He played Crown Prince Rudolph in *The Secret of Mayerling* (1951) and began a series of swashbucklers with *Nez de Cuir* (1952). He played opposite Michele Morgan, * then perhaps the most popular actress in France, Alida Valli, * Dany Robin, Maria Schell, Catherine Deneuve, Danielle Darrieux, Nadja Tiller, Lilli Palmer, and Ingrid Bergman.

Souvenir (1950), *Inside a Girls' Dormitory* (1956), *Royal Affair in Versailles* (1957), *White Nights* (1961), *Patate* (1964), *Provocation* (1969), and *Peau d'Ane* (1970) are others of his pictures shown in art houses.

Warner Brothers offered him a contract but he declined because it would have prevented him from appearing in plays in France, something he has done throughout his career as a film star. The regret of his professional life is *Nude in His Pocket* (1957), a film he believes

Richard Lamparski

Jean Marais three months before his seventy-second birthday.

was his worst because of its direction by Pierre Kast.

In late 1984 he played in Paris in *El Cid*. He has for years done a one-man show of Marais as Cocteau. He has toured Canada, Japan, Italy, and France in this vehicle in which he speaks only lines the artist either wrote or uttered.

The scene in *The Last Metro* (1980) in which Gerard Depardieu attacks a pro-Nazi theatre critic was based on an incident in the life of Jean Marais.

In 1985 he made *Le Lien de Parenté* in which he appears in a wheelchair as the grandfather of a delinquent black boy.

Marais has two large dogs on his property in Vallauris on the Côte d'Azur. After Pablo Picasso, who lived near by, praised his sculpture, Jean started a line of pottery under his name, some handmade and some mass-manufactured, which is sold throughout France.

Chain-smoking and speaking through an interpreter, he said during an interview in September, 1985: "When I am in my house I am cooking because I am one of my favorite cooks. When I am working I am amusing and pleasuring myself. I feel wonderful. Life is very good!"

115

To journalist David Del Valle, an authority on horror films, Marian Marsh is the "perfect storybook heroine. Her innocence, delicate beauty, and vulnerability made audiences want to protect her from the lascivious, lustful fiends who were drawn to her."

Marian Marsh

The leading lady of the thirties was born Violet Ethelred Krauth on October 17, 1916, on the island of Trinidad. Her maternal grandfather, an English engineer, had settled in the British West Indies after being sent there on royal commission to oversee a building program. Mr. Krauth, a chocolate manufacturer, moved his wife and two daughters first to Massachusetts and then to New York before settling in Hollywood. He died shortly after the final move.

Her older sister began acting in pictures under the names Jean Morgan and Jean Fenwick after their father's death. It was she who took Marian to Pathé where she was placed under contract.

Under the name Marilyn Morgan she appeared briefly in *Hell's Angels* (1930), was featured in over thirty of the comedy shorts that starred James Gleason and his wife Lucille, and was loaned out to other studios, where she made features.

When Pathé during a change in administrations neglected to pick up her option she was free to accept an offer to appear in the Los Angeles production of the play *Young Sinners* with the silent star Molly O'Day. After she was singled out by critics a two-reeler she had made with Carole Lombard was screened for executives at Warner Brothers and she was placed under contract. Her studio, she was told, had "big plans" for her and asked her to change her name. She chose Marian Marsh.

The three years she spent on the Warner lot began very promisingly. She was named one of the Wampas Baby Stars of 1931 and John Barrymore approved her to play "Trilby" in his starrer *Svengali* (1931). Marian had a dreamy quality that was just right for a young woman who was supposed to be under a spell during most of the film. The picture was extremely successful at the time and it has since developed a large cult. The chemistry between her and the star was just as strong in *The Mad Genius* (1931), which was almost a reprise of their first picture. Although it, too, has a large following among buffs, the film did not do well at the box office when it was released.

Eventually, Marian Marsh played leads in movies opposite such stars as William Powell, Edward G. Robinson, Richard Barthelmess, Joel McCrea, Joe E. Brown, Van Heflin, and James Cagney. She is known today, however, as the virginal heroine of the two Barrymore vehicles and two others, *The Black Room* (1935) with Boris Karloff and *Crime and Punishment* (1935) as Peter Lorre's sister. The former, like all of Karloff's works, is of great interest today. The latter, which did not fare well with either critics or the public at the time, has grown in prestige over the years because it was directed by Josef von Sternberg.

Marian made *Over the Garden Wall* (1934) and *Love at Second Sight* (1934) in England. Then she played opposite the Continental star Luis Trenker* in *The Prodigal Son* (1935), which was filmed in the German and Swiss Alps.

Among her Hollywood features are: *The Road to Singapore* (1931); *Five Star Final* (1931); *Beauty and the Boss* (1932); *Notorious But Nice* (1933); *I Like it Like That* (1934) with Gloria Stuart;* *Come Closer, Folks* (1936) with the late James Dunn; [8] *The Great Gambini* (1937); *Prison Nurse* (1938) with the late Henry Wilcoxon; *Fugitive From a Prison Camp* (1940) with Phillip Terry;* and *House of Errors* (1942).

Her personal favorite is *The Girl of the Limberlost* (1936) because as a young girl it had been one of her favorite stories.

"I loved acting, but I had become a professional because we needed the money," she remarked in 1985. "In 1938 I married a businessman and just drifted away from my career. I had two daughters, which kept me occupied for quite a while. I did appear on TV in the fifties in a teleplay with Gary Merrill and I made a pilot with John Forsythe, but I found I didn't much like the work anymore and I knew I had never really missed it."

Marian was a widow when she married aviation pioneer Clifford Henderson in 1960. She worked closely with him in the development of Palm Desert, California, and, since his death in 1984 at the age of eighty-eight, has presided over his many civic, charitable, and financial interests. She is also active in the Girl Scouts of America and her Roman Catholic parish church. Her home, one of the first built in Palm Desert, has the largest swimming pool in the entire Coachella Valley.

Chris Dietrich

Marian Marsh is the founder and director of Desert Beautiful, an organization concerned with the environment and conservation of resources in the Coachella Valley of California.

Eddie Mayehoff was the blustery father of Jerry Lewis in the film That's My Boy (1951). *He repeated his characterization in the TV show of the same title that ran during the 1954–55 season and was brought back in reruns on CBS for the summer of 1959.*

Eddie Mayehoff

The spade-jawed comedian was born on July 7, in Baltimore, Maryland. His father was a Ukranian Jew who thrived as a clothing manufacturer in Norwalk, Connecticut. Both parents were converts to Christian Science and their only child graduated from Principia High School and College.

The young Eddie Mayehoff was intensely interested in music. He graduated from the Yale School of Music in 1932 with a teaching certificate and spent the next two years selling advertising in and writing for a magazine called *The Musician.* For a few years during the thirties he led the Eddie Mayehoff Orchestra that toured the Knott Hotel chain.

He credits Norman Corwin with the change in his career and his gradual emergence first as a comedy writer and then as a comedian. Corwin was impressed with the lyrics in the songs Eddie penned but couldn't get published. By 1939 Mayehoff had joined the writing staff of Corwin's production unit at CBS Radio. When his bent proved to be comedy Corwin encouraged him to perform his own material on the air. "He was my mentor," insists Eddie. "Everything I did came from what I learned under Corwin."

The Mutual Broadcasting Company carried the radio show *Eddie Mayehoff on the Town* during the 1940–41 season.

He was heard regularly on radio's *The Edgar Bergen and Charlie McCarthy Show* and toured the supper clubs in the Statler Hotel chain doing stand-up comedy.

Eddie Mayehoff was seen on Broadway in ten short-lived plays, among them *Rhapsody 1944, Concert Varieties* (1945), and *Rainy Day in Newark* (1963). His two hits were *A Season in the Sun* (1950) and *Visit to a Small Planet* (1957). Hal Wallis saw him on stage and felt the character Eddie portrayed so well, a loud-mouthed Rotarian type, would be very effective in movies.

Wallis produced his screen debut, *That's My Boy* (1951) in which Eddie played a middle-aged nine-letter man who is determined to turn his wimpy son into an athletic hero. It was a comedy with very poignant undertones of the generation gap and lack of communication within families. The well-meaning, if insensitive father was constantly trying to get his son to enter into activities that he himself would enjoy and excel at. But the boy, though wanting very much to please his dad, has totally different interests and capabilities.

The characters and situation worked equally well in the series that began on CBS-TV in 1954. On it Gil Stratton, Jr.,* played "Junior Jackson" and Mayehoff repeated his role of "Jarring Jack Jackson."

He was in two other films with Jerry Lewis, *The Stooge* (1953) and *Artists and Models* (1955). In *Off Limits* (1953), he supported Bob Hope and Mickey Rooney. He played a lawyer in *How to Murder Your Wife* (1965) and again in *Luv* (1967), his last. In both features he supported Jack Lemmon.

He made a television pilot for a proposed situation comedy called *See America First.* His costar, had it sold, would have been Terry Thomas.

Mayehoff says he walked away from his career because he just didn't want to perform any longer. "For every laugh you get from the audience or the crew there's a jealous, hateful thought from someone you're working with," he recently explained. "Funnymen are the most competitive people alive. They would will you to fail if they could. When I admitted to myself how much it bothered me I decided to get into another business."

Eddie became a partner in a sales promotion and advertising firm that represented nationally distributed products. The only time he was seen on camera was in television commercials, usually as "The Old Pro," spokesman for Falstaff Beer. He appeared in their print and television ads and on their radio spots for eleven years.

Mayehoff still does monologues at sales conventions and banquets, writing all of his own material.

He has no children from any of his four marriages and considers only one, which lasted for eleven years, to have been "serious." He lives in a luxury apartment building overlooking the Pacific Ocean, but has neither a telephone nor

Richard Lamparski

Eddie Mayehoff has been married four times but now lives by himself in an ocean-front apartment in Ventura, California.

an automobile. "I'm a cycle freak," explains Eddie, who rides his bicycle all over Ventura, California, where he lives.

Although well-read and soft-spoken in a one-to-one situation, Eddie Mayehoff thinks of himself as being very much like the boisterous jock he always played. "I should have been a small-town, back-slapping politician," he said recently.

Another part of him, however, identifies with the son of his character. Although he loved and greatly admired his father, the senior Mayehoff had no understanding of Eddie's early interests. For Eddie the emotional high point of their relationship came the night of the premiere of *That's My Boy.* As Mayehoff tells it: "We were standing on the street after the movie ended and he looked up and pointed to my name in lights on the marquee. Then he told me that I had made him very proud. Those were the happiest words I've heard in my whole life."

Crash of Silence (1952) was released in England under the title Mandy, *which is the name of her character, a disturbed deaf girl.*

Mandy Miller

The British child star of the fifties was born in Somerset, England, on July 23, 1944. Her original name was Carman Isabella Miller. She has been called "Mandy" from birth.

She was six years old when her father, a BBC Radio producer, took his two daughters to watch a film being made at Ealing Studios. Mandy believes they were taken at the request of her older sister. Like Mandy, she took dancing lessons, but she also went to acting classes and had done some commercial modeling.

During lunch in the commissary that day Mandy was noticed and offered a small role in what turned out to be the hit Alec Guinness starrer, *The Man in the White Suit* (1951).

She made ten more features and for a brief time in the fifties held the sort of popularity that Hayley Mills achieved in England in the sixties. Her biggest picture was *Crash of Silence* (1952) in which she played a disturbed deaf girl called "Mandy." It was such a success in England, where it was released as *Mandy,* that for a while afterward she was billed simply by her first name.

In *Background* (1953), Mandy, as the child of parents in the process of a divorce, was the center of attention. In *Dance Little Lady* (1954), her father tries to make her a Hollywood child star. Her mother in the film was Mai Zetterling.* *Adventures in the Hopfields* (1954) was a children's picture with Mandy the star. In the domestic comedy *Raising a Riot* (1955), Kenneth More was her father. She was the lead in the thriller *The Secret* (1955). She shared top billing with Phyllis Calvert* and the late Stanley Baker in the tearjerker *Child in the House* (1956).

Her movie swan song was *The Snorkel* (1958) in which she leads police to her mother's murderer, played by Peter Van Eyck. After a guest appearance on television's *The Saint* and one on *The Avengers* the public never saw her again.

Recently, she explained the abrupt end to her career: "As I got into my teens the competition for parts became quite keen. I'd had no training. I was an instinctive actress, which is probably why I seemed so natural."

"I was always made to understand that there was nothing special about me," she said in an interview. "I was told that I was just another little girl who sometimes played in a movie. Several times while I was starring in films people would turn to my mother and remark about how much I looked like Mandy Miller. She'd look at me and say, 'Yes, she does.'"

When she was eighteen Mandy became an *au pair* in a home in New York State. No one recognized her during that entire period and she never mentioned her career to the family she lived with. Only some of her friends and acquaintances know of her childhood. She does not bring up the subject.

In 1965 Mandy became reacquainted with a young man she had first met when she was seven and he was twelve years old. They were married the same year and have lived in Spain, rural Scotland, and in Aberdeen. Their oldest daughter is a graphic designer. Their youngest is already acting in grammar school plays. The son has just entered college.

Mandy's husband is the architect Christopher Davey. The couple lives in the rectory of a seventeenth-century church in East Sussex, England.

She insists she would not consider a return to acting because "I have absolutely no technique. I'm an amateur." Now, however, since only one of her three children lives with her and her husband, Mandy would like to become involved outside her home. Although she quickly adds that her recent efforts to master gourmet cooking consume much of her spare time and that she is taking a refresher course in French. She describes being a wife, mother, and homemaker as "absolutely fulfilling." The women's movement in general and Germaine Greer in particular are anathema to her.

"I never really wanted a career," she once explained. "That's probably why I never worked at it. I'm glad I did those pictures because everyone was very nice to me. I recently saw *Mandy* for the first time since it was made. My husband and I sat up in bed and both cried.

My children watch my films, but they roar with laughter over them. The only really sad aspect is it was my sister who really wanted the chance that I got."

Bill Tangeman

Mandy Miller on a recent visit to London for lunch with the author at the Hyde Park Hotel. She lives in East Sussex, England.

121

"The Menace to Mason" and "the Young James Mason" is how the press described Kieron Moore early in his career.

Kieron Moore

The young leading man of British films was born on October 5, 1924, in Skibereen, Cork, Ireland. The Anglicized version of the name he was baptized is Kieron O'Hanrahan. All the O'Hanrahan children were given Gaelic names and became fluent in the ancient language. It was taught to them by their father, a Gaelic scholar, and an active participant in Irish politics.

While studying medicine at St. Mary's College Kieron appeared in several plays performed in Gaelic at small Dublin theatres. One of the producers of the Abbey Theatre suggested he audition. He did and won the title role in *Everyman*.

The following year he became a member of the Abbey Players. There, while coaching Maureen O'Hara's sister, who was preparing for a screen test, he was noticed by an executive of Associated British Films. He was offered a contract but on the advice of an agent decided to free-lance instead. Kieron received a lot of attention in the play *Red Roses for Me,* a little-theatre production that proved so popular it was moved to the West End.

Paramount, Twentieth Century–Fox, and Alexander Korda offered him contracts but only the latter had a script that was to his liking. In *A Man About the House* (1947) he played a volatile Italian. It is one of his favorite parts. The other is that of a blind deaf-mute in *The Green Scarf* (1955).

Kieron Moore made pictures in England, on the Continent, and in Hollywood. Some, such as *Mine Own Executioner* (1947), *David and Bathsheba* (1951), *Darby O'Gill and the Little People* (1959), and *League of Gentlemen* (1960) were international successes. Others were: *Anna Karenina* (1948) opposite Vivien Leigh; *Ten Tall Men* (1951) with Gilbert Roland; * *Woman in Hiding* (1950) with Peggy Dow; * *Blue Peter* (1955) with Greta Gynt; * *The Day They Robbed the Bank of England* (1960); *Crack in the World* (1965) opposite Alexander Knox; * *The Key* (1958); *The Naked Heart* (1955) with Michele Morgan; * *I Thank a Fool* (1962) with Susan Hayward; *Arabesque* (1966) with George Coulouris; * and *Dr. Blood's Coffin* (1961) with Hazel Court. *

Although Moore did not quite fit the mold of what at the time was considered material for Hollywood stardom, he had a dashing quality, and a no-nonsense acting style that should have kept him in demand, indefinitely. His name and face were well known to audiences around the world. All of this made his abrupt disappearance from screen and stage all the more baffling. After *Run Like a Thief* (1967) and *Custer of the West* (1968), Kieron seemed to drop from sight.

"I have a great love of literature and the scripts I was being offered seemed worse and worse," he explained recently. "Also, due to the influence of a priest I knew and admired, I became acutely aware that I had to a great degree fallen away from my faith. I joined an organization of Catholic laymen concerned with hunger throughout Third World nations. I produced, directed, and narrated a documentary about conditions in Peru and another on Senegal. I wrote some articles and did radio broadcasts about what I found during trips to the Middle East and Asia. I didn't turn away from the theatre and pictures, I just became so involved in my work I never thought about my former profession."

In 1984 he admitted that he was out of touch with everyone he had ever worked with and saw very few films. His recollection of his own screen work was sketchy. On rare occasions he talks with his agent but has turned down every role that has been offered him for over a decade. "I'm still available," he insists, "but it would be the picture, not the part, that would attract me. I'd have loved to have been in *The Tree of the Wooden Clogs,* for instance. I would have to believe I was making a real contribution to a movie that made a positive, uplifting statement."

His wife is Barbara White, an actress who left her career when they were married in 1947. The Moores live outside London in Surrey. One of their four children is a Roman Catholic nun.

Since 1983 Kieron Moore has been associate editor of *The Universe,* a Roman Catholic newspaper with 140,000 weekly readers. Feature stories and editorials appear in it frequently under his byline.

Before medicine and acting he had seriously considered a religious vocation. He says that the work he does now he finds "very fulfilling. I'm helping my church and humanity in the best way I know, yet I have the great blessing of my own family. I hope I don't sound pious, because I've given much of myself to Catholicism not because I'm so good, but because I'm a sinner."

Richard Lamparski

Kieron Moore is the associate editor of The Universe, **the most widely read Roman Catholic publication in the United Kingdom.**

Lois Moran starred in silents, talkies, and on Broadway in Of Thee I Sing *(1931), but F. Scott Fitzgerald buffs know her as the inspiration for the character "Rosemary" in his novel* Tender Is the Night.

Lois Moran

The actress who inspired F. Scott Fitzgerald was born Lois Darlington Dowling on March 1, 1909. Her father, who was Irish, died in 1910. Her mother, who was related to the German poet-dramatist Friedrich Schiller, detected in Lois an interest in dancing. From a very early age she was given lessons and when she was ten years old mother and daughter moved to Paris to study.

Lois danced for several years at the Paris National Opera, was photographed by Man Ray, and made two films, one opposite the Continental star Ivan Mosjoukine.

Samuel Goldwyn wanted Lois for the lead in *Romeo and Juliet,* which he intended to produce. She then had to choose between the Hollywood contract, which began at $200 weekly, and the Marc Connelly play, which was offered to her at the same time at the same salary. Her mother, acting in the teenager's behalf, contracted her services to Goldwyn, but for only one film. That picture turned out to be *Stella Dallas* (1925). A huge success financially and critically, it made Lois Moran an extremely desirable property as soon as it was released. Free of commitments, she was in a position to command a top salary for all of her subsequent work in pictures and on stage.

Lois spent two years under contract to Fox Films and then free-lanced.

She made over two dozen features, including: *Reckless Lady* (1926) with Ben Lyon;[8] *The Road to Mandalay* (1926) with Lon Chaney; *Don't Marry* (1928) with Neil Hamilton; *Mammy* (1930); and *The Men in Her Life* (1931).

Blindfold (1928) was one of four pictures in which she was costarred with George O'Brien. She also played opposite Edmund Lowe, Warner Baxter, John Gilbert, and Al Jolson.

Lois studied voice in Paris and Hollywood before the advent of sound and was well prepared for her debut in talkies. She sang in several before going to Broadway where she starred in the musical *Of Thee I Sing* (1931) and its sequel, *Let 'Em Eat Cake* (1933).

The late film historian Don Miller wrote of Lois Moran that she had "a freshness, a naturalness that most young actresses lacked. In *Behind That Curtain* (1929) she manages to partly overcome the stilted screenplay and situations largely on her own merits. However, with the exception of *Transatlantic* (1931), the talkies she appeared in were not distinguished."

In 1935 she became the wife of Clarence M. Young, assistant secretary of commerce under Presidents Hoover and Roosevelt. He was one year younger than her mother. According to Lois, they were "wonderfully happy" until his death in 1972. After leaving government her husband served as vice-president of Pan American World Airways.

"I loved my career," she explained in a 1985 interview. "But I had always intended to give it up when I married. Actually, even after we settled in San Francisco, I continued to act. I discovered on the last day of the run of *The Petrified Forest* with Conrad Nagel that I was pregnant with my son. And when he was in his teens I did several plays at Stanford and in Berkeley."

The last time Lois Moran acted on film was as Preston Foster's leading lady on *Waterfront,* a television series that ran from 1953 to 1956 and featured Douglas Dick,[8] Harry Lauter,[9] and Pinky Tomlin.[8]

The *Red Rock News,* the local paper of Sedona, Arizona, carries a weekly column by "Lois Young." She had moved there shortly before she was widowed. Her son lives on the premises. Lois shares her house with a cat. The house contains a lamp made from part of the propeller of the original *China Clipper* and photographs signed to her and her husband by Colonel Charles and Anne Lindbergh, tenor Richard Crooks, baritone Lawrence Tibbett, President Herbert Hoover, and F. Scott Fitzgerald.

Of the rumors that persist concerning her relationship with F. Scott Fitzgerald, Lois Moran has said: "'Rosemary' in *Tender Is the Night* was based on me. Scotti even described my mother in that book, in words she did not like at all, I should add. People believe we knew each other in Paris, but I met the Fitzgeralds in Hollywood and I never really knew them very

Tim Young

Lois Moran celebrating her seventy-fifth birthday in her Sedona, Arizona, home.

well. He might have kissed me on the cheek a few times when I was leaving his home. I can't recall ever being with him when Zelda wasn't there, too. She was always sweet to me, by the way, and never seemed a bit peculiar."

Noel Coward wrote in his diaries: "Anna Neagle is and has been for years one of the greatest box office draws in the English theatre. She has a vast and idolatrous public."

Anna Neagle

The onetime First Lady of the English Cinema was born Florence Marjorie Robertson on October 20, 1904, in the London suburb of Forest Gate.

She used to sing along with the records played on the family's phonograph and pleaded successfully to be allowed dancing lessons after she was taken to see the legendary ballerina Anna Pavlova. By Christmas, 1917, she was in a children's play.

She danced in nightclubs and stage musicals and understudied Jessie Matthews in *Wake Up and Dream* (1929). It was during that show's run on Broadway that Anna came to realize she wanted very much to be a star.

After a few movie parts one of England's biggest stars, Jack Buchanan, accepted her as his leading lady in the stage musical *Stand Up and Sing* (1930). Her second and biggest break came when she played opposite Buchanan in

Magic Night (1932). It was the first of thirty-two features in which she was directed by Herbert Wilcox. Their partnership soon became the most successful in the British film industry. They were married in 1943.

Their second effort, *The Little Damozel* (1933), was such a hit that Anna was offered a Parmount contract but chose to remain with Wilcox. After *Bitter Sweet* (1933), a film its author Noel Coward preferred to its Hollywood remake, Anna played with her brother, Stuart Robertson, who was a successful singer in his own right, in *The Queen's Affair* (1934). The title roles in *Nell Gwyn* (1935) and *Peg of Old Drury* (1936) got Ms. Neagle a great deal of attention outside of Great Britain, but it was *Victoria the Great* (1937) that brought her undisputed international stardom. It was Britain's offering at the 1937 Paris Exhibition and opened in the United States at the Radio City Music Hall. It was a critical success, made a great deal of money, inspired a sequel, *Sixty Glorious Years* (1938), and brought Anna a letter from the exiled Kaiser Wilhelm in which he complimented her on a striking resemblance to the monarch, who was his grandmother.

She seemed to her countrymen and countrywomen the personification of the British ethos. *Picturegoer,* a magazine that awarded five of her movies its coveted Gold Medal, editorialized that no other star could "touch the hearts of the ordinary British cinemagoer as she can. She is as much a part of Britain as Dover's White Cliffs."

Some of Anna's English pictures had done very well in the United States, although American moviegoers seldom pronounced her name correctly (Nee-gul). When the Wilcoxes came to Hollywood to make features at RKO they brought with them their own scenarist and cameraman. *Life* magazine did a cover article and *Irene* (1940), the musical she did after *Nurse Edith Cavell* (1939), was a hit. *No, No Nanette* (1941) and *Sunny* (1941), however, did disappointing business domestically. Her one regret about this period is that she had to turn down Hitchcock's offer of the title role in *Rebecca* because she was firmly committed at the time.

Among the pictures she made after returning to England are: *The Yellow Canary* (1943) with Nova Pilbeam;* *Piccadilly Incident* (1946); *The Courtneys of Curzon Street* (1947); *Spring in Park Lane* (1948); *Maytime in Mayfair* (1949); *Odette* (1950); *Derby Day* (1952) with Suzanne Cloutier;* and *The Lady Is a Square* (1959), her last.

The Wilcoxes are credited with introducing Michael Wilding, her leading man in six of her pictures, to the public. When he married Elizabeth Taylor in 1952 Anna and her husband stood up for them.

She also personally produced three movies that featured her "discovery" Frankie Vaughan.

But films in general were hard hit by the new popularity of television. In 1964 Herbert Wilcox, who once admitted to having spent 25 million pounds in the making of movies, declared bankruptcy.

Approximately one-half of the hundreds of thousands of pounds Wilcox owed was the salaries that his company had failed to pay his wife. Anna, like a character she might have portrayed in one of her screen vehicles, immediately put her jewelry and real estate up for sale to pay the remaining debts.

Her appearance in the play *Charlie Girl* was one of the most dramatic comebacks in the history of the London stage. It earned her a place in the Guinness Book of World Records as the "Most Durable Leading Actress." Although the show was panned by critics when it opened in December, 1965, her fans kept it running until 1971. Anna played the part an all-time record of 2,062 performances and then took it on tour to Australia.

Perhaps the most remarkable aspect of the

Amaryllis Bierne-Keyt

Dame Anna and "Penny," one of the three cats that shared her house in the St. John's Wood area of London. She was made a Dame of the British Empire in 1969.

careers of Anna and her husband is that they were genuinely liked by those working for and with them. Noel Coward, upon learning of the death of Wilcox in 1977, commented on the "unimpaired 'niceness' of the both of them."

Anna leases the first floor of a mansion and its garden from the famed Harrow School, which owns the property. Alan Bates lives across from her. The rooms of her quarters are dominated by large glass cabinets in which are displayed the many awards garnered over the years by the Wilcoxes.

In a 1984 interview Anna Neagle spoke of the phenomenal appeal her pictures once had for the English public: "My husband and I were both doing exactly what we'd always wanted to do and doing it with the person we trusted most in the world. Ours was always a happy set. We felt we were working with real friends. We strived to make pleasant films about decent people. We wanted to give our audiences a lift. If we succeeded, if what we did touched people it is because what we ourselves felt came over on the screen."

(Dame Anna died on June 3, 1986.)

127

Effete and slightly sinister, John Newland struck just the right note as the host of One Step Beyond *and its sequel* The Next Step Beyond. *He was also the director of both TV series, which dealt with documented cases of psychic phenomena.*

John Newland

The former actor-director best known as the host of *One Step Beyond* was born in Cincinnati, Ohio, on November 23, 1917. Of his family background, he has said: "It was scandalous, ugly, and sordid; therefore, I never discuss it."

The day after his high school graduation, he left his home on a Chicago-bound bus. "I was tall, blond, and not a bit shy," he recalls. "I got a job with the trio that backed Ada Leonard, the fabulous stripper. Then I became one of the Ben Yost's Vikings, a group of twenty out-of-work actors who could sing. Milton Berle put us in the variety show he took all over the States and Canada."

Newland left the American Academy of Dramatic Arts after two days, feeling he already knew more than the instructors were capable of teaching.

After being singled out by reviewers in a little-theatre production of *The Moon in the Yellow River,* John went under contract to Warner Brothers. But when his screen test was run for Jack Warner, the studio head said, "That's no movie star. Pay him off."

Almost immediately afterward, he took over the lead in the Los Angeles company of *Lend an Ear.*

In 1950, when John Newland returned to New York City, all live TV drama emanated from that city. He appeared, usually in the lead, on virtually all the video playhouses.

In 1954, after his second season as a member of the cast of Robert Montgomery's summer replacement series, John asked the actor-producer-director for an opportunity to direct. He quickly became alternate director of the prestigious dramatic series *Robert Montgomery Presents.* One of his efforts on that show won a Peabody Award and was made into the feature film *That Night* (1957) that starred John Beal. [9]

"That movie should have changed my career," he said in 1986. "But for the good reviews it was still a 'little picture.' In those days, no major distributor bothered with 'art' films. My next, *The Violators* (1959), was even better, but it meant nothing professionally for the same reasons."

It was Loretta Young[8] who established him as a director. He was her leading man in fifteen of her TV shows and directed ten. From those credits, he was hired to direct *Bachelor Father,* *The Thin Man,* and *Police Woman.* He continued to act but with decreasing frequency.

David Del Valle, historian of the horror genre, credits Newland as having directed three of the best segments of the TV series *Thriller.* Brandon deWilde* starred in the first, *Pigeons from Hell,* during the 1960–61 season. John was the star as well as director of *The Return of Andrew Bentley* and *Portrait with a Face,* both during the 1961–62 season.

Newland is still recognized frequently and always for his role of host on the series first seen on television as *Alcoa Presents* from 1959 to 1961. The half-hour shows, dramatizations of reported cases of psychic phenomena, ran for years in syndication under the title *One Step Beyond* and developed a large and loyal audience.

John has coproduced and directed the made-for-TV movies *A Sensitive Passionate Man, Overboard,* and *The Suicide's Wife,* all three of which starred Angie Dickinson. He has, however, given up directing as well as acting.

He has never missed acting because: "I knew where I was headed. Soon I'd have been the one they hired if Ralph Bellamy wasn't available. And, too, I never found it very gratifying. The qualities I have were never used fully in the craft. My real talent is in understanding 'the game,' as it's called in Hollywood, and playing it well."

The greatest disappointment of his professional life was over what would have been a miniseries on the series of Los Angeles sex murders known as the "Hillside Strangler

Shelly Davis

**John Newland now concentrates solely on producing made-for-TV movies and miniseries. The Execution, Arch of Triumph, *and* Time Stalkers *are some of his recent network credits.*

Case." Newland and his partner held the dramatic rights and had been given the go-ahead by NBC, but then the project was abruptly canceled. John believes the deal was killed after pressure had been brought to bear by a religious group headed by the Reverend Jerry Falwell.

In his opinion: "The only performers who achieve any kind of recognition are the stars who usually play themselves throughout their careers and the truly great actors who can *become* any character they choose. That's because they have no idea who they are."

Newland has been married five times, twice to the same woman, but has no children. He and his present wife have been together for twenty years. The couple live in a large house with a black tile pool surrounded by a high wall in the Nichols Canyon area of Los Angeles, a city he has "always loathed."

The NEW Sound Of
RUTH OLAY

Because of Pete Ruggalo's recommendation to the record company Ruth cut Olay! *for the Mercury label in 1955. Red Norvo, Sy Zentner, and Shelly Manne were among the musicians who backed her on that, her second album.*

Ruth Olay

The jazz singer—chanteuse was born on July 1 in San Francisco. Her father, a rabbi of Reform Judaism, and mother were divorced when Ruth was seven years old. Her family name is Lissauer.

She was brought up by her mother, a trained lyric soprano, in Los Angeles. From a very early age, she studied piano and vocal technique. About the time she entered high school, Ruth ceased taking piano lessons when the teacher slapped her hands "just once too often."

Her brother's large collection of jazz records had a strong influence on her musical tastes and her vocalizing.

As a little girl, she often sang at the top of her lungs to and from school. One day two people in a parked car leaned out the windows and applauded.

"That was one of the most wonderful and important moments of my life," she said forty years after the occurrence. "I had no idea anyone was listening. I was singing because I love to sing. But I'd met the public, and it seemed they liked me."

When she was twenty, she married the writer Lionel Olay and moved with him to New York City for a few years. She describes her first husband as "very prolific and quite unsuccessful." When they divorced, she kept their daughter and his surname.

The divorcée returned to Los Angeles and took a secretarial job at Paramount Pictures. During her vacation, Ruth made her professional debut with her musical idol Benny Carter. For a month she sang with his group in San Diego. At the conclusion of the month-long engagement, she went back to the studio job. Then she worked for a while as a production assistant on Ralph Edwards's shows.

Ruth Olay became a name within the profession during the mid-fifties. She had been working as a waitress-singer in Los Angeles at the Cabaret Concert Theatre when Zephyr Records released her first album, *It's About Time.* That was followed by a year-long engagement at Ye Little Club, an intimate Beverly Hills nitery frequented by celebrities. Axel Stordahl came to hear her, as did Frank Sinatra and Judy Garland. Songwriter Jimmy McHugh brought Louella O. Parsons and Marlene Dietrich brought Rosemary Clooney.

Steve Allen and others gave her exposure on network television, but it was the seventeen appearances on the *Tonight* show that really established Ruth Olay nationally. Jack Paar,* who hosted *Tonight,* and the syndicated columnist Jack O'Brian became her greatest enthusiasts.

She began playing top niteries such as The Cloisters in Chicago, the Flame Show Bar in Detroit, and New York's Blue Angel.

During a play-date in Indianapolis, Indiana, she met a businessman who became her husband after a three-week courtship. She moved to Indiana, but after a year realized the relocation and the marriage were both mistakes. But the momentum of her career had been slowed, and she found herself involved financially with a hostile ex-husband.

While playing the Living Room in Manhattan, she signed with a personal manager who shortly afterward became her husband. By him, she had a son, but he raised her price so high she got almost no work.

After they were divorced in the early seventies, while on a visit to Copenhagen Ruth scored such a hit working with Ben Webster that she moved to Denmark. She stayed altogether over three years, appearing in the Tivoli and the Montmartre, the city's premiere jazz club. Between engagements, she supported herself as a presser in a dry-cleaning establishment.

"Europe is such a different life for a performer," she said in 1986. "They admired me for how I survived between bookings. Here, I'd have been known for the rest of my life as a pants presser."

In the mid-seventies, Ruth Olay returned to the United States to be with her two children. She admits she might have never reactivated her career had it not been for Gregg Hunter, a local newspaperman, radio personality, and Ruth Olay enthusiast. When he learned she had no agent, he arranged showcasing for her at several Los Angeles night spots. Another fan got her a booking at the Royal York Hotel in Toronto.

"I don't blame anyone, including myself," says the singer. "When I married those men and made the moves, I never considered what effect any of it might have on my professional

Stanton Z. LaVey

Many Ruth Olay fans, who know her only from recordings, believe her to be black because of her sound and choice of material. In this photo, taken in her Glendale, California, apartment, she is holding Watch What Happens, *the only one of her eight albums still available.*

life. Now, I'm at an age that I *must* think about security, so I'm back working during the week as a secretary in a bank. Weekends, I usually have local gigs. I never made it into the really big money, and what I did make seemed to wind up with my husbands. But both my kids are my friends. We really *like* each other, so on one front, I'm a big success."

Charles Champlin wrote of her "crystal-pure certainty of intention" and described her as a "rare, tasteful, and electrifying singer" in the *Los Angeles Times* in 1977. The same review called her voice, "a marvelous instrument, capable of a kind of fluting scat-song well up in the octaves and also a harsh growl south of alto when she chooses to be a belter on a bitter lament like 'Free Again.'"

Ms. Olay believes her life experience has enriched her artistry: "What I've been through over the years I use in my work, just as an actress or a writer would. Pain has compensation for creative people."

131

Peter Ostrum played "Charlie Bucket" in the movie Willie Wonka and the Chocolate Factory *(1971). It was based on Roald Dahl's novel* Charlie and the Chocolate Factory.

Peter Ostrum

The star of *Willie Wonka and the Chocolate Factory* (1971) was born in Dallas, Texas, on November 1, 1957. Peter has two older brothers and a sister, but he is the youngest in the family by ten years.

Peter was taken to a children's theatre presentation of the Cleveland Playhouse shortly after the Ostrums moved to Ohio. Soon afterward when the same group put on a show at his school the boy learned that the prestigious Playhouse offered Saturday classes for youngsters.

Peter appeared in several plays for children and then in three of the regular productions at the Cleveland Playhouse. Marian Dougherty, a New York casting agent, saw him in one and recommended him to play the key role in *Willie Wonka and the Chocolate Factory,* "Charlie Bucket."

The picture was made from the Roald Dahl novel *Charlie and the Chocolate Factory.* Not long before the casting agent noticed him Peter had read the book at the recommendation of a classmate.

When it was agreed that he would play the part Peter was offered a contract calling for an additional three features, which the Ostrums refused.

"I really wanted to play 'Charlie' because I'd liked the book so much," he explains. "But when I understood that David Wolper, the producer, could cast me in anything he wanted afterward I balked. My folks explained it to me and I didn't like the idea of not being free."

The movie was made in Germany and the twelve-year-old boy was accompanied by Mr. Ostrum for part of the time and his mother for the last months of the shooting.

He did almost no publicity when the picture, a major hit, opened in the United States. He has never had an offer for another acting role. His first and only interview was given in late 1985.

"When the picture was over it was like it had never happened," he said. "I returned to school and by the time it was in the theatres I'd changed a lot so I wasn't even recognized much. So, when I was, it was always a nice experience because of people like 'Charlie.' He's a nice kid. My parents told me to look on it as an experience, which is what I did. Acting was something that interested me. It still does, but not as a profession. The only time I ever considered it again was when I heard they were holding auditions to replace Peter Firth in *Equus* on Broadway. My thinking was that, perhaps I should at least present myself. Getting that part would have been like lightning striking twice. But I didn't get it. So I continued in school with the same majors—animal husbandry and veterinary medicine."

The entire experience of making the film was to Peter, "better than enjoyable. It was really interesting. But I had a chance to see what everyone's job entailed and I knew I didn't really want to do any of those things for a living. Including being stars like Gene Wilder and Jack Albertson. When it was over I was anxious to become just another kid again."

In 1985, after an internship at the University of Florida, Peter Ostrum, D.V.M., opened a practice as a veterinarian in Upstate New York. Ninety-five percent of his patients are cows.

The only one he is in touch with from his movie is Frawley Becker, who was the dialogue director. He considers Becker, who is now a screenwriter, to be his closest friend.

"My mom and dad were not at all stage parents," he has said. "They made sure I had a clear choice about what I did for a living. I'm really grateful to them because being a veterinarian is very gratifying. My dad was especially great because he had done a lot of acting in high school and college, but he never influenced me either way. And now that he's retired from the Bell System he's in New York City, trying to establish himself as an actor."

He never volunteers that he played "Charlie Bucket," the poor but honest boy who finds "Willie Wonka's" golden ticket, thus winning a lifetime supply of candy. If, however, someone recognizes his name and asks he is glad to talk about it. He has not seen the feature in "a long time," has not seen it more than "four or five times," and does not own it on video cassette.

Peter Ostrum, a bachelor, believes the best part of his one-movie career will be: "Watching *Willie Wonka* with my grandchildren."

Dr. Peregrine Wolff

Peter Ostrum with his Chesapeake Bay retriever "Lupine" near his home in Lowville, New York, where he practices veterinary medicine.

Korla Pandit had a definite mystique to those who saw him on early television. His appearance and much of the music he played seemed exotic to viewers. In over five hundred TV appearances the organist never once spoke.

Korla Pandit

The musical personality of early television was born in New Delhi, India, at the stroke of midnight, September 16/17th.

When he was two years and four months old, as the Pandit family story goes, Korla was discovered seated at the piano playing melodies. His mother, who was of French descent, had trained as a coloratura soprano, but neither she nor anyone else in their home had any idea how the child had learned to play.

He had been studying classic composition for two years with an English instructor when he was asked to perform before a large gathering of musicians. Reaction to the seven-year-old prodigy was so positive that Korla's father, an educator of the Brahman caste, decided his son should study abroad.

Mr. Pandit took him first to England and then to Chicago where he entrusted the boy, who was not yet thirteen, to the care of a close family friend.

At the University of Chicago he studied orchestration, piano, and string bass and practiced on the huge organ in the Rockefeller Hall on campus.

For a brief time after coming to Hollywood he played Mexican and Spanish music exclusively and was billed as "Juan Rolando."

Korla Pandit was appearing on *Hollywood Holiday,* a local radio program that emanated from Tom Breneman's restaurant at Sunset and Vine when he was "discovered" by Klaus Lansberg, the highly innovative director of KTLA, the first television station on the West Coast.

Korla did the music for Mutual radio's *Chandu the Magician,* and briefly had his own program on the local CBS station. When he guested on Rudy Vallee's show, the host predicted that television would be his medium. Vallee had seen how fascinated the studio audience was by the dark-skinned young man in the jeweled turban.

In late 1949 he was hired to do *The Korla Pandit Program* three times a week, provided he would also do the music for the children's show *Time for Beanie.*

At first there was only one camera, which was operated by the same man who also acted as the engineer-director. "It was just the two of us," recalls Pandit, "and we were always live. But eventually we became proficient and the audience was able to see me in close-ups, something that really brought me into their homes in a very personal way. Television showed my physical image to anyone tuned in, but as I played I was able to project my innermost thoughts and feelings from the heart as well. When I meet old fans they seldom fail to mention how I communicated with them. And, don't forget, in over five hundred TV shows, I never spoke one word—ever!"

The picture on the early television sets was frequently jiggly. Mad Man Muntz[8] once told the musician that his customers often said Korla, stationary and serene, was the easiest to watch for lengthy periods.

A program such as Pandit's could be produced for a relatively small amount of money and would bear repeated airings in the same market. But when he was approached, as he was several times, to sign a long-term exclusive contract to film and syndicate shows worldwide, it was with terms the artist found completely unacceptable.

"My compositions past, present, and future were all to be theirs, forever," he stated in 1985. "I explained that my services were for hire, but I was not for sale. 'We don't need you. We'll get Liberace,' they told me. My lawyer was informed that if I would not work for them, I would not work—ever. As it turned out, that was the case."

In the judgment of most television programmers, Pandit and Liberace appealed to essentially the same audience. Many believe that the early popularity of the exotic and somewhat mysterious Korla paved the way for so fey and flamboyant a personality as Liberace.

Most of Korla Pandit's fifteen albums are on the Fantasy label. In his personal appearances

Scott Dean Davis

Korla Pandit was billed as "The Prince of the Wurlitzer" when he concertized in November, 1985, at the Old Town Music Hall in El Segundo, California.

he plays music of all nations, periods, styles, and creeds while wearing a Nehru suit and the familiar jeweled turban. At times he plays the piano with one hand and the organ with the other. By foot pedal he operates the drums and a large gong.

Korla and Corliss, his wife, live in Calistoga in California's Napa Valley, along with an assortment of chickens, rabbits, and five cats. He has never smoked or drank and is an almost total vegetarian.

"I was not one of the flash acts who receive so much exposure today," he said in a 1985 interview. "Unlike Prince or Michael Jackson, no one styled me. I didn't even have a producer. I appeared exactly as I am. Without accompaniment or color I spoke the universal tongue—the language of music. Frequently my programs were televised late at night. What better time for my message through sound, which is always 'harmony, peace of mind, loving thoughts'? What better way to conclude one's day?"

"Porky" debuted with Our Gang *in* Little Sinner *(1935), playing Spanky McFarland's little brother. He appeared in forty-two of the shorts, which are now known as the* Little Rascals.

Eugene "Porky" Lee

"Porky" of *Our Gang* was born on October 25, 1933, in Fort Worth, Texas. He was adopted in infancy by a mortician and his wife, the chief stenographer for the Rock Island Railroad. His original name was Eugene Lee.

He has described his adoptive mother as, "the original liberated woman. She could drive a motorcycle, run a business, do anything, and do it well."

When her son was eighteen months old, Mrs. Lee sent his photo to producer Hal Roach along with a note pointing out his resemblance to Spanky McFarland, the most popular member of *Our Gang.* The studio replied, agreeing about the likeness and suggesting that some movie film be shot on the toddler by a local cameraman. Instead, the Lee family moved to Hollywood.

The nineteen-month-old boy proved to be both cooperative and photogenic. He was under contract to Hal Roach for the next four years, during which time he was featured in forty-two of the comedies. More than likely, he would have continued as a member of the "Gang" had he not grown so quickly. In his last in the series, *Auto Antics* (1939), he was almost as tall as the gawky "Alfalfa."

Both parents, but especially Mrs. Lee, were impressed by Gordon Douglas, who directed many of the *Our Gang* pictures. Although he was always billed as Eugene "Porky" Lee, he was called Gordon at home and has always used that name.

When the studio failed to pick up the option of their son's contract, Mrs. Lee offered his services to other studios. When there were no offers, they moved to Oklahoma City. Eventually, the Lees returned to Texas, where Gordon lived until 1971.

Gordon Lee remembers the making of the one- and two-reelers as a very happy time. He was almost five years old before he realized not all children made movies. "All the kids I knew were in pictures," he said in 1986. "I just thought it was something little boys and girls did when they weren't at home with their families. Because we played together, too. My very best friend then was 'Buckwheat.'"

By the time he reached tenth grade, however, he had begun to resent the "Porky" tag. "Kids can be very mean," he explained recently. "About that time, boys don't take well to teasing. So, I left 'Porky' behind completely. My wife knew about my background, but by then the shorts were no longer in the theatres and not yet on TV. Our son knew the little boy on the screen was his daddy, but he didn't seem to much care about it."

In 1971, Gordon, his wife, and son moved to Colorado. Until recent years, not even his best friend knew he was "Porky." After some local publicity, that friend talked him into appearing, along with Spanky McFarland, at the Trivia Bowl held annually by the University of Colorado at Boulder.

In 1984, Eugene Gordon "Porky" Lee filed a $1,950,000 lawsuit against the Hanna-Barbera Corporation, charging that their animated version of *The Little Rascals* featured a cartoon version of "Porky" without his consent. Within a year, he received a sizable out-of-court settlement.

Gordon's wife is a librarian and teacher. He teaches sociology, modern European history, and political science at an alternative school for high school dropouts near his home in Longmont, Colorado.

His hobby is buying, rebuilding, and selling postwar European sports cars. He is actively involved in the Democratic Party in his state.

The former "Porky" screened some of his films and talked about them to one of his classes in late 1985. It all went well until the students began asking the whereabouts of the other members. When told of those who were deceased, they seemed, to Gordon, "shocked and depressed."

On January 21, 1986, "Porky" attended the *Our Gang* reunion at Sidney "Woim" Kilbrick's Desert Shadows R.V. Resort in Cathedral City, California. Afterward, he commented: "The more of these get-togethers I go to, the more I understand what those comedies

Morgan Amber Neiman

William Thomas, Jr., the son of the late "Buckwheat,"[8] and "Porky" are friends and business partners. Thomas is a parole officer and lives in Cypress, California.

meant to people. I'm grateful to my friend who made me see that being 'Porky' was a responsibility. I hadn't seen Mickey Gubitosi in forty-five years when he reappeared as Robert Blake, movie and TV star. Aside from seeing the old friends, I've made a new one in Bill Thomas, Jr. We've formed a company that licenses the 'Buckwheat' and 'Porky' images for commercial purposes. The sole regret I have about all that has happened is that over the years I lost touch with his dad who had died before 'Porky' was 'found.' "

Devil in the Flesh, the film that brought Micheline Presle to world attention, was a sensation in Europe in 1947, but was not seen in the United States until three years later. Subsequently, she costarred in Hollywood films opposite John Garfield, Tyrone Power, and Errol Flynn as Micheline Prell.

Micheline Presle

The Continental star was born Micheline Chassagne in Paris on August 22, 1922.

She was seven years old when her father, a businessman, took her to a stage musical. Shortly thereafter she saw her first movie, *Trader Horn* (1931) with the late Duncan Renaldo and Edwina Booth. * She says that she never considered any life but that of an actress after.

During the summer of her fifteenth year Micheline, through the efforts of her godfather, was considered for a part in a film that starred Charles Trenet. * At that point she was doing so poorly in school that permission was granted

for her to study by correspondence. She immediately enrolled in acting classes.

When she was singled out of a group of extras and brought to G. W. Pabst he tested her for *Young Girls in Distress* (1939). She came over so well he allowed her to choose which of the two key roles she would play. Micheline picked the one she felt was most unlike herself. The picture was not a success, but to have been chosen, as she was, by the once great director gave her a definite professional cachet. Even before the picture was released Abel Gance heard of the new "discovery" of Pabst and hired her for a dual role in *Paradis Perdu* (1939). The Pabst picture brought her the Suzanne Bianchetti Award, a French film industry honor for promising new actresses.

Micheline continued to make films during the Occupation and by 1947 was considered the most important young female star in the French cinema. When she signed a two-picture-a-year contract with Twentieth Century–Fox, a Gallup poll taken in France showed her to be the one thought of as the "Best Actress in Films." All of this was the direct result of *Devil in the Flesh,* which was released in 1946 in Europe as *Le Diable au Corps.*

At her insistence Gerard Philipe was cast as the boyish lover to her somewhat older woman. It catapulted him to stardom.

She came to Hollywood with an agreement that promised her two features a year with co-star billing and the freedom to do other films. The man she had just married, William Marshall, was an American actor-turned-producer who had recently divorced another French star, Michele Morgan. But little in the film capital appealed to her.

"I signed that contract," said Ms. Presle in 1985, "because I was in love with Bill Marshall and wanted to be with him. I could have done almost anything I wanted in France then. My Hollywood pictures were all flops. I'm grateful because, although I have a lovely daughter by

In mid-1985 Micheline Presle, now blonde, had just made **Roast Chicken** *in France.*

the marriage, I was unhappy as his wife and I never took to Hollywood. To leave was very easy.''

In one of her first interviews the French star complained to columnist Hedda Hopper that people who took walks in Beverly Hills were considered peculiar and were frequently stopped by police.

"And I don't swim, so pools don't impress me," she added forty-five years later. "And I missed the changing seasons."

After viewing her first Fox feature *Under My Skin* (1950), she met with Darryl F. Zanuck for two hours. The producer listened to her complaints and promised that she would next act under the direction of Fritz Lang.

The picture, *An American Guerrilla in the Philippines* (1951), was in her words "quite awful." Her next, *Adventures of Captain Fabian* (1951) was produced and directed by her husband, and was even worse.

Micheline Presle returned to Paris with her daughter who is now known as the actress Tonie Marshall.

The few movies she made in the United States did not diminish the prestige she had and still holds in her homeland. Madame Presle has appeared without interruption on both stage and screen in France.

A longtime live-in affair with a painter recently came to an end. She now shares her large book-filled apartment on Paris's Left Bank with a cat. Her collection of elephants is displayed throughout the rooms.

Among her pictures are: *Boule Suif* (1945), *Twilight* (1949), *The French Way* (1952), *House of Ricordi* (1956), *Royal Affairs in Versailles* (1957), *The Bride Is Much Too Beautiful* (1958), *Demoniaque* (1958), *If a Man Answers* (1962), *Seven Capital Sins* (1963), *The Prize* (1964), *King of Hearts* (1967), *The Magic Donkey* (1970), and *La Téte à Ca* (1980).

139

December Bride *with Spring Byington and Frances Rafferty was on CBS-TV for six seasons beginning in 1954 and then was syndicated. Other cast members were Harry Morgan and Dean Miller.**

Frances Rafferty

The Mary Tyler Moore of the sixties was born on June 26, 1922, in Sioux City, Iowa. Out of work because of the Depression, her father took the Raffertys to Los Angeles in 1931 in hopes of finding employment.

In 1932 Frances won a scholarship to the Edith Jane Dancing School. The previous year Alexis Smith had been the winner. The two became friends, danced together in local productions, and are still in almost daily communication.

Frances dropped out of UCLA after one day to understudy Vera Zorina* in the film *I Was an Adventuress* (1940) under George Balanchine who choreographed the dance sequences.

During a performance of *The Firebird* at the Hollywood Bowl Frances fell, injuring her knee so badly she was forbidden any dancing for at least eighteen months. "Until then," she said recently, "I was committed to dance. It was Alexis who suggested I try acting while I was on the mend."

Frances Rafferty's photo collection includes a portrait of a monocled Mme. Maria Ouspenskaya, the Russian actress who was her drama coach.

At age nineteen she went under contract to Metro-Goldwyn-Mayer.

Although she is known chiefly for her work in television, Frances has appeared in over thirty features. In *Presenting Lily Mars* (1943) she danced only, but she had parts in *The War Against Mrs. Hadley* (1942) with Richard Ney* and Jean Rogers,[8] *Thousands Cheer* (1943), *Girl Crazy* (1943), *Barbary Coast Gent* (1944) with Binnie Barnes,[8] *Mrs. Parkington* (1944), *Bad Bascomb* (1946), *Lost Honeymoon* (1947), *The Hidden Eye* (1945), and *Abbott and Costello in Hollywood* (1945).

Her most memorable performance in a movie was as the daughter of Walter Huston in *Dragon Seed* (1944). Her character, an Oriental girl, is raped and then murdered.

Peggy Ryan* arranged the blind date with an air force colonel from Texas that led to marriage in 1948. They have a son and a daughter. The latter is married to actor John Ashton and is the mother of their grandson.

Frances was cast in *December Bride,* the role for which she is best known, because Lucille Ball remembered her from their days together at M-G-M. Desilu, the production unit she owned with her then husband Desi Arnaz,* produced the series that ran for six seasons beginning in 1954. On it she played "Ruth

Henshaw," daughter of Spring Byington who had the title role. The sitcom was very popular while it was on CBS-TV and then the 187 half-hours did well in syndication.

Today she says of the program: "My salary the first year was $100 a week. There were raises each season, but I certainly never made much money. I'm not complaining because $28 a day was what most actors were paid when I began on TV and a lot of shows were shot in one day. But Spring and I became great friends and we all worked in a lovely atmosphere. I enjoyed the experience tremendously, but when we were canceled I couldn't wait to move to the ranch we owned and completely disappear."

Actually, she remained on television for one more season, 1961–62, as "Nancy," the next-door neighbor on *Pete and Gladys*. The show was a spin-off of characters from *December Bride* and had Harry Morgan and Cara Williams[9] in the title roles. Morgan and Frances still speak frequently on the telephone.

Frances and her husband raised quarter horses on their forty-three-acre spread in Paso Robles, California. During the years since her retirement she has turned down the leads in several series on television, including one in which a complete unknown was cast instead. That actress, who Ms. Rafferty declines to have mentioned, became and has remained one of the most popular personalities on television.

Earlier in her career Frances Rafferty rejected an opportunity to play the ingenue role in the original company of *All My Sons*. Her reason: "I couldn't bear the thought of living in New York City."

When her husband became the general manager of Los Alamitos racetrack they moved back to Beverly Hills. Their apartment building is directly behind the one Frances and her family lived in when they went to California over fifty years ago.

Robert Mitchum and his wife were neighbors

Frances Rafferty-Baker and her Maltese, "Rocky." The collection of Oriental rugs she inherited are throughout her Beverly Hills apartment.

during her years on the ranch and lived in the apartment above her until recently. The couples are still close friends. Robert Paige,* a movie actor of the same period as Frances, is an old acquaintance of her husband.

Asked if she might consider returning to her profession, Frances Rafferty replied: "I couldn't. I've completely forgotten the craft of acting. It was all great fun, but retirement is even nicer. I never had any ambition other than to keep working as long as I had to. Now neither my husband nor I have to work and we don't."

She was frequently referred to as "the young Loretta Young"[8] during her heyday but says her role model as an actress was really Myrna Loy. Frances' language is quite at odds with the refined, Waspy image she projected.

A convert to Episcopalianism, Frances declares, "God and I are on very good terms."

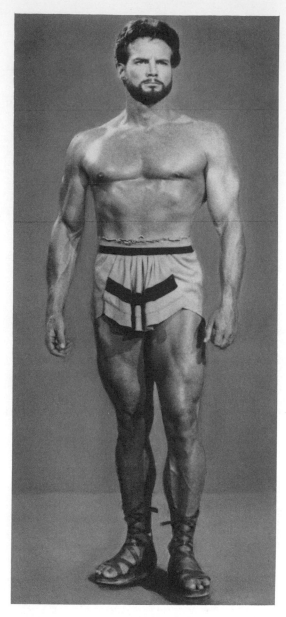

Steve Reeves was Mr. Pacific Coast, Mr. America, Mr. World, and Mr. Universe before acting in movies. For a few years in the early sixties he was considered the biggest male box office star in the world.

Steve Reeves

The muscleman movie star was born S. Lester Reeves in Glasgow, Montana, on January 21, 1926. He was six months old when he won his first title, "The healthiest baby in the county." After his father died when he was three years old Steve went to live on his uncle's ranch. He was ten when he moved with his mother to Oakland, California.

Steve's paper route required that he ride his bicycle up and down steep streets and he soon developed exceptionally muscular thighs and legs. When at seventeen he started lifting weights much older bodybuilders were struck by how quickly Reeves's body responded to the exercises. While serving with the United States Occupation forces in Japan he used rope climbing and tension exercises to further develop himself.

Steve Reeves first came to public attention when he won the "Mr. Pacific Coast" title. Six months later he was "Mr. America of 1947." Although that contest had been held since 1939 when Bert Goodrich became the first to win the title, many credit Steve Reeves with making it really well known. Three years later he was voted "Mr. Universe." He had an appeal that went beyond his physique and, although it took him years, he was the first "Mr. America" or "Mr. Universe" to become a movie star.

Reeves had a considerable following before he ever made a movie. His picture had appeared on the covers of literally every bodybuilding and nutrition publication, as well as a few that were merely concerned with males as sex objects. Exercise and health foods, however, had not yet gained acceptance by Middle America.

Cecil B. DeMille put him under contract and seriously considered Steve for the lead opposite Hedy Lamarr* in the film spectacle *Samson and Delilah,* but finally cast Victor Mature.* Many thought him the ideal "Li'l Abner," but Peter Palmer* played the role on

Broadway and in the movie version.

Director Pietro Francisci, at the suggestion of his thirteen-year-old daughter, saw Steve in the screen musical *Athena* (1954) in which he played Jane Powell's boyfriend, a small role, and signed him. Francisci, an Italian, had auditioned actors all over Europe, but had not found one who had both perfect body proportions and a heroic face to play the title role in *Hercules*.

The picture was a success when it was released in Europe in 1957, but nowhere near the smash hit it became in the United States two years later. It was followed by *Hercules Unchained* (1960), *The Giant of Marathon* (1960), *Goliath and the Barbarians* (1960), *Morgan the Pirate* (1961), *Thief of Baghdad* (1961), *The Trojan Horse* (1962), *The Slave* (1963), and *Sandokan the Great* (1964), all Steve Reeves starrers. In these costume epics he battled horses, raging bulls, Amazons, and former World Champion Heavyweight Primo Carnera. These exploitation features drew critical pans, but huge audiences at theatres and drive-ins.

The popularity of the Steve Reeves costume-action films spawned many imitators. None, including Richard Harrison* and Ed Fury,* his closest competitors, ever became the box office draw he was around the world.

Steve was the first choice for the role in *A Fistful of Dollars* that made Clint Eastwood an international star.

He was paid only $10,000 each for his first two starring features, but as soon as he became aware of the money they were making his price sky-rocketed.

Reeves says he does not miss acting, but neither does he rule out a comeback. He still gets offers such as a featured role in a "James Bond" film. He liked the part, but the producers would not meet his salary requirements.

In 1986 Reeves explained his absence from the screen: "I guess show business is an exciting profession, but for me the best part was the travel. I found acting very stressful. I never liked it. The most enjoyable time I had was making *A Long Ride From Hell* (1970). However, along with starring in it I was the cowriter and coproducer. I ended up with an ulcer. That was my last."

For over twenty years Steve has been married to a Polish-born woman who has acted at times as his press representative and agent. They frequently drive to Hollywood in their twelve-cylinder Jaguar, but seldom have any contact with film makers anymore.

He has a gym on his property, where he spends at least an hour each day. His supplemental exercise is aerobic walking, which he has described and promoted in his book *Power Walking*. In 1986 his weight was just over 200 pounds and his arms, calves, and neck each measured seventeen and a half inches.

Steve Reeves grows most of his own food organically on his fourteen-acre estate, Hacienda del Sol, near Mount Palomar in Valley Center, California. He has several boxer dogs, eight Morgan horses, a goat, and orchards of lemons, oranges, and avocados.

Richard Lamparski

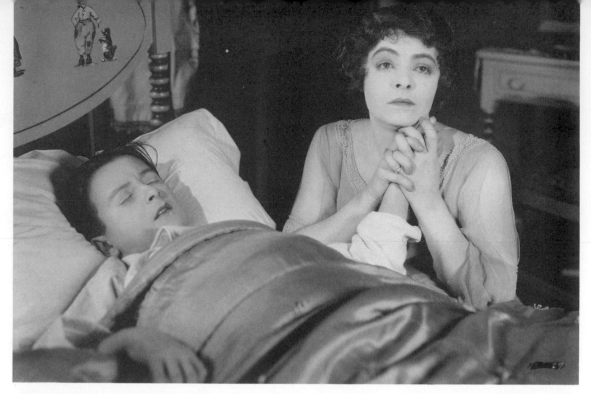

The scandal of her husband's death was still fresh in public memory when Dorothy Davenport Reid appeared in Human Wreckage *(1923), an anti-drug exploitation movie. Wallace Reid fans jammed the theatres where she made personal appearances to see and hear the widow of the stalwart star who had died of narcotics.*

Dorothy Davenport Reid

The motion picture pioneer was born on March 13, 1895, in Boston, Massachusetts, while her parents were on tour. Her mother was Alice Shepard, leading lady to her husband, Harry Davenport. Later in his career he became a familiar face to moviegoers for the characters he portrayed in such films as *Gone With the Wind* and *The Ox-Bow Incident.* His father, E. L. Davenport, was very well known in the theatre at the time, as was Dorothy's aunt, Fanny Davenport.

Dorothy Davenport had been in pictures since 1910 and was well established as a leading lady when she met Wallace Reid. They played together in *His Only Son* (1912) and were married in 1913 with Ruth Roland, queen of the serials, as the bride's attendant.

Reid became what today would be called a superstar, as sure a box office draw as Douglas Fairbanks, Sr. They built a home that had the first backyard swimming pool in Hollywood. After Dorothy bore a son, the couple adopted a daughter. The Reids appeared to have everything. The secret they shared was the knowledge of his addiction to morphine and alcohol.

"Stout-hearted" would best describe the sort of hero Reid portrayed in most of his pictures. His fans thought of him as the "picture of health" and "a man's man." When the truth about his condition was revealed, the public was stunned, but not unsympathetic. Many a World War I doughboy came home like Wallace Reid, a "dope fiend." The screen star died

January 18, 1923, while in a clinic trying to break his habits.

Dorothy maintained throughout her life that Wallace Reid had become addicted to morphine when he was injured during the making of *The Valley of the Giants* (1919) and given the drug to ease his pain.

According to Mrs. Reid, as she was usually addressed, neither she nor her husband had ever used drugs, nor were they aware that narcotics were about as plentiful then in Hollywood as they are now. Her son commented recently: "She had an image to protect—two, actually. Because the movie business itself was threatened. This wasn't Hollywood's first dope scandal. It was just the biggest."

Dorothy Davenport Reid remained active in the motion picture industry for many years, although her maiden name was sometimes given in the credits. On other pictures she was simply Dorothy Reid.

Within months of Reid's death *Human Wreckage* (1923), a picture about the "evils of narcotics," was in the theatres. She supervised the production and received top billing. One of the most successful exploitation films of the era, it contains a scene in which drug addict Bessie Love tries to quiet the baby she is nursing by rubbing heroin on her breast.

Her friend Adela Rogers St. John scripted *Broken Laws* (1925) and *Red Kimono* (1925) for her. The former was a warning to indulgent mothers. Dorothy headed the cast of both. *Red Kimono* purported to expose prostitution, then referred to as "White Slavery," and featured Priscilla Bonner.[9]

The Satin Woman (1927) was one of her final screen appearances. Henceforth, she worked behind the screen in the studios as producer, screenwriter, and director into the fifties.

In *Sucker Money* (1933), which she codirected, it was the fake mind readers who were being exposed.

Road to Ruin (1934) was based on her original story of high school boys and girls corrupted by "loose" morals.

Dorothy and Wallace Reid had helped founder Carl Laemmle turn the first spades of earth in the ceremony that commenced construction on Universal Pictures in 1914. Until a few years before her death in 1977 she lived only two blocks from the studio's main gate. Her house was strewn with mementoes of the two careers. Each yuletide she put up the small, artificial Christmas tree that Cecil B. DeMille and Will H. Hays had brought to her husband weeks before his death.

Mrs. Reid's daughter predeceased her by several years. The son, William Wallace Reid, made several screen appearances as a young man, but is now an architect.

Dorothy Davenport never remarried. "I wanted to," she once told an interviewer. "But no one came around. He (Wallace Reid) was the kind of man that men tried to be like and I guess they didn't feel up to following him. I expect Mrs. Clark Gable knows what I'm talking about."

Dorothy Davenport Reid was a Christian Scientist. She died on October 12, 1977, at the Motion Picture and Television Country House and Hospital.

Richard Lamparski

Her autobiography was published in 1971. Shortly afterward Liz Renay had what she describes as a "big romance" with Glenn Ford. She is now writing the sequel, *My First 2,000 Men*, which names Burt Lancaster as one of the best lovers of her life and Jerry Lewis as the "all-time, absolute worst."

Liz Renay

The life that resembles a Hugo Haas movie began in Mesa, Arizona, on April 14, 1926. Her ancestry includes one-eighth Iroquois Indian. Her original name is Pearl Elizabeth Dobbins.

Mrs. Dobbins, a Pentecostal, brought up her daughter very strictly, but Pearl's grandmother advised her to "feel free—most of life's rules are bunk."

At age thirteen she decided she would "totally ignore what I'd learned in our church and what Mama had tried to teach me at home. I drank, smoked, and petted. I did everything but go all the way."

When she was fifteen Pearl married a soldier. She and her husband, the first of seven, parted after one week. Then there was a brief marriage to a marine.

The next husband brought her east, promising to take care of Liz and her two children. But she very quickly became one of Eileen Ford's top models. He then quit his job and insisted she turn over all her earnings. When he beat her son, Liz walked out with the boy, her daughter, and only $20 to her name.

She continued to model during the day, but got a second job performing in one of the small nightclubs on West 52nd Street. She had recently won a Marilyn Monroe look-alike contest and was the idealized form of a type that was extremely popular at the time. The underworld characters who frequented the nitery took to her immediately.

She was kept by one hoodlum who introduced her to others such as Frankie Carbo, "Little Angie" Carfono, and Albert Anastasia. Liz acted as hostess whenever the gang gave parties and was seen around Manhattan with the kingpins of crime. She wore clothes that were expensive, if flashy, and a fortune in jewelry, either given or loaned to her by shady friends. Columnist Walter Winchell noted the company she kept and her eyes, which are green, flecked with hazel. It was he who dubbed her "The Girl with the polka-dot eyes."

She appeared as a contestant on *You Bet Your Life*, acted on a *Sugarfoot* episode, and starred with Harry Lauter[9] in the movie *A Date with Death* (1959). She believes that Cecil B. DeMille was seriously considering her for the lead in one of his epics when her friend, crime boss Albert Anastasia, was a victim in a gangland murder in 1967. When she was called before a New York grand jury, all her hopes for an acting career were dashed forever.

Mobsters trusted Liz Renay to carry messages and money. She asked no questions and never betrayed a confidence. When she was tried on a conspiracy charge with her boyfriend, West Coast racketeer Mickey Cohen, she was defended by a prestigious law firm and press agent Shelly Davis was retained to affect her image. Though Cohen went to jail, Liz was given probation. But it was soon revoked.

Liz explains: "Bobby Kennedy who was then Attorney General, was furious that I walked. He hated Mickey like poison and saw to it that I was set up for parole violation."

She served twenty-seven months without incident and has avoided any connection with criminals ever since. The underworld element in Las Vegas, where she lives, considers her "very cool." As one said recently, "Those luscious lips kissed but did not talk. She never told anything and this is appreciated. Renay is respected and looked after."

Her home, near Caesar's Palace, is surrounded by twenty-two fruit trees and is shared by the Pekinese dogs she raises.

Ms. Renay is not in love and has had no therapy. Yet she describes herself as a "very joyful person. I like myself and my life."

She feels she has been a good mother and is still puzzled by the suicide of her daughter. After she shot herself on her thirty-ninth birthday in 1981, Liz took charge of two grandchildren. She also has two great-grandchildren.

Liz says that she has never smoked nor used any drug and drinks only a "little white wine now and then." She does not have a physician and claims never to be ill. Her second book, *Staying Young,* in 1981, was a personal endorsement of natural foods, cosmetic surgery, and the vacuuming of cellulite.

"I'm Rehearsing a Risqué Comedy Act" is her current project, a show she plans to open soon in Las Vegas. She describes it as "One hour of solid comedy—very sexy and blue. I have an entire six minutes on Joan Rivers where I pick her apart the way she does others, only with more taste. Much to say about sex changes, sex operations (the Flexifat implant, etc.), transvestites, S. and M., etc. The act ends with an audience participation in a wild sex game. The closing song is *Don't Call Him a Cowboy 'til You See Him Ride.* At the close I invite the whole audience to my place for an orgy."

Raised under the strictures of the Assembly of God church, Liz is now an agnostic. Guilt to her is "a big waste of time." Her goal is to "Have fun and be fun. I want to *enjoy* my life." She does not think about old age or dying because: "I may never reach old age and no one knows what dying is like, so what's there to think about?"

Courtesy of Liz Renay

Sylvester and Frank Stallone with Liz Renay at a Las Vegas party during the summer of 1985. The sexagenarian dates Frank Stallone and is painting him as a Roman gladiator.

To Richard:
I've never enjoyed
an interview more than
Marjorie

In the movies Marjorie Reynolds danced with Fred Astaire, was sung to by Bing Crosby, and had leads opposite Bob Cummings, Boris Karloff, Ray Milland, the late George O'Brien, and Abbott and Costello. On TV she played the wife of William Bendix in "The Life of Riley."

Marjorie Reynolds

The leading lady of movies and television was born Marjorie Goodspeed on August 12 in Buhl, Idaho. Her parents were well into middle age and had two other daughters, the youngest of which was seventeen years older than their baby.

Marjorie was brought up in Los Angeles where she took dancing, singing, and acting lessons. In her youth Mrs. Goodspeed had wanted to be an opera singer and started taking her little girl to studio casting offices when she was four years old.

As Marjorie Goodspeed she played small parts in many silent films. When she entered her teens she began using the name Marjorie Moore. In 1936 when she married Jack Reynolds, Samuel Goldwyn's casting director, she took his surname.

For a while she had a stock contract with Paramount Pictures and appeared in *Murder in Greenwich Village* (1937). There is a glimpse of her in the scene in *Gone With the Wind* (1939) in which "Rhett Butler" and "Scarlett O'Hara" see each other for the first time.

Then Marjorie Reynolds was signed by Monogram Pictures, where she had the leads in their low-budget features such as *Mr. Wong in Chinatown* (1939), *Doomed to Die* (1940), and *Top Sergeant Mulligan* (1941).

Her break came when someone at Paramount thought of her when Mary Martin became unavailable to play in *Holiday Inn* (1942). At the audition when Irving Berlin, who wrote the music for the picture, asked her to sing, the only song she could think of was "The Hut Sut Song." Even though she stepped on Fred Astaire's toes, he and his costar Bing Crosby approved her as their leading lady. It is the film for which she is best remembered and is her personal favorite. Her songs in it were dubbed by Martha Mears.

Marjorie never got to know Crosby well, but reasons he must have liked something about her because he accepted her to play the girl he marries in *Dixie* (1943).

"The Bing that we saw on the screen was very different from the person I worked with," is all she will say about the star.

Some of her other screen credits are: *Star Spangled Rhythm* (1942), *Up in Mabel's Room* (1944), *Ministry of Fear* (1945), *Duffy's Tavern* (1945), *Monsieur Beaucaire* (1946), *That Midnight Kiss* (1949), *The Great Jewel Robbery* (1950), *His Kind of Woman* (1951), *Models, Inc.* (1952), *Juke Box Rhythm* (1959), and *All the Marbles* (1981).

In 1948 Marjorie took over the costarring role in the West End production of *Burlesque* when Mary Martin left the cast.

In 1953 as soon as her divorce was final she married John Haffen who had acted under the name John Whitney. By then he had become a film editor.

Along with *Holiday Inn,* the other highlight of her career was the part of the patient, good-hearted "Peg Riley" on *The Life of Riley.* The half-hour TV shows were filmed between 1953 and 1958 with William Bendix in the title role and are still being shown.

Marjorie would like to hear from Wesley Morgan who played "Junior Riley," but has no idea where he is. She and Lugene Sanders, * her daughter "Babs" on the show, have remained close friends. She is not, however, in touch with anyone else she worked with, something she has come to somewhat regret.

"My second husband and I were very, very close," she explained recently. "Neither of us felt the need for anyone else. He died in 1985 after a lengthy illness and since then I have come to realize that I should have developed relationships outside of my home. Fortunately, my daughter who is by my first marriage works at Twentieth Century–Fox, which is close by. She stops by frequently and sometimes stays with me."

Occasionally Marjorie appears on a TV commercial, usually playing a grandmother. She finds, however, that those who cast for commercials neither know nor care about her background.

"The crews and production people are all very young," she says. "When we're not shooting I'm left completely to myself. It's all so different today. In the old days I never felt so alive as when I was on a set. It was wonderful fun making pictures. People ask me now if I didn't want to be a star. I never really thought about it because I always felt very lucky to have gotten as far as I did. Just look at the competition that was around then."

Marjorie does volunteer work at the Jules Stein Eye Institute on the campus of UCLA. She narrates video cassettes that are shown to patients prior to eye surgery.

Widowed in 1985, Marjorie shares her Cheviot Hills home with three stray dogs.

Jordan Lee-Benner

Patricia Roc was one of the British film industry's foremost stars in the forties. She also appeared in international productions and was brought to Hollywood by Walter Wanger for one picture, Canyon Passage (1946).

Patricia Roc

The star of British films was born in London on June 7, 1915. Her original name was Felicia Riese. No one in her family was connected with

theatre or movies, but when she told them of her acting ambitions they were very supportive.

While growing up her sister frequently brought to their home her best friend, Joyce Howard,* who years later became a British film star.

Patricia made her debut in *Nuts in May* (1938) in the West End. A scout for Alexander Korda saw her in the stage production and she was immediately cast in *Rebel Son* and then *The Gaunt Stranger,* both in 1938. Her first appearance on film was as an extra in *The Divorce of Lady X* (1937), a Merle Oberon starrer.

While still a student at the Royal Academy of Dramatic Art, she was singled out and tested for the leading role in *La Bête Humaine* opposite Jean Gabin. Simone Simon* got the part in that picture. Patricia was told that she photographed too young, a drawback she was to endure for several years of supporting roles.

Her films include *A Window in London* (1939) with Sally Gray;* *Three Silent Men* (1940); *My Wife's Family* (1941) with Joan Greenwood;* *We'll Meet Again* (1942) with Vera Lynn;* *2,000 Women* (1944) with Phyllis Calvert;* *Madonna of the Seven Moons* (1944) with Jean Kent;* *The Wicked Lady* (1945) with Margaret Lockwood;* *When the Bough Breaks* (1951) with Rosamund John;* *Circle of Danger* (1951) with Ray Milland; *Something Money Can't Buy* (1952); *The Hypnotist* (1957); and *Bluebeard's Ten Honeymoons* (1960) with Corinne Calvet. *

There were two other features that she wanted and was tested for but did not do: *First of the Few* in which she would have played opposite Leslie Howard and *Hatter's Castle* with Robert Donat, which was a hit on both sides of the Atlantic.

Under contract for much of her movie career to J. Arthur Rank, Patricia Roc is to fans in her own country a "Gainsborough lady."

When her name was changed for the screen

she chose her surname from the Roc Studios that had recently been built in Elstree, London.

Patricia was first married to a Canadian physician, a union she describes as a "wartime marriage." It ended in divorce. She was widowed by her second husband, a French cameraman who was the father of her son. When she married her present husband over twenty years ago he didn't recognize her name or her face. "He simply liked pretty ladies and at that point I still qualified," she has said.

One of the last performances she gave was as guest star on the first episode of the television series *The Saint*.

When she retired it was without regrets, although she insists she enjoyed every one she ever worked with and the making of all of her films. "I wouldn't have missed any of it for the world," she said in 1985. "But then I wanted a different life, which is what I've had. I feel that I've had two lives, both wonderful. Most people have to make do with only one. I've been very fortunate."

After her husband retired from the shipping trade the couple did a lot of traveling. In recent years they have given up their London flat to settle in a condominium in Locarno, Switzerland. Its decorations include original works of Dali, Boudin, and Toulouse-Lautrec, and Patricia's collection of seventeenth- and eighteenth-century fans, snuffboxes, and pomanders made of gold and silver. The only photograph of Patricia Roc on view is one taken with Ronald Reagan when he visited her set when she was making *Canyon Passage* (1946). She corresponds with Margaret Lockwood and Phyllis Calvert and occasionally sees Paulette Goddard who has a home in Ascona, Switzerland.

Richard Lamparski

The apartment Patricia Roc and her husband share with a stray cat overlooks Lake Maggiore in Locarno, Switzerland, near the Italian frontier.

151

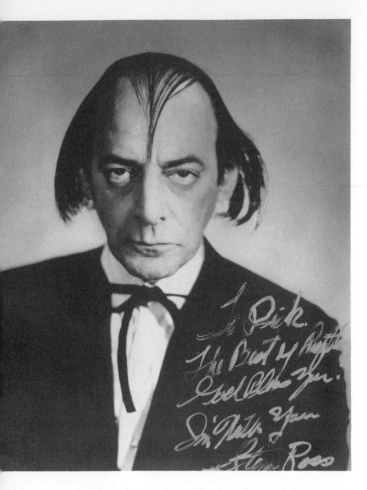

"I'm with you!" the line so closely identified with Stan Ross, was written by the team of Norman Lear and Ed Simmons. He received his greatest exposure in TV appearances with Jackie Gleason, a man he has called "the lowest, cheapest, meanest man I've ever known in my life."

Stan Ross

The man Jackie Gleason called "the world's greatest living sight-gag" was born Abraham Schiller in Brooklyn. His birthday is February 14, 1926.

One of nine children, he sold newspapers on a street corner while still in grammar school to supplement the meager living his father made as a tailor. Whenever he had the price of admission Stan went to movies and vaudeville shows. He imitated his idols, stars of the day, for the amusement of his customers. He dreamed of becoming an entertainer, but could never muster the courage to do his impressions at amateur shows until one day a man took him into a bar and promised to buy all of his papers if Ross would do "Eddie Cantor" for the house.

"That was it," remembers Stan. "My dad hit the ceiling when I announced I was going into show business. My brothers and sisters called me a bum, but my mother, may she rest in peace, she understood. She'd slip me a little money whenever she could."

Until he was drafted at the outbreak of World War II Ross worked in nightclubs and presentation houses with the comedian Archie Robbins.

For three of the years that Ross served with the United States Army Signal Corps he was stationed in the Aleutian Islands along with Bernard Kalb and Dashiell Hammett, members of the same unit.

Stan had his heyday during the early fifties when live comedy shows proliferated on television. His specialty, physical comedy, was much in demand and he was used frequently by most of the big-name comics. Milton Berle, "Mr. Television" at that time, hired him for forty of his shows. Jackie Gleason used him over a hundred times when he reigned on the medium as "Mr. Saturday Nite."

Stan Ross goes out of his way to emphasize his bitterness over the way he feels he has been treated. "I'm a stooge, a bit actor," he has said. "The lowest rung on the comedy ladder. All big-time comedians are sadists and monsters. Berle, Jerry Lewis—all of them except Jack Haley treated me like dirt. I was on nineteen shows with Jonathan Winters who couldn't even bring himself to speak to me except in a skit. But the worst of all is Gleason. Over a hundred times I worked for him, but when I had a coronary years ago my wife, desperate with worry, called him. He wouldn't even come to the phone. 'The Great One' had his secretary tell her to go to the union if we needed a loan. He never hired me that an insult didn't go with it. He calls small-timers like me 'Pal,' only the way he says it sounds like 'scum.'"

It was in 1950 on Jack Haley's[8] show that he first uttered the line that became his trademark. "I didn't think too much about it at the time," the comic said recently. "I was suppose to pop out of a box or something and say 'I'm with you!' I did it. It got a laugh and I was paid $75. I would never have given it another thought, but the very next day a cab driver yelled out his window at me, 'Hey, I'm with you!' People looked at me and laughed. A few of them repeated it and everyone laughed some more. I thought it was a fluke, but it kept up everywhere I went. Right away I got calls to do it. Usually, that's all they wanted—the line and the take I delivered it with. It always worked. People screamed."

Stan Ross never made a great deal of money at his craft. Even when he was appearing almost weekly with Gleason he worked as a salesman at the showroom of a wholesale garment firm. His wife was employed until her death in 1980 as a salesperson at Giorgio's in Beverly Hills. He supports himself still with occasional bit parts and walk-ons, and receives a pension from the Screen Actors Guild.

In May, 1985, he received a residual check for the small role he played in the television dramatization of *Requiem for a Heavyweight*. It was the sixty-third time he had been paid for the show, which had originally been televised in 1956, and it amounted to a net of $9.00.

Ross never aspired to stardom, but sought to establish himself as a respected character actor. He is proud of his work in *How to Murder Your Wife* (1955) and *Beyond the Valley of the Dolls* (1970). Usually, when he acts today, it is as a derelict, a role he has played on *Fantasy Island, Starsky and Hutch,* and *Vice Squad.* There is a brief glimpse of him as a pirate in the David Lee Roth video *Just a Gigolo.*

Sarah Richardson

"I live alone and look it," Stan Ross likes to lament. Actually, he shares a West Hollywood apartment with his son, Marlon.

153

"I would never cut off my nose to spite my race" was one of the lines Benny Rubin used in his vaudeville act. Between 1920 and 1932 he played the Palace Theatre in New York City twenty-six times.

Benny Rubin

The Jewish dialect comedian was born in Boston, Massachusetts, on February 2, 1899. He learned clog dancing by watching other boys in wooden shoes entertain people on street corners. He was ten years old when he left school and ran away from home briefly to dance for the prize money in amateur shows. Much later he fought in forty-eight boxing matches, again for prize money. As Benny tells it: "My parents had seven sons and we were poor as hell. In those days all boys did whatever they could to bring home a buck." Fred Allen, later one of radio's most popular comedians, was one of the boys he grew up with.

His first professional engagement as an entertainer was as part of *Billy Hall's Revue* when it opened in Rhode Island in 1914. By 1916 Benny was in *English Dandies,* a tab show that was performed on showboats that cruised the Ohio and Mississippi rivers.

Rubin developed comedic timing and some ethnic dialects during the time he spent touring the burlesque wheels. He is best remembered for his Yiddish characters, but impersonations were part of his act and he had a specialty slip-and-slide dance that was very popular with vaudeville audiences. Occasionally, he played a trombone.

By 1923, working both as a single and at times with a partner, Benny was playing all the key vaudeville theatres in the nation. He wrote much of his own material and usually produced his own act. Max Baer and Cliff "Ukelele Ike" Edwards were two of those he was teamed with. He was probably at his best when he appeared with Jack Haley.[8] The duo got top billing at the Palace Theatre, where they also were co-emcees. It was during this engagement that Rubin became ill and Milton Berle filled in for him, a booking that was to be pivotal in Berle's career.

Rubin was on Broadway in 1927 in *What a Widow!* and took over when Willie Howard left the cast of *Girl Crazy* in 1930.

M-G-M placed him under contract at $2,500 a week. He was the star of shorts such as *Naughty Boy* (1927) and *Benny Rubin in Seven Minutes of Your Time* (1928) and of the feature *Sunny Skies* (1930). He supported Marion Davies in *Marianne* (1929), Joan Crawford in *Montana Moon* (1930), and Irene Dunne[8] and Ken Murray* in *Leathernecking* (1930).

He wrote comedic dialogue, routines, and entire scenarios: *The Girl Friend* (1935) for Jack Haley and Ann Sothern,* *Bright Lights* (1935) for Joe E. Brown and Ann Dvorak, and *On Again-Off Again* (1937) for Wheeler and Woolsey.

In his book *The Vaudevillians,* Anthony Slide quoted the comedian as stating his belief of how his fate was sealed: "It wasn't a case of my giving up the business, it was the business that gave me up. Dialect comics were considered out. This was announced at a meeting of the entertainment bigs back in 1938. Pressure within banished us, not the general public. Ethnic groups were becoming hypersensitive and a section of the industry thought it knew what was best for the nation."

Over the years he was able to make a good living doing small parts in features such as *Here Comes Mr. Jordan* (1941), *Torch Song* (1953), *A Hole in the Head* (1959), *A Pocketful of Miracles* (1961), *Thoroughly Modern Millie* (1957), and *Coma* (1978). In between pictures he worked in women's ready-to-wear clothes, as a manager of a smart restaurant, and as a stockbroker. Jack Benny, who had been his friend since 1923, frequently found small parts for him on his radio and television shows.

During the Great Depression, when Benny Rubin could command $2,500 weekly, he had a ranch in Encino with its own baseball diamond. He claims to have gone through three fortunes: "One on the first wife, another on the second, and gambling took the third."

He admits that having his own program dur-ing the very early years of television gave him a real opportunity for a comeback, but that his drawback was "this foul temper of mine. I did myself in and ended up doing bit parts when I should have been really making a contribution in a very creative capacity."

He says he lives only for his grandchildren and he considers himself retired. In 1973 his autobiography, *Come Backstage with Me,* was published by a vanity press. He sees none of his contemporaries, explaining, "They are all either dead, like my dear friend Jack Benny, or are people I do not choose to be around."

(The comedian died on July 15, 1986.)

Benny Rubin lived by himself in a Hollywood apartment. Of his personal life and career he has said, "I regret nothing!"

She had been named Germany's most popular actress five times before M-G-M brought her to Hollywood amidst a blaze of publicity to make The Brothers Karamazov *(1958).* Time *magazine observed: "Perhaps not since the full-blown Garbo has the old world offered to the new such a prepotent image of the eternal feminine as can be seen in the mysteriously soulful face of Maria Schell."*

Maria Schell

The once queen of the German-language cinema was born in Vienna, Austria, on January 5, 1926. Her mother is Marguerith Schell von Noé, a well-known actress in central Europe. Her father, the author Herman Ferdinand Schell, tried to discourage her passion for acting, but by age sixteen Maria had made her first motion picture, *Steinbruck* (1942).

Maria Schell had one of the screen's most dazzling smiles. Yet when she was the reigning queen of central European cinemas, most of her vehicles were accurately described as "tearjerkers." Until the emergence of Romy Schneider in the sixties Maria was the undisputed first lady of movie houses in central Europe.

In Germany, Austria, and Switzerland there was no actress more popular or more active than Maria Schell in the fifties. When she came to Hollywood to play "Grushenka" in *The Brothers Karamazov* (1958), it seemed she was destined to become an important international star. No one faulted her performance or said the film was not good, but somehow neither Maria nor the big-budget, color production caught on with the United States public. Again, in *The Hanging Tree* (1959), she seemed quite right opposite Gary Cooper, but United States fans showed little enthusiasm. Maria and Glenn Ford costarred in a remake of *Cimarron* (1961), she in the role that had made Irene Dunne[8] a star. No one faulted her performance, but the lavishly produced western was a failure at the box office.

Playing the part Ingrid Bergman originated in the movie, Maria appeared in the prestigious two-part television dramatization of *For Whom the Bell Tolls* in 1959. When the live show ended she was handed a telephone with Ernest Hemingway at the other end. The author had called from Cuba to congratulate her on her performance.

In 1957 she married Horst Haechler, a German film director. She says she turned down the leads in *Ben-Hur, Spartacus,* and *El Cid* because: "My man came first with me and he objected to my leaving him for many months. It was all right that I was a star in Germany where he, too, was well known. More than that would be too much—for him. Now he is gone from my life. We are divorced. But I have no regrets, because without him I would not have my fantastic son, Oliver."

Madame Schell points with pride to her work in the pictures *The Magic Box* (1952), *So Little Time* (1953), *The Heart of the Matter* (1954), *The Last Bridge* (1957), *White Nights* (1961), and *The Mark* (1961). The definitive Maria Schell film and performance is *Gervaise* (1957) for which she was chosen Best Actress at the Venice Film Festival. The picture was nominated for an Oscar as the Best Foreign Film.

Among her other screen credits are: *Nach dem Strum* (1948); *The Affairs of Dr. Holl* (1950); *Napoléon* (1954); *Dreaming Lips* (1958), a remake of the Elisabeth Bergner* starrer; *The Sins of Rose Bernd* (1959); *As the Sea Rages* (1961); *Who Has Seen the Wind?* (1965); and *Lust in the Sun* (1972).

Maria sometimes acts under the auspices of her present husband, Veit Relin, the director of the avant-garde Tor Thaurm-Theatre. They were married in 1966, a year after she divorced Haechler.

Of her younger brother, Maximillian Schell: "I love him dearly. He is a splendid actor, but for me to be directed by him is agony. He wants from me what he has never seen me do. I think what I do I do very well. But always he wants something else."

United States audiences are unaware of her frequent appearances on German television and the features she makes in her native language. Her scenes in such pictures as *The Odessa File* (1974), *Superman* (1979), and as David Bowie's mother in *Just a Gigolo* (1978) were brief. *Christmas Lilies of the Field*, a 1979 made-for-television movie, was to have been her comeback, but it did not, as planned, become a series.

She held Paul Scofield in very high esteem after costarring with him in *1919*. Filmed mostly in Sigmund Freud's Vienna apartment in 1985, they play patients of the great psychiatrist.

If she has a regret it is that she was not more aggressive about screen roles. "I was very ambitious, but I was also very busy," she said in 1985. "If only I had found the time to write to the great directors asking for parts in their films. I longed to work for Ingmar Bergman, but, foolishly, I never communicated that to him."

"I have no tears for what might have been," she insists. "I consider at least ten of my films to be excellent. How many artists can honestly say that?"

Maria Schell lives on "Herberthal," her estate forty-five miles from Munich. She is a Swiss citizen and maintains a home there, as well.

Helmut Neuper

Billed usually as "The Silvery-Voiced Buckaroo," Fred Scott starred in over one dozen westerns during the thirties. Several of these low-budget features were produced by Stan Laurel.

Fred Scott

The singing cowboy of the screen was born Fred Leedom Scott in Fresno, California, on February 14, 1902. Both his parents were descendants of early American settlers. His mother, who came to California in a covered wagon, was related to President John Adams.

Fred learned to ride horseback and herd cattle while growing up on ranches near Fresno that were owned by his maternal grandfather and in the Mojave Desert. "I've long thought that cowboys began playing guitars and singing for lack of something to do," explained Scott recently. "Once the sun went down, you didn't even have chores to keep you occupied and a lot of the fellows couldn't read, even if they were lucky enough to have enough light to read by."

The chef on the ranch had a phonograph on which Fred learned to sing by listening to the recordings of Enrico Caruso and the Irish tenor John McCormack. By the age of twelve, he was singing publicly; by his teens, he was acting and singing in local theatricals.

Scott went to Hollywood in the early twenties for a fencing championship in which he won a bronze medal. He joined an acting school. His screen debut was in support of Dolores Costello in *Bride of the Storm* (1926).

At the time the studios were converting to sound, he was studying voice with the same teacher that Bebe Daniels[8] had. After the star heard him sing, she recommended him for a part in her talkie debut, *Rio Rita* (1929). From his appearance in that early, successful musical, he was placed under contract to Pathé.

While making *Beyond Victory* (1931), his third and final picture with Helen Twelvetrees, Scott formed a friendship with William Boyd, another member of the cast, which endured throughout Boyd's later career as "Hopalong Cassidy" and until his death in 1972.

Fred was introduced to movie audiences as a singing cowboy in *The Last Outlaw* (1936), a Harry Carey starrer. It was done as a film-within-a-film in which Carey, an old-time cowpoke deeply upset with the changing times, enters a theatre just as Scott comes on the screen warbling "My Heart's on the Trail."

Fred Scott was neither the first western star to sing nor the most popular, but he is considered by some to have been the best. After leaving Pathé, he sang in many light operas as well

158

as on the stage of the San Francisco Opera with the legendary soprano Maria Jeritza. He had a beautiful, trained voice, was an excellent horseman, and had a real understanding of the Old West. He achieved neither the fame nor the rewards of the other singing cowboys because his features were made by low-budget producers operating on what was known as "Poverty Row."

Scott readily admits that the production values in his films were low and rates *The Singing Buckaroo* (1937), the one that got him his billing, as "the worst of all." "It was never how good, but how quick," he has said. "You did everything in one take because the schedule and budget allowed for no more. As a professional I took pride in the fact I could get through a scene or a song without a flub, but everything was done on the cheap and it often showed."

Al "Fuzzy" St. John, who had been prominent as a comic in early slap-stick silents, made a second career of the character he created in the Fred Scott pictures. The comic Stan Laurel, who produced some of the features, worked closely with St. John on his routines.

Fred Scott westerns often contained almost as much music as action and appealed more to adults than to children for that reason. Among his films were *Romance Rides the Range* (1936), *Melody of the Plains* (1937), *Rangers Roundup* (1938), *Two Gun Troubadours* (1939), and *Ridin' the Trail* (1942). His last starring role was in *Rodeo Rhythm* (1942).

During World War II, Scott sang at Nils T. Granlund's Florentine Gardens on Hollywood Boulevard, which he also managed. He then became a realtor . It is through his sales of and investments in Los Angeles properties that Fred and his wife were able to retire to Palm Springs in the early seventies. Mrs. Scott, a dancer, had been featured in the *George White Scandals of 1929,* but left the profession when they married in 1936. Both are lifelong Christian Scien-

Shelly Brodsky

"The Silvery-Voiced Buckaroo" in his Palm Springs home holding the plaque commemorating his installation into the Great Western Heroes Hall of Fame.

tists. One of their two daughters is also a realtor. The Scotts have eight grandchildren.

Scott has remained in touch over the years with his former leading lady, Lois January. * He hears frequently from old friend Sunset Carson[8] and has coffee several mornings every week with Gene Autry, the man Fred credits with originating the singing western hero. The Scotts breakfast almost every morning at the Gene Autry Hotel in Palm Springs.

159

Gabe Essoe in his book Tarzan of the Movies *stated: "Although Scott was handsome and possessed a superb physique, he lacked the winsome, primitive air manifested by Weissmuller and, to a lesser degree, Lex Barker."*

Gordon Scott

The screen's eleventh Tarzan was born Gordon Werschkul in Portland, Oregon, on August 3, 1927.

The public first became aware of him when he was "discovered" for the movies while working as a lifeguard at the Sahara Hotel in Las Vegas.

Once he became Gordon Scott he gave out widely varying accounts of his background. In one he had worked for a while as a fireman. Another had him a rancher.

Signed to a contract with producer Sol Lesser, Scott played the ape man in five feature films.

His debut was in *Tarzan's Hidden Jungle* (1955) with Don Beddoe and Jack Elam.* A romance developed during the filming with leading lady Vera Miles that led to marriage in 1957.

The actress understood that theirs was Scott's first marriage. It subsequently developed that he had a daughter by his first marriage. There was also a son by a second wife. About the time Vera Miles learned she was in fact his third wife she had become pregnant. Not only were the Scotts not getting along, but there was strong indication that by marrying him she had distanced herself socially from many people who could help her career.

Gordon Scott and Vera Miles were divorced in 1960. Although legally bound to support their son, he has contributed very little financially. His mother repeatedly juggled schedules so the boy could spend time with his father, but he was canceled at the last minute or just stood up.

A Hollywood press agent who remembers the actor from the fifties says: "He was known for standing people up and for not paying his bills. Bad news!"

Gordon Scott portrayed the Edgar Rice Burroughs character four more times on the screen. *Tarzan and the Lost Safari* (1957) was made in England and had George Coulouris* in the supporting cast. In *Tarzan's Fight for Life* (1958), he was pitted against bad-guy Harry Lauter.[9] In *Tarzan's Greatest Adventure* (1959), Sean Connery played the heavy. Jock Mahoney* and John Carradine* were in *Tarzan the Magnificent* (1960) with him.

He had become enough of a name playing "Tarzan" to be starred in a string of costume and muscle movies made mostly in Italy. The most notable was *Duel of the Titans* (1961) in which Steve Reeves played "Romulus" to Scott's "Remus." Most of the others never received distribution in United States theatres. Among them were: *Zorro and the Three Musketeers* (1962), *A Queen for Caesar* (1962), *Hercules Attacks* (1963), *Buffalo Bill* (1964), *Hercules and the Princess of Troy* (1965), *Top Secret* (1966), *The Tramplers* (1966), and *Nest of Spies* (1967).

During the years he lived in Rome Gordon developed a reputation very similar to the one he left behind in Hollywood. One of his contemporaries, an American actor who resides abroad, remembers him as "someone with a compulsion to please and impress, but lacking any real sense of responsibility about appointments or financial obligations. He reveled in being talked about, which unfortunately, he seemed to confuse with popularity."

Scott has been a natural foods enthusiast for years. He still wears a size 51-long jacket and, in the circle in which he travels, is considered a ladies' man. In the last job he held, selling children's books, he was working for the woman he was living with. That relationship and position came to an end in 1985.

In early 1986 Gordon was very much a part of the social scene in affluent Marina Del Rey where he was living on a friend's houseboat. "An out-of-work actor doesn't threaten the men who live here," explains one matron. "And the women just love having this big guy around. Let's face it, what female has not given serious thought to 'Tarzan'?"

Jack Gaunt/Los Angeles Times

Gordon Scott has moved about a great deal in recent years. As of early 1986 he was the guest of a friend who owns a boat docked in Marina Del Rey, California.

Heather Sears received a lot of press coverage for her portrayal of Joan Crawford's blind, deaf, and dumb ward in The Story of Esther Costello *(1957). For her performance she was awarded the "Stella," the English equivalent of the Oscar.*

Heather Sears

The former screen ingenue was born in the East End of London, giving her claim to being a Cockney, a form of reverse snobbery currently popular in England. Her father was a physician. Her birthday is September 28, 1935.

At the age of four years Heather was sent to boarding school in northern Wales to safeguard her during the Blitz of World War II. She was cast as the youngest boy in her school's production of *Peter Pan*. "Everyone clapped when I came on," she remembers. "And that was it."

When she was sixteen she was an *au pair* for a family in Brittany, but soon moved to Paris on her own. Unbeknownst to her family, she supported herself by modeling and dubbing French films into English, while reduced to sleeping in a broom closet.

After her return to London she attended the Central School of Speech and Drama. From a student production she was signed to a contract with Romulus Films. Their only other contractee was Laurence Harvey, who immediately dismissed her as "utterly boring."

Although not generally known, her first screen role was a small one in *Dry Rot* (1956).

The publicity and ads for *The Story of Esther Costello* (1957) featured "and introducing Heather Sears." Joan Crawford, however, was very much the star of the picture. She is remembered by Heather as: "A thorough professional and a very generous star. She went out of her way to make me comfortable. We were in touch until she died. I respected her very much and have warm, loving memories of her. But to that I must add that I feel strongly that had I really been her child our relationship would have been much different."

Heather was much less impressed with her official screen debut than when, before the film's release, she was chosen to replace Mary Ure* in the original West End production of *Look Back in Anger*.

"It wasn't merely because I so much prefer the stage to film," she explained recently.

162

"That my name was next to Joan Crawford's didn't mean I was making any more money. My husband and I were sent to represent the picture at the Venice Film Festival with our expenses paid, but we returned to the bed-sitter that was our home then."

Heather was in Hollywood to appear in some live television dramas, including a memorable *Playhouse 90* production of Tad Mosel's *A Corner of the Garden* in 1959. She says of that period: "I really wasn't pretty by Hollywood standards. What I was offered was usually characters who were crippled, either physically or emotionally or both."

She returned to England to make *Room at the Top* (1959) and *Sons and Lovers* (1960). The former was a major international success. She more than made up with Laurence Harvey and recalls dissolving in laughter with him and the late Simone Signoret during the filming.

Twenty years after the sequel, *Life at the Top* (1965), was made she explained her absence from the cast: "It was either that I was pregnant and so they got Jean Simmons or that they wanted her originally and I was the substitute the first time. I've forgotten which."

Heather Sears played the lead opposite Herbert Lom in the second remake of *The Phantom of the Opera* (1962).

Most of the remainder of her career has been on British television or the stage. She had a running part in the series *The Informer* and has played Brecht, Ibsen, Strindberg, and Shakespeare in English productions. After being cast repeatedly as a heavy she asked a director why. He replied, "But darling, that's just what you are—fat and heavy!"

She admits that while raising her three boys she stopped even considering acting jobs for long periods. Her eldest is a film editor. The others are draftsmen. Still, she is not concerned that she is not acting. For about ten years she has been writing and has completed one play and parts of a second.

"When I'm not traveling with my husband, which I enjoy very much, I'm happy to be at home," she said in 1985. "I write fiction, though I've not been published nor produced yet. I have pugs and labradors and a large garden."

At present the only parts that would tempt her are in *Phaedra* and "any" picture with Robert Mitchum, her favorite movie actor.

Nan Hogan

Heather Sears lives in a house on an acre and a half of land in Surrey, England. She is the wife of Tony Masters, the art director of such films as Dune and Taipan.

It was the role of "Sgt. Bilko," the fast-talking schemer on The Phil Silvers Show, *that brought the bald, bespectacled comedian his greatest fame. In the mid-eighties, thirty years after the programs were filmed, they were among the most popular shows on television in the United Kingdom and Italy.*

Phil Silvers

The comedic star of Broadway and television was born Philip Silversmith on May 11, 1912, in Brooklyn, New York. He was the youngest of eight children born to Russian Jewish par-

ents. Mr. Silversmith was a tinsmith.

As a boy soprano not yet in his teens, he began earning money singing in neighborhood movie houses whenever the projectors broke down. Impresario Gus Edwards put him in his *School Days Revue,* which played in New York's Palace Theatre and a vaudeville chain throughout the country. For five years, Silvers was a stooge with the comedy team Morris and Campbell.

When he could not find work in vaudeville, Silvers did improvisations at hotels in the Catskill Mountains in what is known as the "Borscht Belt."

By 1934, he was working for the Minskys, touring their burlesque wheel doing low comedy. In the vernacular of the professional, Phil began as a "third banana," but by the end of five years, he had moved up to "top banana." It was during this period that he perfected the takes and timing for which he later became famous. The horn-rimmed glasses that were thought of as his trademark were as common to burlesque-comedy attire as baggy pants.

It was *Yokel Boy,* a Broadway musical of 1939, that got Phil out of burlesque. Although the show had a very short run, he was signed from it to an M-G-M contract.

Phil Silvers made over twenty features. Among them were: *Hit Parade of 1941* (1940) with the late Kenny Baker; * *Tom, Dick,* and *Harry* (1941) with George Murphy; * *Roxie Hart* (1942) with Iris Adrian; 8 *All Through the Night* (1942) with Humphrey Bogart; *Footlight Serenade* (1942) with John Payne; * *A Lady Takes a Chance* (1943) with Jean Arthur; * *Something for the Boys* (1944); *Don Juan Quilligan* (1945); *Summer Stock* (1950) with Gloria De Haven; *Lucky Me* (1954) with Martha Hyer; * *Forty Pounds of Trouble* (1962) with the late Jack La Rue; 8 *It's A Mad, Mad, Mad, Mad World* (1963); *A Guide for the Married Man* (1967) with Polly Bergen; and *Buona Sera, Mrs. Campbell* (1969).

It was the Broadway hit of 1947, *High Button Shoes,* that made Phil Silvers a star. He followed it with *Top Banana,* which brought him the musical star Tony of 1952, playing the title role that he knew so well. He repeated his performance in the 1954 movie version.

Songwriters Saul Chaplin and Sammy Cahn were his closest friends; Milton Berle was his oldest. Their relationship survived over half a century as well as an intense professional rivalry in the mid-fifties when Phil's TV show on CBS topped Berle's in the ratings in the same time period.

When the *Phil Silvers Show* returned for its second season, Berle, who until then had been considered "Mr. Television," had been moved by NBC to another night.

It was as "Sgt. Ernie Bilko," the ingratiating swindler on the *Phil Silvers Show,* that he became a familiar face and name throughout North America. The "Sarge" of fictional Fort Baxter, Kansas, was a quick-thinking con artist who, upon close examination, was basically decent and quite likable. Between 1955 and 1959, when the series was first aired, Phil was nominated five times for Emmys. He won two in 1955 as Best Actor in a Continuing Series and as Best Comedian.

The Phil Silvers Show was notable for being one of the first integrated sitcoms on TV. It also had some of television's best comedy writing and featured some excellent character acting.

A role he enjoyed enormously was in *A Funny Thing Happened on the Way to the Forum* (1972). The revival brought him another musical star Tony award.

In 1945, the comedian married Jo-Carroll Dennison, who had been Miss America of 1942. The two remained friends after their divorce in 1950, and she was one of the mourners at his funeral.

In 1956, he entered into a ten-year marriage to actress Evelyn Patrick, which produced five daughters and ended in divorce. Nancy,

Phil Silvers shortly before he died in his sleep in his Century City apartment in 1985 at the age of seventy-three.

Candy, and Cathy Silvers are actresses.

On November 1, 1985, Phil Silvers was going over some fan mail with an assistant when he excused himself to take a nap. He never awoke.

It was at Silvers's request that Milton Berle delivered the eulogy. His audience included Sid Caesar, Steve Allen, Danny Thomas, Carl Reiner, Red Buttons, Morey Amsterdam, and Nanette Fabray.

His oldest daughter, Tracy, said of her father: "He was a great dad to all of us and a wonderful grandfather to Jaclyn, his only grandchild. Two things we always knew: that he loved us and show business. All five of us are in it. He had a stroke in 1974, and although he made a remarkable recovery, he didn't want to tax himself, so he turned down many offers. His idea of sport was gambling, and he was always betting on something. Fun to him was taking Jaclyn to the beach. He died a happy man."

To Richard,
Thanks for a
very pleasant
interview,
Penny
Gloria Winters

"Sky King" threatens to cut the ponytail of his niece "Penny" in this mid-fifties publicity photograph. They are wearing on their kerchiefs sterling silver rings that bear wings and a crown, the insignia of their Arizona ranch, "The Flying Crown."

"Sky King"

"Out of the blue of the western sky comes Sky King" was the opening of the series that dramatized the adventures of television's hero of the modern West. The show, which began in 1951, is still in syndication.

Kirby Grant played the wealthy gentleman rancher who pursued evildoers in his twin-engine Cessna, the "Songbird." Before stepping into the role he had leads in low-budget westerns and a series of features as a Canadian Mountie. Born in Butte, Montana, on November 24, 1911, Grant was a lifelong aviation enthusiast who had been taught to fly by barnstormers when he was in his teens.

The morals and methods of the character "Skylar King" were his own—or at least he aspired to be the high-minded man he played. No matter how dangerous the culprit, extreme violence was never used to apprehend him, nor did he ever take a life. "The whole thing had a tendency of making a better person of me," he once told an interviewer. "I tried to live up to the character I portrayed."

Gloria Winters, who played the flying cowboy's niece, "Penny," was born in Los Angeles on November 28. Since childhood she had acted in movies in small parts and was "Babs," Jackie Gleason's daughter, on *The Life of Riley,* a television series that ran during the 1949–50 season. *Sky King,* however, was the most enjoyable experience of her career. She made extensive personal appearance tours with Grant, who was delighted when her dates with their show's sound engineer led to marriage.

Gloria rode her own horse on the show and often was a pivotal part of the plot. Teenage girls strongly identified with her and bought her book *Penny's Guide to Teen-Age Charm and Popularity* by the thousands.

Today she says: "I'm one former child performer who never felt frustrated or traumatized by my career. Now that we know a lot of celebrity books are ghost written, I take special pride that mine was not. I wrote *every* word of it."

For the first twenty-five programs, "Sky King" had a nephew, also. Ron Hagerthy, who played "Clipper," was drafted during the Korean War and was never replaced. He has been retired from acting for over twenty years and lives with his family in Encino, California. Hagerthy is in the real estate investment business.

After filming 130 episodes, Kirby Grant spent several years touring with the Carson and Barnes Circus. He retired in 1970, settling in Winter Springs, Florida, with his wife and three children.

Grant bought the title and rights to the show and for a while ran the "Sky King Youth Ranch," which at one point provided food and shelter for nine homeless children. But the nonprofit enterprise led to his eventual bankruptcy, which was followed by two heart attacks and bypass surgery.

For the past few years Kirby acted as the goodwill ambassador for Sea World.

The highlight of the entire *Sky King* experience for both Grant and Winters was meeting astronauts Scott M. Carpenter, "Deke" Slayton, Alan B. Shepard, Jr., and "Gus" Grissom, who stood in line with their children to get Kirby's and Gloria's autographs at an appearance in Houston.

The strong avuncular feeling "Sky King" had toward "Penny" accurately described the relationship of Grant and Gloria off-camera as well. "If anything," she has said, "we became closer over the years, even though it was by telephone. When I last spoke with him, he told me all the things he had been active with and his many projects coming up. I made some comment about how busy he was and he said, 'Well, I intend to die with my boots on.''

Less than a week later, wearing duplicates of the western hat and boots that were his television trademarks, Kirby Grant was driving his car to Cape Canaveral when he was involved in a collision that sent him off the highway and into a ditch. Television's flying good guy drowned in several feet of water before help arrived on October 30, 1985. He was on his way to watch a space launch of *Challenger* at the personal request of the astronauts who as young boys had been inspired by *Sky King* to study science.

Kirby Grant, age seventy-three, was on his way to watch the launching of space shuttle Challenger *when he was killed as a result of a car crash on October 30, 1985.*

Courtesy of Gloria Winters

Gloria Winters lives with her German Shepherds "Holly" and "Happy," her mother, and husband in Northridge, California. She is an executive of their family firm, which rents sound equipment to movie and TV studios.

Donna Schaeffer

Of the cast of Space Patrol *only Ed "Commander Buzz Corey" Kemmer and Nina "Tonga" Bara (both on right) are living. Lyn "Cadet Happy" Osborn (lower left) died in 1958. Virginia "Carol Karlyle" Hewitt died in 1986, Ken "Major Robertson" Mayer in 1985.*

Space Patrol

"Space Patrol: High adventure in the wild reaches of space . . . missions of daring in the name of interplanetary justice. Travel into the future with Buzz Corey . . . Commander-in-Chief of . . . the Space Patrol!" were the words of the opening of the early TV series set in the thirtieth century.

Space Patrol began as a local Los Angeles show, moved to the ABC network in June, 1951, and was, for a while, a radio program as well. There were *Space Patrol* comic books and official shirts, helmets, and the "Paralyzer Ray Gun." Gary H. Grossman wrote in his book *Saturday Morning TV* that Los Angeles police had to be called when over 30,000 children and parents jammed into a department store in response to an advertisement for

"Space Patrol" merchandise and a chance to see the full-scale replica of the "interplanetary battle cruiser 'Terra'" seen on the show.

Another mock-up "Terra" toured the country as a promotion for the program's sponsor, Ralston-Purina. Eventually, the thirty-five-foot-long vehicle, which can sleep eight people, became a prize in a giveaway contest.

The shows were kinescoped at what is now the ABC Prospect Avenue studios. The cast wore the same costumes that had been used in the film *Destination Moon*.

Ed Kemmer, who played the lead, "Commander Buzz Corey," and the late Lyn Osborn, who took the part of "Cadet Happy," originally made $8 per episode. "And," Kemmer recalls, "we were the highest paid of the regulars. Of course, when the network picked up the program, we got substantial raises."

The late Virginia Hewitt played "Carol Karlyle," the blonde daughter of the "Secretary General of the United Planets," a part taken by Norman Jolley, who was also one of the scripters. "Carol" was clearly shown to be smitten with "Buzz," but while he seemed interested, the feelings of the steel-jawed commander were always in check.

Marvin Miller, who later became a television star on *The Millionaire,* played the diabolical "Mr. Proteus." He died in 1985. Gene Barry played another of the show's heavies. "Prince Baccarratti," also known as the evil "Black Falcon," was acted by Bela Kovacs.

"Tonga," formerly of the dark forces of the universe, but who had been shown the "path of truth and justice," was played by Nina Bara and was on most of the early episodes. Now Mrs. Linke of La Canada, California, she raises champion Siamese cats. After retiriing in 1986 as head librarian and chief legal researcher at Blue Cross, Nina has been "reactivating my theatrical career."

After playing "Buzz Corey" on *Space Patrol's* last telecast on February 26, 1955, Ed

Kemmer portrayed an astronaut on the TV soap opera *The Clear Horizon.* Since then he has had a running part on other daytime dramas, *The Doctors, Somerset,* and *As the World Turns.* During the five years he spent on the latter, playing attorney "Dick Martin," he met actress Fran Sharon, whom he married in 1969. They live in Manhattan with their two sons and a daughter.

The early 1950s was an era acutely aware of the ominous potential of nuclear power, yet *Space Patrol* never depicted serious violence. The most serious punishment the crew of the "Terra" ever deployed was to subject their captives to the "Brainograph," a machine that rehabilitated them. The workings of the fictional machine sounded very much like the processes of deprogramming used by some of the personal development movements of the seventies.

Argentine-born Nina Bara has written three books on Space Patrol. She sells her works, which she also publishes, at science-fiction conventions where she receives added interest for having played a role in Missile to the Moon *(1958).*

Ed with his daughter, Kim, in the Kemmer apartment on Riverside Drive in Manhattan. He delivered the girl himself in the back of a taxi in front of Tiffany's.

169

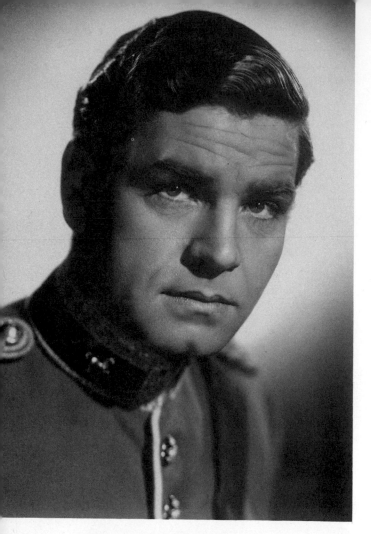

One of Anthony Steel's many military roles was in Storm Over the Nile *(1955), a remake of* Four Feathers, *with the late Mary Ure.**

Anthony Steel

The English leading man was born in Cumberland on May 21, 1919. His original name was Anthony Maitland-Steel. He is distantly related to the late Raymond Massey. [8] Until he was eight years old he lived in India where his father served as part of the British military.

At Cambridge Anthony took no classes in theatre, nor did he ever participate in amateur plays. His intention was to make a career of the army, which he joined in 1938.

Ten years later Major Anthony Maitland-Steel was given a leave of absence. He had mastered three European languages and was contemplating a post that was open to him at the Foreign Office.

He had served during World War II with the actors Hugh Williams and Guy Middleton. Both had returned to their profession and urged Anthony to be tested by J. Arthur Rank, a studio that was looking for athletic leading men. He photographed very well and was placed under contract.

In *Saraband* (1948) both Steel and Christopher Lee had small parts. Others followed in *Poet's Pub* (1949) with the late Joyce Grenfell, and *The Mudlark* (1950) with Irene Dunne. [8]

He considers his first important role to have been in *The Wooden Horse* (1950), which he did on loan-out to Alexander Korda. The picture was such a hit Rank gave him a new contract. He was to remain with the studio for twelve years. *Laughter in Paradise* (1951) was another boost to his career. When he signed for *Another Man's Poison* (1951), he was to have played Gloria Swanson's lover. After illness caused the star to withdraw, she was replaced by Bette Davis. He had another great success in *Where No Vultures Fly* (1951) in which he played the warden of a game reserve. He then played opposite Claudette Colbert* in *Outpost in Malaya* (1952) and was Errol Flynn's brother in *The Master of Ballantrae* (1953).

When he made *Storm Over the Nile* (1955), a successful remake of *Four Feathers,* Anthony Steel was thought to be the male among the Rank contractees most likely to achieve international stardom.

Steel's career never lived up to its potential.

He was not cast in the big pictures that might have put him over to the world market, and he got much attention in the press from his romance with and eventual marriage to Anita Ekberg. As one of the world's most photographed and talked-about couples in the fifties, they were frequently on the front page of tabloids. Whether he was being arrested, as he was several times, for drunk driving or being separated in a public brawl over the blonde star, he always got second billing. Art Buchwald devoted an entire column to their carryings-on entitled "Bodyguard Husband." Until taking up with the Swedish beauty, Anthony had a stalwart, dashing image. After several years of such publicity, it was difficult for audiences to take him seriously.

For some years after their 1959 divorce, Steel continued to live and work mostly on the Continent. In the mid-seventies he became a familiar face again in England with regular appearances on *Crossroads,* one of the nation's top-rated evening soap operas. He has lived in London mostly ever since, making an occasional appearance on television, as in 1985 when he guest-starred on *The Swords of Wayland.* In 1982–83 he toured the United Kingdom and Canada in the play *Conduct Unbecoming.*

Steel was in the news in 1981 when, asked why he had refused a movie part as a homosexual, he snapped, "I've never been a fairy and I'm certainly not going to start now."

Anthony Steel is a heavy coffee drinker and a chain smoker, but no longer takes any alcohol. When he drank, which he did very heavily for many years, he occasionally described to other men marriage to Ekberg as "like being possessed. I saw what was happening to my career and my image of myself. But the sexuality was overwhelming. Eventually, thank God, the fever broke."

He lists his recent movies as *The Story of O* (1977) and *The Mirror Crack'd* (1980) "and a lot of rubbish I never see nor refer to." Several of his credits during the last few years have been soft-porn films.

Richard Lamparski

Anthony Steel has an apartment on the thirty-seventh floor of the Shakespeare Tower of London's Barbican Center and a house in the Austrian Alps that he uses for skiing holidays.

171

Marjorie Steele was married to multimillionaire Huntington Hartford when she made No Escape *(1953) with Lew Ayres [8] and Sonny Tufts (above).*

Marjorie Steele

The Cinderella story began in Reno, Nevada, on August 27, 1930. The first nine years of her life she lived in one of the log cabins her father, a contractor, had built in the Santa Cruz mountains. On her mother's side she is Russian and Swedish. Mr. Steele was German and Sioux Indian.

The family moved to a two-room apartment in San Francisco in 1939. In her teens she worked part-time in a store and took acting lessons at a studio noted for its left-wing sponsorship. When she was seventeen she won a scholarship to the Actors Lab in Hollywood.

Marjorie Steele had not gotten on well among her family or with the other students during grammar and high school. "I half believed that something was wrong with me," she said in 1985. "Another part of me suspected that maybe they were ordinary people destined to live ordinary lives. Whatever was right, I knew I wasn't meant for an ordinary life."

While studying acting she supported herself as a cigarette girl at Ciro's, then a top nightclub. There, she began meeting people who confirmed her suspicions about herself. Sydney Chaplin found her "intelligent" and introduced her to his father, who agreed. Charlie Chaplin arranged for her to study with the noted drama coach-actress Constance Collier.

It took multimillionaire Huntington Hartford several weeks to get a date with Marjorie and he probably would never have succeeded if the club's owner, Herman Hover,* had not interceded, waiving the rule that employees of his nitery could not go out with the customers. During their courtship the thirty-eight-year-old playboy signed Marjorie to a contract with a motion picture production company he owned. In 1949, shortly after her nineteenth birthday, she became his wife. At the time he was reputed to be worth seventy million dollars.

During the twelve years they were together Marjorie took up painting and developed a good reputation as an actress, especially as a stage actress. He strongly encouraged all of her creative instincts.

While the wife of the heir to the A&P grocery fortune, she also made the movies *Tough Assignment* (1949) with Don Barry,* *No Escape* (1953) with Lew Ayres,[8] and *The Bride Comes to Yellow Sky* (1953).

When they were divorced he set up trust funds for their son and daughter. Marjorie received a $385,000 cash settlement plus a

172

$60,000 yearly alimony. She waived the latter shortly afterward when she married the actor Dudley Sutton. The marriage lasted only a few years.

In 1954 she drew excellent notices in the title role of *Sabrina Fair* and played it in London for over six months. On Broadway Marjorie took over the lead from Barbara Bel Geddes in *Cat on a Hot Tin Roof*. When she came with the play to San Francisco she was made to realize how much of her acting motivation had been as revenge for her early, unhappy years in that city.

"I really got over acting right then," she has admitted. "I never had anything less than 'very good' in any review for what I did on stage. The movies were not my thing, but I don't think I was a bad film actress. Spencer Tracy asked for me for a film that was eventually shelved and *he* knew something about screen acting. I don't rule out a play as something I would never do again, but I know that I no longer need to be up there. I never even think about acting."

In 1967 she was in Greece on her honeymoon with author Constantine FitzGibbon when she decided to sculpt. Within eighteen months she had her first show from which she was commissioned to do fourteen heads for the Royal Dublin Society Library. Her works are on display at the Common Market Museum, the Old Vic, the Tyrone Guthrie Theatre, and in the Vatican.

Marjorie FitzGibbon, as she is now known, lives in a Dublin mews house with her son by Dudley Sutton and her daughter by her third husband, who died in 1983. They have four birds, twenty fish, a dachshund, and a mongrel. A citizen of the Republic of Ireland, she has been accepted into the Royal Hiberian Academy.

"My late husband wrote *When the Kissing Had to Stop* and was Dylan Thomas's friend and biographer," she explained recently. "The Irish take writers and artists very seriously. I'm a big fish in a little pond, which I am enjoying immensely."

Richard Lamparski

In the Republic of Ireland, where Marjorie Steele lives, she is known as the widow of the distinguished author Constantine FitzGibbon and for her sculpture. The bronze statue in the photo was commissioned by the relief organization African Concern.

This photograph of Jan Sterling was taken after she had her nose reshaped by plastic surgery. It was done in 1951, the year The Big Carnival *was released. Most of her fans consider her performance in that feature to be her best. The film was also released under the title* Ace in the Hole *and brought her a Best Actress award from the Film Board of Review.*

Jan Sterling

The Oscar nominee was born Jane Sterling Adriance on April 3, 1921. Her father, who was a prominent advertising executive, and mother were divorced when she was eight years old. Her father later married Gladys Cooper. Her mother then married a man who represented an American oil firm abroad. They lived first in Brazil and then in Paris.

Although both parents frowned on her burning ambition to become "just like Jean Harlow," she was allowed to study acting in England. Later they agreed that she could try her luck in New York, but her father forbade her to use the family name.

She was waiting for a friend who was auditioning when Milton Shubert noticed her. She was asked to read for the role of a fourteen-year-old girl in *Bachelor Born* (1938), a show he was producing. During its run she married the actor Jack Merivale. The marriage ended shortly in divorce. In that first play and in three subsequent ones she did on Broadway, Ms. Sterling played English girls under the name Jane Sterling. It was Ruth Gordon who convinced her to become Jan when she was signed to play an American in *Over 21* (1944).

When in 1942 Virginia Field decided to marry Paul Douglas Jan took over her part in *Panama Hattie*. By 1950 that marriage had been dissolved. Shortly afterward Jan and Douglas got married.

The Douglases appeared together on some television shows and in a revival of *Born Yesterday*. Paul Douglas died suddenly in 1959 and his widow has not remarried. Jan was carrying their son, her only child, when she filmed *1984* (1956) in which she was a militant member of the "Anti-Sex League." Adams Douglas is a programmer at NASA.

Jan Sterling acted in plays, most notably in *Present Laughter,* which she did on Broadway opposite Clifton Webb in 1946. After making her movie debut in *Johnny Belinda* (1948), she returned to the New York stage in *Two Blind Mice* (1949) with Melvyn Douglas. She has been in several Broadway plays since then, such as *Small War on Murray Hill* (1957), but most people know her for the films she has made.

The work she did in Hollywood is frequently singled out still in the reviews of her pictures when they play on television. If she had a specialty it was playing floozies, but Jan Sterling had many opportunities in which to show how wide her range was. In *Caged* (1950) she portrayed a prison inmate who describes herself as a "common prostitute." In *Mystery Street* (1950) she played a B-girl and in *Union Pacific* (1950) she was a gun moll, but in *Rhubarb* (1951) she was equally convincing as a nice girl from a good family. After being thoroughly unscrupulous in *Flesh and Fury* (1952) she played another nice girl, but one who was down on her luck in *Split Second* (1953). In *Pony Express* (1953) Jan was the hoyden who gets into a slugfest with Rhonda Fleming. She was a stripper in *The Human Jungle* (1954), a murderess in *Female on the Beach* (1955), and a madam in *Man with the Gun* (1955). In *The Harder They Fall* (1956) she was Humphrey Bogart's last leading lady. Her part in *Slaughter on Tenth Avenue* (1957) was a drab one and was followed by *The Female Animal* (1957) in which she was a former celebrity forced to pay for the company of young men. She was a teacher in *High School Confidential* (1958), a gossip columnist in *Kathy O'* (1958), and in *Love in a Goldfish Bowl* (1961) she played Tommy Sands's* swinging mother. She was a victim in *The Incident* (1967).

The press picked Jan Sterling as the likely recipient of the Best Supporting Actress Oscar of 1954. "It was the longest minute of my life," the actress said recently. "And when the envelope was opened and it was Eva Marie Saint who had won, my heart sank. I really believed then that my place on earth would be complete if only I could have an Oscar. But Claire Trevor was nominated in the same category and the vote split because we were both up for parts we played in the same picture, *The High and the Mighty*."

In an interview in her home in the Knightsbridge area of London Jan Sterling spoke of her absence from screen and stage and her life today: "You really have to be in

Richard Lamparski

Jan Sterling in her London mews house where she has lived since the late sixties. It had belonged to the English actor Cyril Raymond.

Hollywood or New York to be thought of for parts. Then, too, I can't play the roles I once could and I'm not old enough for many of the others. I've lived in London for many years and I couldn't work here, either, because I did not have a work permit until very recently. Even when I was married to Paul we lived a very quiet life. Sam Wanamaker is my fella now and has been for a long time. He works a lot and when he doesn't have to be out we like it to be just the two of us."

Jan usually accompanies Wanamaker when he makes a film on location. She has let her house to Richard Gere and to old friend Robert Mitchum while the stars were making pictures in London.

She has admitted that other reasons for her professional inactivity are "my almost total lack of ambition and the fact that I enjoy my life now very much. I'm not aware that I'm missing anything." One of her rare appearances in recent years was in a minor role in *First Monday in October* (1981).

175

Binky Stuart was starred in movie musicals that were popular in England, where they were made, and in many parts of the British Empire. She sang and danced in her pictures and was frequently referred to by her fans as "our Shirley Temple."

Binky Stuart

England's Shirley Temple was born Alison Fraser in Kilmarnock, Scotland, on March 11.

Shortly after her parents moved to London their only child won a "Most Beautiful Baby" contest. On the advice of one of the judges she was enrolled in dancing classes given by Euphan McLaren. His school was frequently called by studios when kiddie dancers were needed in a scene of a movie. McLaren was at first reluctant to send the little girl because she

was not quite three years old. It was at the urging of the mother of her best friend and classmate Jennifer that McLaren finally relented. Jennifer was the great-granddaughter of Charles Dickens.

At her first audition she caught the eye of the director Monty Banks. He hired her over the objections of the producer, who felt she was too young to learn the part and would be disruptive.

"The producer quickly admitted to Banks that he had been wrong," Binky said forty-nine years after making that film, *Keep Your Seats, Please* (1936). "I always did exactly as I was told. That, coupled with the fact that I loved to dance and act made me perfect for pictures."

In England, as elsewhere in the late thirties, child performers were huge box office draws. Binky supported the American stars Richard Cromwell and Noah Beery in *Our Fighting Navy* (1937), released in the United States as *Torpedo*. In what she now considers to be her most important picture, *Moonlight Sonata* (1937), she supported Ignace Jan Paderewski, one of the world's most renowned musical artists of the period.

Binky remembers Paderewski's knee as "boney, but very nice to sit on." She recalls, also, that during a session of publicity photos she was placed on the lap of Gracie Fields: "I didn't want to be there. I didn't know why, but I wanted very much to be away from her."

It was thought that she "stole" *Rose of Tralee* (1937). She was signed as a featured player, but when it was released, Binky Stuart was clearly its star. *Little Miss Somebody* (1937) followed with her name over the title. The late Cathleen Nesbitt was one of those who supported Binky in the musical vehicle *Little Dolly Daydream* (1938). Her last was *My Irish Molly* (1938), which had Maureen O'Hara and Philip Reed* in secondary roles.

Binky's father had been a musician until she clicked in movies. Thereafter he acted as her manager. Her most vivid recollection from her career was when she refused to be locked inside a suitcase. "They begged, they pleaded. They gave me pennies and candies, but I was terrified and just wouldn't do it. Then my dad was called onto the set. As scared as I was of that trunk, I got into it. I was even more frightened of him. And he made me give back all the money and the sweets."

It was not until she was fifteen that Binky rebelled. After costume fittings and rehearsals, she would not go on a road tour her father had booked. He made her, instead, take a job as a receptionist in a dental office.

Three days after her twenty-first birthday she left the home of her parents. It was almost the last time she ever saw her father, who subsequently divorced her mother and remarried. Binky got none of the money from her career. Along with salaries from screen appearances, there were large fees for endorsements and personal appearances. At the height of her popularity, theatres in the British Isles advertised "Binky Stuart will *positively* appear at . . ." Yet when she once got up the courage to ask about her earnings, her father told her: "You made no money. Who would pay you to do anything?"

Her mother, who was as tyrannized as Binky, consulted an attorney at one point with the intention of leaving her husband, but was advised that, most likely, a court would award him custody of the child. Binky is again friendly with her "mum," who she describes as "quite bitter and not at all well off."

She now works at the Farnham Park Rehabilitation Centre in Berkshire as a nurse. "My work has greatly helped me," she said recently. "By learning to understand people in pain, I've come to forgive my father."

Because she was never allowed to see her press clippings or view her pictures, Binky Stuart was an adult before she fully realized that she was well known to many people. Today she is "humbled" by the fans who vividly remember identifying with her as a child.

Her husband, a television engineer who died in 1980, is the father of her two sons, John and Alstair, and one daughter, Fiona. It is through raising them, she has said, that she came to understand "what childhood is *supposed* to be like."

Binky Stuart on a recent visit to London with her daughter, who is the wife of a U.S. Marine. Fiona and her brothers, John and Alstair, have recently begun calling their mother "Binky."

After winning the Rodeo Cowboy Association's highest honor, the title of World's Champion All Around Cowboy in 1951, Casey Tibbs's name and picture appeared in advertisements endorsing Lee Riders and Wrangler jeans.

Casey Tibbs

The nation's most famous rodeo cowboy was born near Fort Pierre, South Dakota. His birthday is March 5, 1929. His father homesteaded his ranch, which had been part of the Cheyenne River Territory. Casey was the youngest of ten Tibbs children.

He broke his first colt at ten years old and within two years was considered a wrangler. When he was fifteen Casey "rode away from home" because his father looked down on horsemen who rode for prize money. But when he returned with over $3,000 in winnings, Mr. Tibbs, says his son, "changed his mind right quick about me being a saddle tramp. Dad remained my biggest fan until he died."

Life, Saturday Evening Post, and *Time* magazine are just a few of the periodicals that devoted large picture spreads to Casey. He was young, good-looking, and had the "Ah, shucks" attitude that made good copy. The publicity and his long winning streak in competitions established him as the number one star of rodeos, which in the fifties were coming into their own as major attractions at arenas from Calgary, Canada, to New York's Madison Square Garden. In 1951 his income was over $80,000.

Not all the publicity was welcome. In 1959 a young woman, who three years before had been the official "Round-Up Queen" at a rodeo where Tibbs had performed, brought a paternity suit. At his side throughout the proceedings was Miss South Dakota of 1955, whom he had married the year before. The judge found in Casey's favor.

Casey and his first wife were divorced after nine years. His second marriage was very brief. He acknowledges a daughter by a woman he knew only slightly. By her he has a granddaughter.

Casey works almost daily breaking horses. He has sixty-three on the 6,000-acre ranch he leases in Ramona, California. Casey Hannun, his nephew and protégé, is frequently there with him.

Casey was named World's Champion All Around Cowboy twice. He still owns the saddles and belt buckles he was given by the Rodeo Cowboy Association when he won their highest honor in 1951 and again in 1955. An international rodeo organization, which no longer exists, chose him as their top cowboy three times. His buckle commemorating that title is displayed in the Cowboy Hall of Fame in Oklahoma City, Oklahoma.

After leaving the rodeo circuit in 1959 he came back briefly in 1967, winning twenty-two of the twenty-seven contests he entered that year.

Since then he has promoted many events and has twice produced wild west shows that were major grossers in Japan.

Beginning in 1952 Tibbs worked in and around movies. He was paid $2,500 for doing a complicated and dangerous stunt on his first picture, *Bronco Buster* (1952), with John Lund.* He doubled for Don Murray in *Bus Stop* (1956) and had one line. He played a part in *The Lusty Men* (1952) and acted as technical adviser.

He had the manner and lanky good looks of a star of western movies and was enough of a name to be the lead in a film. In 1985 Casey explained: "The movies were willing to pay big money to me for stunts, but they only take a day or two. When you play a part it takes weeks and months of your life. I could make more riding broncs and have the freedom you don't get on a picture. And the contracts were always with options. I don't like being in a position where someone else has the power to decide what you may or may not do."

When Casey turned to movie-making he remained independent. After his documentary *Born to Buck* (1967) did well at theatres in the western United States and Canada, Tibbs produced, directed, and acted in *The Young Rounders* (1973). The star of the picture was Joel McCrea[8] who was supported by Monte Montana. Casey quickly turned a profit with both features, but finally was disheartened by the fraudulent business practices he found rampant in the distribution and exhibition of movies. The videotapes of these films are pirated.

Walter Alexander

Casey Tibbs in his Ramona, California, home holding the issue of Life, **October 22, 1951, that carried a cover story on him.**

He is especially proud of *Sioux Nation* (1969), the documentary he made which is still shown at schools and universities.

His health, his physicians assure him, is excellent, and he suffers no ill effects from any of his many injuries. All of his ribs have been broken, some several times. Complicated knee surgery has healed perfectly.

He is working on his autobiography in which he intends to tell how he and some other cowboys and Indians were left stranded in Europe after Gene Autry sensed financial disaster for the troupe he brought to the international exhibits in 1958 in Belgium, usually referred to as the Brussels World's Fair.

179

*Burr Tillstrom's arms from the elbows out were all that were seen of him during **Kukla, Fran, and Ollie** shows. Sometimes, however, he would appear briefly at the end of the program. Its concept, puppets, their voices, and dialogue were all his creations.*

Burr Tillstrom

The television pioneer and puppeteer par excellence was born on October 13, 1917, in Chicago, Illinois.

Tillstrom began playing with hand puppets during a long convalescence from diphtheria. The disease, which he contracted when he was five years old, left him with a heart condition that exempted him from the draft during World War II.

His mother accompanied him on the piano when Burr put on puppet shows from the windowsill of their home. The neighborhood children developed favorites among the characters that he endowed with human personalities. He made his professional debut when the sister of the marionette artist Tony Sarg presented the fourteen-year-old Burr Tillstrom in her garden.

The first of his most famous puppets emerged in 1936. The ballerina Tamara Toumanova named him "Kukla," the Russian word for doll. He was bald with a bulbous polka-dot nose, had a whimsical nature, and eyebrows that suggested a constantly worried state.

Next came "Mme. Oglepuss," a diva of endearing pomposity and ample bosom. "Ollie," the creature with alligator-like jaws, leopard-like spots, and a single tooth, was third. Over the years, Tillstrom introduced others such as "Fletcher Rabbit," "Cecil Bill," "Werner Worm," and "Beulah Witch."

In 1935, he won a scholarship to the University of Chicago, but chose instead to develop his skills with the WPA–Chicago Parks Theatre. He also appeared with his puppets at state fairs and in vaudeville and nightclubs into the forties.

A demonstration of television in 1939 convinced Burr that the new medium was the ideal one for what he did. The following year, he was part of the first ship-to-shore telecasts ever attempted by RCA. Shortly after that, he appeared on the premiere presentation seen over KBKB, Chicago's first TV station. On his thirtieth birthday in 1947, *Kukla, Fran, and Ollie* debuted as a regular program on the same station.

For dedicated fans, *Kukla, Fran, and Ollie* never lost its charm or freshness. They followed it through several series of programs, into syndication, and onto PBS.

Tillstrom, without any of the Kuklapolitan Players, as he called them, appeared on *That Was the Week That Was*. His hand ballet about the emotional conflicts caused by the Berlin Wall Crisis brought him a special Emmy in 1966.

Burr and Fran Allison,[9] the human intermediary on the show, first met during a Defense Bond rally in front of the Wrigley Building prior to Pearl Harbor. The rapport they had through his puppets was almost as strong off-camera. They remained in close touch over the years and frequently spent holidays together. They last spoke on November 20, 1985, when "Kukla," "Ollie," and Fran's other friends called to wish her a happy birthday.

On December 6, 1985, Burr Tillstrom was found dead sitting beside his swimming pool with a newspaper in his lap. His Palm Springs home, where he intended spending the winters, was a recent purchase. Warm months he lived in Saugatuck, Michigan. His companions, two dogs he had rescued from the pound, were taken by Dom DeLuise. When the comedian's animals refused to accept either of them, Burt Reynolds gave both a home.

Tim Doherty

Kukla, Burr, and Ollie during their appearances along with Fran at the Museum of Broadcasting in New York City in March, 1985, nine months before Tillstrom's death.

Tillstrom was the recipient of over fifty awards, including five Emmys, but the most cherished compliments of his career came from Fran Allison. Twice she spoke to "Ollie" off-camera as though he were a person.

"Burr made them as real for me as for the millions who watched us," said Ms. Allison in 1986. "That was the magic he had."

When he was inducted into the Television Hall of Fame in March, 1986, Fran Allison appeared in his stead.

The famous Tillstrom puppets were willed to the Historical Society of Chicago. Shortly after the death of their master, Tom Shales wrote of the Kuklapolitans in the *Washington Post:* "They were as gifted an acting troupe in their own way as any that ever trod the boards of any theatre on Earth. . . . They were live in the fullest sense of the term . . . real in the fullest sense of the term. It was maximum minimalism."

Burr Tillstrom, bachelor and Christian Scientist, was one of the very few, and perhaps the only, artists the medium of television has ever produced.

Audrey Totter, an Illinoisan, was the official hostess for the University of Illinois football team when they played UCLA in the Rose Bowl Game on January 1, 1947. Her side won.

Audrey Totter

The leading lady of the screen was born on December 20, in Joliet, Illinois. She was the eldest of five children born to an Austrian father and a Swedish mother. From an early age Audrey consciously studied both accents so she could mimic them.

After seeing her first circus when she was seven years old Audrey decided on a career in show business. Her mother, however, insisted that she learn to cook and sew. "She wanted to make me into a home girl," she says today with a laugh. "And I *knew* I was destined to be a star!"

She did manage to play bass fiddle with her school band. Eventually her parents relented somewhat and she was allowed to do some amateur dramatics during high school.

Audrey spent a year with Ian Keith's repertory company and then did some radio acting in Chicago. After touring in *My Sister Eileen* she moved to New York City and quickly established herself in radio as an actress who could imitate almost any accent.

Because of her striking looks and throaty voice movie studios took an immediate interest in the young actress. But, after two screen tests brought no contract offers, she was rather nonchalant about her third try. A month later, on the same day that another studio approached her and a Broadway part was offered to her, M-G-M signed Audrey Totter.

Her first taste of life in Hollywood came when she attended a party at Louis B. Mayer's home. Wanting to make a good impression she had bought a dress that she felt was very extravagant. Within minutes she was introduced to Joan Bennett and then to Nancy Sinatra whose gowns were identical to hers.

In her first picture, *Main Street After Dark* (1944), she played a character who rolls servicemen. She was only an off-screen voice in *Bewitched* (1945) and did not have a single line in *Her Highness and the Bellboy* (1945). Her ability with accents was put to good use in *Dangerous Partners* (1945) in which she played a Viennese chanteuse and in *The Sailor Takes a Wife* (1945) as a Rumanian siren.

Some of her other parts were in: *The Postman Always Rings Twice* (1946); *The Unsuspected* (1947) with Hurd Hatfield*; *The

Saxon Charm (1948); The Blue Veil (1951); and My Pal Gus (1952) with George "Foghorn" Winslow. [8]

The two films for which Audrey Totter is best known are also her personal favorites. In Lady in the Lake (1946) she played the leading role to the camera rather than Robert Montgomery, who is seen only reflected in mirrors. Because Montgomery, who also directed, used the unusual screen technique of placing the audience in the position of the film's hero Audrey delivered her kisses as well as her lines to the camera's lenses. Some think the performances of Audrey and Robert Ryan in The Set-Up (1949) were the best of their entire careers.

She made Adventure (1945) and Any Number Can Play (1949) with Clark Gable and dated him, but it never became serious. She went out with Cary Grant, also.

Filmologist Doug McClelland has called her "a specialist in big city, hard-boiled dame types," but she also played a nurse, widow, fashion editor, and psychiatrist. Probably what kept her from becoming a star was her versatility. The public knew her only as an actress who could always be relied upon to give a good performance. She forged no strong image on the screen or in her publicity.

When Audrey married Dr. Leo Fred in 1952 it was with the understanding that she would not accept any parts that interfered with their life together. She says that the work she has done since the birth of her daughter in 1954 has always been secondary to her family life and she has no sense of frustration because of that.

"Before I got married I considered myself a very ambitious actress," she said recently. "But once I made the commitment it was very easy to keep. Now my husband's retired and would be happy to see me acting again, and I do something once in a great while. We do just about everything together, so when I'm on a picture I miss his company. But when I'm with

Mea Fred-Lane

Audrey Totter photographed recently in the garden of her West Los Angeles apartment.

him I never think about my career."

She was a regular on Cimarron City from 1958 to 1960, Our Man Higgins during the 1962–63 season, and came back as "Nurse Wilcox" on Medical Center during the seventies.

The Apple Dumpling Gang Rides Again (1979), a feature, and The Great Cash Giveaway Getaway (1980), a TV movie, are her most recent credits.

"I would never have made it in today's Hollywood," says the woman who was so believable playing floozies. "The themes and so much of the language in pictures now are really distasteful to me."

Audrey Totter is a student of Unity.

"Waldo," Darla Hood,⁸ and Carl "Alfalfa" Switzer in 1937. Darla died in 1979. "Alfalfa" was shot to death during a quarrel in 1959.

"Waldo" Darwood Kaye

The studious member of *Our Gang* was born Darwood Kaye Smith on September 8, 1929, in Fort Collins, Colorado.

His parents loved music and saw to it that their son had singing and dancing lessons at a very early age. When Tom Mix arrived in town for a personal appearance, Mr. Smith brought his boy to the western star and told him how

Darwood had been reading since he was four years old and that he tap-danced so well he had performed several times on the local radio station. Mix advised him to take the boy to Hollywood.

Mrs. Smith believed it was only for a vacation when the family came to Los Angeles in 1935. The casting director at RKO, the first studio the Smiths went to, gave Darwood a part in the Zasu Pitts starrer *The Plot Thickens* (1936). Mother and son remained in Hollywood for the filming, but before it was completed, he had been cast in another feature, *Quality Street* (1937) with Katharine Hepburn. Mr. Smith returned home just long enough to arrange with his employer, Sears Roebuck & Company, to be transferred to California.

Darwood debuted as the pedantic "Waldo" in *Glove Taps* (1937). He played the same bookish character in twenty other *Our Gang* shorts, often winning the affections of Darla, the "sweetheart" of the series, over keen competition from "Alfalfa" and "Butch" (Tommy Bond).⁹ His final appearance in the two-reelers was *Waldo's Last Stand* (1940).

Among the other features he made were *Barnyard Follies* (1940), *The Human Comedy* (1943) with Butch Jenkins,* *Best Foot Forward* (1943), and *Kansas City Kitty* (1944) with Jane Frazee.*

Both of Darwood's grandfathers were clergymen. He was especially close to his mother's father, a minister in the Seventh-Day Adventist church. When he was fifteen years old he was baptized and announced to his family that he did not wish to act again. Shortly afterward he decided that he would make his religion his life's work.

"It's what our boy really wanted and we accepted his decision," said his father over forty years later. "By then we had lived here over ten years and really knew what Hollywood was all about. I'm sure there are very fine people in the studios, but if someone is serious about leading an exemplary Christian life, I don't think he'd gravitate to show business."

Darwood's younger brother, Dennis, worked intermittently in pictures. In *Lillian Russell* (1940) he played Alice Faye as a baby. He is now a bank manager in Haywood, California.

After spending seventeen years in Thailand as a missionary, Darwood and his family returned to California and settled in Tijunga. Two of his sons, like himself, are ordained ministers of the Seventh-Day Adventist church. Another teaches in a South Dakota grammar school. The fourth boy is employed in Christian publishing.

Darwood is known now as "Ken" or "Kenny," although many of the children he teaches at Sabbath School call him "Waldo." He introduces himself to each new class by showing them his personal favorite of the famous two-reelers, *Three Men in a Tub* (1938).

Dylan Cali

"Waldo" is pastor of the Seventh-Day Adventist church in La Crescenta, California.

Jack Warner changed his name to Clint Walker when he cast him in the title role of Cheyenne. *Frequently, throughout the long-running TV series, the actor appeared in scenes stripped to the waist.*

Clint Walker

The "hunk" who became a television star as "Cheyenne" was born Norman Walker in Hartford, Illinois. He and his twin sister were born on May 30, 1927.

He left school when he was fifteen years old and went to work as a bus boy. There followed times during his teen years of "going two, three days not eating, not having a place to sleep."

Eventually, he enlisted in the U.S. Navy, then served in the merchant marine and worked on an oil rigger.

Van Johnson was headlining at the Las Vegas Sands Hotel when he noticed the strapping security guard and suggested he try an acting career. Through the star he met an agent who agreed to his potential. Walker moved to Hollywood.

He made his debut in *Jungle Gents* (1954), a "Bowery Boys" feature, using the name Jett Norman. Cecil B. DeMille tested him for a prominent part in *The Ten Commandments* (1956), but he was on the screen only briefly as one of the Pharaoh's bodyguards.

It was the role of "Cheyenne Bodie," western wanderer, that brought national recognition as soon as the show debuted in September, 1955. Exploitation by Warner Brothers of Clint Walker as a sex object resulted in high ratings for the series.

In 1958 he walked off the *Cheyenne* set and was placed on suspension. During the nine months in which he and his studio remained estranged he described himself to the press as a "caged animal" in his frustration over the constraints of his contract. When he returned to the program it was with a raise in salary and the promise that he would make features as well.

He starred in the movies *Fort Dobbs* (1958), *Yellowstone Kelly* (1959), *Gold of the Seven Saints* (1961), and *Night of the Grizzly* (1966). Frank Sinatra was the star and director of *None But the Brave* (1965) with Walker and Tommy Sands* in supporting parts. In *Maya* (1966) he was teamed with Jay North[8] and Sajid Kahn.*

He was also in *The Dirty Dozen,* the top-grossing film of 1967, and *The Great Bank Robbery* (1969).

Throughout his career Clint's height of six feet five and a half inches has been a mixed blessing. Actresses found it difficult to look up that far in two-shots and were, according to Walker, "afraid in a clinch they'd get my tie pin in their eye." Actors, particularly stars, felt threatened when he towered over them.

He made a real effort not to be typecast as the big, rugged man of few words. When the actor guested on Jack Benny's TV show he did so well in a comedy routine he was signed for *Send Me No Flowers* (1964). Rock Hudson and Doris Day were the stars of that feature in which Walker was a Texas millionaire. He played it for laughs and was effective but his image remained the same.

In 1971 he had the lead in a TV movie, *Yuma.* The following season he did *Hardcase,* also for ABC Television. In fall, 1974, he starred in his second series, *Kodiak,* playing an officer of the Alaska State Patrol. When it was canceled after only four weeks he was philosophical.

Three years before *Kodiak,* Clint had been clinically dead. While skiing he fell in such a way that the pole he was holding punctured his heart. Upon arrival at the hospital he had neither pulse nor blood pressure. He believes he had an out-of-body experience during that time that has changed his perspective on life.

In 1979 he again hovered near death as a result of a heart tumor. He calls his survivals his "double miracle."

In 1983 he told *Los Angeles Times* reporter Jerry Cohen: "I was suddenly aware of a lot of things they talk about. That glass that we see through darkly, it's true." The same article quoted Clint as stating: "You remember your younger days. You wanted to impress people. That's a heck of a position to be in. I'm a little more relaxed and I enjoy life more."

John Maxon

Clint Walker has appeared recently on public service television announcements for the care and feeding of cats.

He has a daughter by a 1948 marriage to his childhood sweetheart.

In 1974 he married his present wife, Gigi, who was born in France. While he is building a home on the ranch property they own in Grass Valley, California, the Walkers live nearby in an apartment. They intend eventually to raise horses.

In The Big Bands *musicologist George T. Simon wrote: "Fran Warren came along to bring an even greater emotional depth to the band [Claude Thonhill's]. Fran, a very hip Bronxite, made one recording, 'A Sunday Kind of Love,' that really established her. But she sang numerous other songs, some with far subtler feeling, that showed even better what a good artist she really was."*

Fran Warren

The pop artist considered among her peers a "musician's singer," was born in the Bronx, New York, on March 4, 1928. Her original name is Frances Wolfe.

She grew up listening, along with her parents and brothers, to music on the radio and phonograph. Her father's illness, Parkinson's disease, prevented him from working, which resulted in the Wolfes going on welfare.

The spare change Fran earned singing in her neighborhood was very much needed at home. Her first professional fee, $5, came from singing one night along with a band in a local ballroom. Unbeknownst to her parents, she dropped out of school in the ninth grade to make the rounds of what was then referred to as "Tin Pan Alley," an area in Manhattan where much of the music of the day was written, arranged, and contracted.

She became Fran Warren while backstage at the Apollo Theatre one night when she was fourteen. Billy Eckstine (who then spelled his name Eckstein), who was appearing on the amateur bill as she was, took "Warren" from a wine bottle and suggested it to her.

When she auditioned for Duke Ellington, he told her he liked her sound, but because she was white, he would not even consider hiring her. "I thought it was all about music," she said recently. "I couldn't understand how skin color could be important. But I was sixteen, so there was much I had to learn."

Fran was Art Mooney's vocalist for six months but left when she had offers from Hal McIntyre and Charlie Barnet. A flip of the coin decided her on Barnet. She had been singing with him for over a year when he fired her for substituting blue lyrics one evening at the Metropole.

Next she was songstress for Claude Thornhill's orchestra. For Barnet's music, she had learned to make her voice heard over the music. With Thornhill's soft sound, Fran had to sing much lower. She feels she learned the most while with Thornhill and would have stayed indefinitely, but the group disbanded.

Louis Prima recorded "A Sunday Kind of Love" before Fran cut her version with Thornhill's outfit. Prima's rendition did not sell well, but hers earned a gold record, which Thornhill gave her. She had been paid a flat fee of $50 for the session, which lasted fifteen minutes, including the time it took to record the flip side, "For Heaven's Sake."

A few years later, she was offered "Tennessee Waltz." It did not appeal to her, but when Patti Page recorded it, the song sold in the millions. The other, now a standard, that Fran passed on was "I Apologize." It was one of the biggest hits in the career of her old friend Billy Eckstine.

Fran Warren and Billy Eckstine worked together frequently over the years. Their duets have brought hate mail sporadically. The letter that she received during their engagement at Manhattan's Paramount Theatre threatened her life for "public race-mixing" and brought the police.

When July Garland was terminated from M-G-M, Fran was put under contract. But the studio noted for musicals found no role for the singer. During the year she spent under salary, the only thing she did was on loan-out to Universal, *Abbott and Costello Meet Captain Kidd* (1952).

For ten years, she was married to Harry Steinman, who represented some major performers and who owned Philadelphia's Latin Casino. They had one daughter and adopted another.

Fran Warren has never had a gimmick and enjoyed only the one hit record in 1947, yet, by skillful management and her sheer musicianship was still making between $85,000 and $100,000 a year between 1962 and 1964. She played the lead on Broadway in *The Pajama Game* and worked with Danny Kaye on stage at the Palace Theatre. She cut records with the Mills Brothers and Ezio Pinza. Her album, *Fran Warren Sings Harold Arlen,* did very well. She had a loyal following that turned out to hear her when she played the Copacabana or Caesar's Palace. She was well liked within her profession.

Then, within a few hours in October, 1964, her professional life came to an immediate halt. When the man she had recently married, who she had known only a few months, was arrested, she was taken into custody as well. Eventually, her husband pleaded guilty to attempted grand larceny and served two years in prison. But Fran, who knew nothing of his unlawful activities, had been held and questioned without counsel for nineteen hours, strip-searched, and threatened with an additional drug charge after the police had been through her apartment. Two months later, all charges against her were dropped.

When Fran Warren last played Manhattan's Michael's Pub, Rex Reed wrote of the "bruised quality of her voice," which he described as "full of emotion and depth, capable of range and power when necessary, but always beautifully modulated."

Anyone linked with drugs was anathema to most club owners in 1964, especially in the tri-state area where Fran is best known. Then, after she sued the City of New York for malicious prosecution, the word went out on her that there was "serious litigation pending." Her bookings in 1965 amounted to $8,000.

Fourteen years after she was arrested, a jury awarded her $400,000 in damages for "malicious prosecution."

In recent years, Fran has gone on the road with the late Harry James in *Big Broadcast of 1944,* starred in *Mame* on the dinner-theatre circuit, and played some smart clubs. For eight weeks, she toured with the King Sisters, Alvino Rey, and John Gary. [9]

Fran and her husband are "trying it apart for a while." She lives in what was once songwriter Johnny Burke's apartment in Manhattan's Parc Vendome with "Samantha," a Persian. One of her neighbors is Arthur Tracy, "The Street Singer."

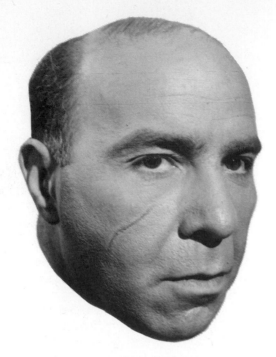

Ben Welden never played the leading part in any of his many films, but he would have been the ideal actor to portray Al Capone.

Ben Welden

The screen tough guy was born Ben Weinblatt in Toledo, Ohio, on June 12, 1901.

He worked his way through his first year at Carnegie Institute of Technology and then won a scholarship. He had gone to the university to study engineering, but soon switched to the drama school. His parents, who were sending him a $4 weekly allowance, were dismayed.

Ben Welden acted in road companies and in several unsuccessful New York productions before going to London as part of the cast of the smash hit *Broadway* in 1926. In one of the plays, *Arabesque* (1925), which ran less than two weeks, he was Bela Lugosi's understudy. Sara Sothern, who later became Elizabeth Taylor's mother, was another member of the cast.

During the years Ben lived in London he appeared in plays and films. *On the Spot* (1930), which starred Charles Laughton, ran in the West End for over a year. *Amongst the Wolves* (1928), *Little Accident* (1929), and *Brothers* (1929) are some of the other plays he did there.

Edgar Wallace, a popular and prolific playwright of the time, thought highly of Ben's work and frequently engaged him. Welden was deeply disappointed when the British censors refused permission for a production of *The Last Mile.* He was set to portray "Killer Mears," the role that had brought stardom to Spencer Tracy.

He came back to New York to support Claudette Colbert* in the play *Tin Pan Alley* (1928) and again in her movie *The Hole in the Wall* (1929). When neither was a success he returned to London, where he lived until 1936.

When he accepted a part in *Silent Barrier* (1937) it was because it was to be filmed in Canada. Welden had intended to visit his family and then return to England, where he was well established professionally. But he stopped off in Hollywood to see his former college classmate Arthur Lubin who had become a movie director. An agent brought him to Warner Brothers and he was assigned a part in *Another Dawn* (1937). The same studio used him in *The King and the Chorus Girl* (1937) and then *The Marked Woman* (1937).

Ben Welden made an indelible impression in *The Marked Woman.* To this day fans insist they remember him coming at Bette Davis with a knife. There is no such scene in the picture. When he is ordered by his boss to "take care of her" Ben breaks into a big toothy, sadistic smile. The next time the star is seen her face has been badly cut. Welden believes he was the screen's first smiling heavy and was unique until Richard Widmark came along.

That chilling performance in *The Marked Woman* earned him a studio contract and

190

movie immortality, but it also firmly typecast him. As a trained and experienced actor he hoped to play many different character parts. He was cast in sympathetic roles on a few occasions but in the minds of moviegoers as well as casting directors, Ben Welden is trouble. His appearance on the screen meant danger—usually for the hero or heroine.

The one time he had a real chance to change his image was in *The Life of Emile Zola,* but when Paul Muni, who played the title role, objected to Ben's portrayal of the artist Cezanne, he was replaced by Vladimir Sokoloff. Ben was to work with Muni on a picture after that, *Angel On My Shoulder* (1946), but the star never spoke a word to him during its shooting.

"Thug," "gangster," or "enforcer" is how his characters were often described. Even in scenes in which he did not speak, his menacing presence was strongly felt. As horror and crime film historian David Del Valle said, "When it came to looming in the background, nobody could be scarier than Ben Welden."

He made dozens of movies. Among them were: *The Missing Rembrandt* (1932), *Along Came Sally* (1934), *The Triumph of Sherlock Holmes* (1935), *Kid Galahad* (1937), *Tenth Avenue Kid* (1938), *Rose of Washington Square* (1939), *City for Conquest* (1940), *Men of Boys Town* (1941), *Manpower* (1941), *All Through the Night* (1942), *Shadows in the Night* (1944), *Sorrowful Jones* (1949), *Buccaneer's Girl* (1950), and *The Lemon Drop Kid* (1951).

He was also in the serials *The Desert Hawk* (1944) with Mona Maris and *Adventures of Captain Africa* (1955). Fans of *The Adventures of Superman* know him from his frequent appearances on the series, always as a bad guy.

Although he worked steadily Ben never became a big enough name to command a large salary. He can afford to live in Beverly Hills because during the fifties he went into the confection business with a product called "Nutcorn."

Richard Lamparski

In his eighty-fourth year Ben Welden said, "I have very few regrets and absolutely no complaints about my whole life—so far, anyway!"

He sold out his interest in 1974, the same year his wife retired as an executive secretary with Universal Pictures.

His last appearance before a camera was as Vincent Price's henchman on *Batman* in 1968.

He considers his best work on stage to have been in *Spread Eagle* (1928) in London with Raymond Massey.[9] *Alcatraz Island,* a box office hit of 1937, contains, in his opinion, his best movie performance. The role he liked best on television was in his words "a slimy double-crosser" on *The Rifleman*. It provided Ben with a touching scene with the late Dolores Del Rio.[8] The part he wanted very much was the old man who was to narrate a fairy tale each week on television. He made the pilot but the series was never sold.

Asked in 1985 if he was retired, the actor responded: "I'd jump at any good part, but I wouldn't get up off this chair to go look for one. Casting people today don't know me and I just can't be bothered re-introducing myself."

He is often recognized by people who don't know his name but who remember him vividly from his movies. He was dining in a restaurant once when a woman had to be restrained from striking him. To her he was "that horrible man who scarred Bette Davis." He considers it his greatest compliment.

Señor Wences appeared forty-eight times on Ed Sullivan's Sunday-evening TV show during the fifties and sixties. He was usually its first act, so very young children could see the ventriloquist and "Johnny" (above) before being put to bed.

Señor Wences

The internationally known ventriloquist was born Moreno Wenceslao on April 20 in Salamanca, Spain. His father, a violinist, frequently took him along when he went to work in the pit at a local theatre. Mr. Wenceslao was a member of the orchestra that accompanied the silent films.

At some of the matinees Moreno attended there were variety acts as well as movies. Moreno became fascinated with the performers who could throw their voices. From an early age he had imitated the speech of playmates and adults. He practiced his art at first in the classroom during roll call, answering "present" for students who were absent in voices very similar to their own. Often, when a student was called on and did not know the answer to the question, Moreno would call out a reply. Sometimes it was the correct answer. Other times it was a clever remark.

One of the many punishments he got for his verbal impersonations was to clean all the inkwells in the school room. When he finished he glanced at one of his ink-stained hands and thought it looked like a face for a cartoon. When he flexed it, the character seemed to move its lips. Thus was born the world's most famous hand-puppet.

At first he was paid with eggs. "Everyone was poor," he said recently. "But I make them laugh or the baby stops crying. People want to give something. I take eggs home. Momma is very happy. We poor, too."

The act that became famous throughout North America, England, and France is essentially the same one honed by the ventriloquist when he graduated from vaudeville houses in Spain to an extensive tour of South America.

At the insistence of an American agent, Wences learned to do his act in English phonetically. Both he and the agent believed his United States debut was, in a sense, starting all over again. So, his first booking was in an amateur show. He won first prize.

"Even if I don't say things so good," he remembers, "audiences know what I mean. They laugh right away."

Using no risqué material and working in tails, Señor Wences was a classy opening act for niteries and supper clubs. Since he appealed to all ages, he could work presentation houses as long as they existed. Although he has never really mastered conversational English, his pronunciation is so precise and his timing so acute the heavy accent actually works in his favor.

Edgar Bergen and Wences became friends and mutual admirers in the mid-thirties when they were both playing small clubs in Greenwich Village. They met when the face of "Charlie McCarthy," Bergen's dummy, was scratched and Wences repaired it.

Wences' long and happy association with Ed Sullivan began during World War II when the columnist-emcee often had him in the shows he took to troop installations and military hospitals. When Sullivan began hosting the early television variety program *Toast of the Town*, Wences was one of his first guests and frequently was at the top of the bill on the popular Sunday evening show.

Television was even more his medium than the stage. On the screen audiences could see close-ups of his hand. The fondness and respect Wences always showed for his creations was even more evident on television. His exchanges with "Pedro," the face in the box, always concluded with Wences' concern for his feelings. "'S-all right?" he would ask. "'S-all right!" was "Pedro's" reply.

Señor Wences appeared with Perry Como on television and was part of the crooner's traveling show that was playing the United States Marine base in Guantánamo, Cuba, during the abortive invasion of the Bay of Pigs. He was part of the Danny Kaye troupe that toured Australia, South Africa, and the United Kingdom.

Wences was a great success at London's Palladium and has had much exposure on television in the United Kingdom. He appeared in Command Performances before King George VI and Queen Elizabeth. In the United States he has performed for Presidents Roosevelt, Truman, Eisenhower, and Nixon. Walt Disney was one of his greatest enthusiasts.

Señor and Señora Wences met and married when they were both in the Folies-Bergère at the Golden Gate International Exhibition in San Francisco in 1940. She was a dancer. Their son is an architect living in Chile.

Señor Wences spends his summers fishing in his hometown in Spain. For five years he was part of the show at the Lido. He went from that Parisian nightclub to another, the Crazy Horse. He has been out of the country for so much of the time in the last fifteen years that Manhattan's Chateau Madrid was inundated with queries when they announced a forthcoming booking recently. Fans wanted to be certain it was the same gentle-humored ventriloquist they remembered.

Wences insists the one change among his "friends" is for the better: "They, even 'Johnny,' no more smoke the cigarettes!" he says.

Señor Wences with "Cecilia Chicken" on a recent visit to Los Angeles.

Paul Schaeffer

193

Jack Wild was nominated for an Academy Award as the Best Supporting Actor of 1968 for his portrayal of the "Artful Dodger" in Oliver. *The British Association of Film and Television Artists nominated him also that year as the "Most Promising Newcomer."*

Jack Wild

The Oscar nominee and television star was born in Manchester, England, on September 30, 1952.

Jack and his older brother Arthur were part of what they describe as a "real working class family." Their father earned a living on the assembly line in a tire factory. The Wilds moved to London when their sons were very young.

Jack and his brother were playing football with Phil Collins when Collins's mother, a theatrical agent, came to pick him up and noticed them. It was through Mrs. Collins that the Wilds were placed in the Barbara Speake Stage School, a training ground for professional children.

Arthur Wild played the title role in the West End production of *Oliver*. Jack was one of the many boys in the show for eighteen months. He auditioned for the "Artful Dodger" role a number of times as boys such as Leonard Whiting* left the part, but was always told he was too short. Only after being chosen for the screen version was he offered the role on stage.

Jack was puzzled by his agent's ecstatic reaction when he received an Oscar nomination for his part in *Oliver* (1968). He had never heard of the Academy Awards and was equally unimpressed with his nomination for the "Stella," the British equivalent of the Oscar.

When he attended the Oscar presentations the night of April 14, 1969, he had the assurance of those around him that the odds of his winning were very strong. Still, he was unaware of the award's importance and when "Jack," the first name of that year's winner for the supporting male actor Academy Award, was announced, Jack Wild stood up as millions of television viewers watched. He sat down just as quickly when he realized that the name announced as the winner was "Jack Albertson."

The telecast ended with a brief pre-taped piece with Jack and Ron Moody, who also had been nominated. Moody and Wild were seen sneaking out the stage door, Oscars in hand,

194

saying, "We didn't get us an Oscar, so we got ourselves an Oscar."

"All I felt was relief," said Wild in 1985. "I hate being extremporaneous in front of an audience and all that winning meant to me was that I'd have had to make a speech. It was at least four years before I fully realized what it would have meant professinally to have won."

Immediately following the enormous success of *Oliver*, Jack Wild starred for three seasons on *H. R. Pufnstuf* over NBC-TV. On it he played "Jimmy," a boy who owned a talking flute. Their adventures were popular with children in the late afternoons from 1969 to 1971. After the feature film of the same name, the show was returned in 1973 to ABC.

Jack guested on such shows as the *Engelbert Humperdinck Show* and won the "8th Annual Gold Star Award" from *16* magazine as the "Best Movie Actor" and "Most Promising TV Star" of 1969.

Jack returned to England where he made *To Love Somebody* (1971) with his *Oliver* movie costar, Mark Lester. Although it did not do well elsewhere, the film was a major grosser in the Orient.

Wild has appeared on English television and has toured the United Kingdom as "Bob Cratchit" in *A Christmas Carol.* Every yuletide he appears in a pantomime.

Jack has been married for over ten years to his wife, who is a backup singer for various artists, including David Essex.

He and Suzi Quatro have developed the plot outlines and characters for a television series in which they hope to star.

Being so well known so early in his career for kid shows he now finds a drawback in his pro-

Martin Norris

Jack and his wife, Gay, with "Chopin" and "Papillon," two of their many companions. Behind their duplex in the Richmond area of London the Wilds have a menagerie of pets, including rabbits, monkeys, and a pair of piranha fish.

fession. Asked if he is thought of as an actor or singer, he replied: "Neither. I'm thought of as a celebrity. Everything I've ever done, with the embarrassing exception of *The Pied Piper* (1971), a film I did with Diana Dors, has been for children. As long as I was working constantly, that was fine, because, although I don't have any children, I do relate better to them than adults."

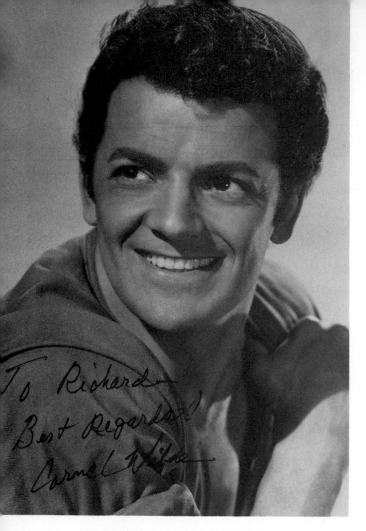

Cornel Wilde became a star and was nominated for the Best Actor Oscar of 1945 when he portrayed the composer Chopin in A Song to Remember. *The same year he headed the cast in the Arabian Nights adventure* A Thousand and One Nights, *a total change of image for him and another box office hit.*

Cornel Wilde

The movie star turned director-producer was born Cornel Wilde in Budapest, Hungary, on October 13, 1915. His father, an officer in the army of Emperor Franz Josef, brought his fam-

ily to the United States shortly after the Communist takeover in 1919.

Cornel was not quite sixteen years old when Columbia University accepted him as a premedical student. At exactly the same time he was awarded a scholarship to Columbia's College of Physicians and Surgeons, he was given another to a dramatic school. While pondering what his choice would be, Wilde auditioned for a Broadway play, *Moon Over Mulberry Street* (1935). When he got that part, he decided on acting as a career.

"I have no regrets," he said in 1986. "I think I would have been a good doctor, but doing what I've done has been much more interesting."

After a few more Broadway appearances, he was chosen to play "Tybalt" in *Romeo and Juliet* (1940) in support of Laurence Olivier and Vivien Leigh. Since she had to be in Hollywood for a film commitment, the play was rehearsed on the West Coast. The prestige of that production brought Wilde a Warner Brothers contract.

He made a brief appearance in *High Sierra* (1941) and was then dropped. By then he had married the actress Patricia Knight and was glad to accept an offer of another term contract. His new studio, Twentieth Century–Fox, used him in *Manila Calling* (1942) and *Wintertime* (1943).

He was loaned to Columbia to play Frédéric Chopin to Merle Oberon's George Sand in *A Song To Remember* (1945). The role brought him an Oscar nomination and immediate stardom. Technicolor at that time was reserved almost exclusively for upbeat musicals. When the picture was first released, audiences were stunned by the vividness of the blood the tubercular Chopin coughed onto the piano keys. It was a huge success.

But forty years after he made it, Cornel Wilde said of *A Song To Remember:* "I'm very, very grateful it came along. I'd been tested and rejected by just about every studio; then it came out and they all wanted me. But really, both Merle and I were quite unsuitable for those parts. We looked nothing like the people we played. It was Chopin's gorgeous music that carried that film."

He returned to his home lot, firmly established as a serious actor and one with strong romantic appeal. His horsemanship and fencing skills made Wilde an obvious candidate for adventure roles. He seemed the heir apparent to Tyrone Power, Fox's most important star.

There followed the costarring assignment opposite Ginger Rogers in *It Had To Be You* (1947), a comedy. And the big-budget color picture *Leave Her to Heaven* (1945), *The Bandit of Sherwood Forest* (1946), *Centennial Summer* (1946), the highly controversial flop *Forever Amber* (1947), and Cecil B. De Mille's *The Greatest Show on Earth* (1952). It is the black-and-white drama *Road House* (1948), however, that is his favorite of this period.

Immediately upon his divorce from Patricia Knight in 1951, Cornel married the blonde actress Jean Wallace. She also became his partner in the movies he produced and directed, and, occasionally, as in *Storm Fear* (1955) and *Sword of Lancelot* (1963), his leading lady.

Five out of the eight pictures he made have been profitable, a relatively high percentage.

Cornel starred in *The Naked Prey* (1966), his own production. The screenwriters were nominated for an Oscar. The picture was a critical and box office hit. He had the lead in *Beach Red* (1967), another of the films his company made, and one that was strongly opposed by the U.S. Department of Defense. Most reviewers, who were not put off by its strong anti-war sentiments, gave it excellent notices.

Other pictures Cornel Wilde appeared in are: *The Homestretch* (1947) with Maureen O'Hara*; *Treasure of the Golden Condor* (1953); *Passion* (1954) with John Qualen* *Omar Khayyan* (1957) with Debra Paget* and

Jim Janisch

Cornel Wilde and his only son, Cornel, Jr., live together in a West Los Angeles condominium. The teenager's mother is Jean Wallace.

Yma Sumac*; *No Blade of Grass* (1971); *The Norsemen* (1978); and *Shark's Treasure* (1975).

The Wilde-Wallace marriage and partnership were both dissolved in 1981. Their only child, Cornel Wilde, Jr., is seriously considering an acting career.

Wilde was offered a role in *The Original,* but did not feel the feature had strong box office potential. From time to time, he makes a rare TV appearance, such as on *The Love Boat.* Almost all of his creative energies, though, have been concentrated recently on a film property he is developing. There are parts in it for him and his son, but neither has the starring role. His other project is his autobiography, *Wilde for Life,* which he hopes to complete in 1986.

Although he was raised a Roman Catholic and admits that he was for many years "fervent," today, he considers the Church, "more of a business than religion." He says, "I worship God by loving my fellow man. I am very concerned about the environment and psychological health of this beautiful planet. Throughout my work is the idea, over and over, that we *must* all learn to respect one another."

In the United States Googie Withers is probably best known for her appearance in **The Haunted Mirror** *sequence of the episodic thriller* **Dead of Night** *(1946) and in a smaller role in Hitchcock's* **The Lady Vanishes** *(1938).*

Googie Withers

The English star was born Georgette Lizette Withers in Karachi, India. Her birth date is March 12, 1917. "Googie" is a term of affection and means "pigeon" in Hindi. She remained in India with her mother, who was of Dutch-French-German descent, and her father, a British naval officer, until she was sent to boarding school in England at age seven.

Her father indulged her in dancing lessons, believing she would soon get over her interest in the theatre. "But," said Googie, "suddenly I was a very good dancer and they just had to take me seriously."

She was seventeen and dancing in a West End show when someone at a film studio spotted her and, feeling she showed potential, gave her a contract. She made quickies such as *The Love Test* (1934) with Louis Hayward* and *All at Sea* (1935) with Rex Harrison.

She supported Dolores Del Rio[8] in *Accused* (1936), was with Ann Todd in *Action for Slander* (1937), and in *Paradise for Two* (1937) with Patricia Ellis, *Kate Plus Ten* (1938) with Genevieve Tobin, *Murder in Soho* (1938) with the late Jack LaRue,[8] *She Couldn't Say No* (1939) with Greta Gynt,* *Busman's Honeymoon* (1940) with Constance Cummings,[9] *One of Our Aircraft is Missing* (1942), which drew two Oscar nominations, and *On Approval* (1944) with Bea Lillie.

Pink String and Sealing Wax (1945) with Sally Ann Howes was a major hit in England. The grim but powerful *It Always Rains On Sunday* (1947) was one of the best British films of all time. *Miranda* (1948) with David Tomlinson* was another box office success. Googie starred in all these, as well as in the Jules Dassin thriller *Night and the City* (1950). She was also one of many stars in *The Magic Box* (1951).

She believes the turning point in her career came when she was offered the lead in J. B. Priestley's *They Came to a City.* Since it was a drama it was thought the name "Googie" was unsuitable. She adamantly refused to change it, but was cast in the play anyway. After a two-year run in the West End during the Blitz, she played in it at Allied troop installations throughout Great Britain and starred in the 1944 movie version.

Her television series *Within These Walls* ran for two years in England, but was not seen in the United States. Based on fact, Googie portrayed the warden of a high-security women's prison.

In 1958 Googie moved with her husband, John McCallum, to Australia where for years he managed the country's largest chain of theatres. *Skippy,* the television series he wrote, directed, and produced in Australia, has been shown in eighty-nine countries.

Her last Broadway appearance was in *The Complaisant Lover* (1961) with the late Michael Redgrave. She played "Queen Gertrude" to his "Hamlet" at Stratford. In 1984 Googie and her husband did *School for Scandal* on a government-sponsored tour of ten countries.

She starred in the Australian movie *The Nickel Queen* (1971) and frequently tours their country and New Zealand in plays opposite her husband.

Bert Newton, Australia's top television and radio personality, said of Googie: "Her name on a theatre billboard is a guarantee of success in not only the major capital cities but anywhere there is a theatre. She is considered here one of our very own."

Because of the great distance and personal commitments, she has lost out on important roles on a number of occasions. Peter Hall wanted to present her in *Cleopatra* at Stratford-On-Avon, but, as Googie puts it, "my family needed me." She could have done the Rosalind Russell role in *Wonderful Town* in London, but again could not get away.

There were two movie roles for which she was considered and wanted to do. After she tested for *A Yank at Oxford* her agent told her it

Googie Withers and her husband, producer-actor John McCallum, live in New South Wales, Australia.

was hers, but Vivien Leigh played it. Googie took over the lead in Terence Rattigan's *The Deep Blue Sea* from Peggy Ashcroft in the West End and won an award when she re-created the character on English television. She was approached about doing the screen version but it, too, went to Vivien Leigh. "I really did feel cross about that one," the actress said in 1985. "The woman was no beauty and never had been. Vivien was still lovely, so the film really made no sense."

The one role she still longs to do is the part Gladys Cooper created in *The Chalk Garden.*

In recent seasons television viewers in the United Kingdom have seen Googie Withers as the subject of *This Is Your Life* and in the made-for-television movies *Hotel du Lac* and *Time After Time.* In the latter, in which she plays a seventy-five-year-old blind woman, she worked with her husband and her actress daughter Joanna Withers.

Dana Wynter had cool and class, but the parts her studio gave her in D-Day, The Sixth of June *(1956),* Something of Value *(1957), and* Fraulein *(1958) failed to make her a star. One of her motion pictures,* Invasion of the Body Snatchers *(1956) has cult status.*

Dana Wynter

The almost star was born Dagmar Spencer-Marcus in London on June 8, 1931. She does not reveal her parentage or background except to say that she is of Rumanian-German descent and that her parents are presently living in a country that is experiencing great internal turmoil.

Raised in England, she was accepted in a South African medical school before she turned seventeen. During her first year her appearances in plays staged by the university's drama department brought her considerable attention on campus and encouraged her to seek a career in acting.

As Dagmar Wynter she appeared in the Googie Withers starrer *White Corridors* (1951), *The Woman's Angle* (1952) with Joan Collins, the Burt Lancaster vehicle *The Crimson Pirate* (1952), and *Colonel March Investigates* (1953) with Boris Karloff.

It was at this time she took the name Dana, which she pronounces "Donna."

An American agent who knew her work in England induced her to go to New York in 1954. Within weeks of her arrival and without any prior television experience she replaced Eva Gabor in the lead on the prestigious *Robert Montgomery Presents.* Martin Manulis saw her on the program and put in a bid for her services for *Playhouse 90,* which he produced.

Her Broadway debut, *Black Eyed Susan* (1954), ran for only four days, but brought her good reviews and a screen test by Universal. After a *Look* magazine article, four studios made offers.

The contract she signed with Twentieth Century–Fox began at $500 a week. Dana, however, was less than pleased with most of her screen assignments and found life as a contractee not to her liking. "The rules seldom made sense to me," she said in 1985. "For instance, I was told not to drive my car on the lot. It seems the studio had some arrangement with a big U.S. automaker and a Talbot Lago was unwelcome." Her reserved quality quickly brought her the label "lady," a category she feels limited her opportunities professionally. As she has said, "In movies, nothing succeeds like sin."

In 1956 she married Greg Bautzer, who up until then was known to the public as a handsome lawyer who dated many movie stars such as Joan Crawford and Lana Turner. Until their marriage he had usually headed each year's listing of filmdom's most eligible bachelors. He was and continued to be for many years, probably the most influential deal-maker in the movie capital. The cachet the union gave her, however, was only social. Bautzer was of no help when Dana refused a role in *No Down Payment* and was placed on suspension. When she turned down the lead in *The Lion* opposite William Holden, the role went to Capucine and thus began an intense and long-running relationship between the two.

Among her pictures are: *The View from Pompey's Head* (1955), *In Love and War* (1958), *Sink the Bismarck!* (1960), *On the Double* (1961), *The List of Adrian Messenger* (1963), and *If He Hollers, Let Him Go* (1968).

The television series *The Man Who Never Was*, in which she costarred with Robert Lansing, lasted only a few months in 1966.

Her best work, she believes, was done on *Playhouse 90* in such productions as *Winter Dreams, The Violent Heart,* and *Wings of the Dove.*

In 1981, after a separation of nearly twenty years, the Bautzers were divorced. Dana spends part of each year with her only child, Mark, who lives in the home she maintains in Beverly Hills. His godmother is Leslie Blanch, the author of *The Wilder Shores of Love.*

She was very taken with Ireland when she first went there to make *Shake Hands with the Devil* (1959) and for years rented a cottage outside Dublin. In 1971 she bought the chimney and ruins of an old house in a glen and built around it. With a cat and a wild pheasant as companions she now considers it her main residence.

Dana Wynter never developed a feeling of camaraderie with other actors and was not ambitious for an acting career. Before she came to the United States, Anthony Quayle suggested that she audition for Stratford, but, says Dana, "The director had made a remark that hurt me, so I never tried. More than likely I misunderstood what he said. The point is, had I been

dedicated, neither a remark nor anything else would have put me off."

"I am no longer an actor," says Dana. She now makes films for television, six of which have been shown on Irish television. The cult of Isis, the author Frederick Forsyth, and the Irish Sweepstakes are among her subjects.

Dana thinks of herself as having been "extraordinarily lucky." If she has a regret, it is not having pursued her original ambitions: medicine and anthropology. The work she has done in recent years, however, more than eased her frustrations. She has written for publications as diverse as Irish women's magazines and the *National Review* on subjects as varied as remaining single to the political situation in Zimbabwe. Although a Quaker, Ms. Wynter has interested herself in the choir school and bellringers of the Roman Catholic St. Patrick's Cathedral.

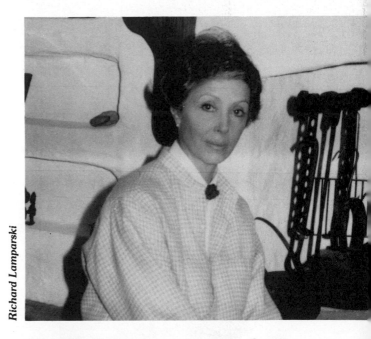

Dana Wynter's thatched-roof house in County Wicklow of the Irish Republic is set in twenty-two acres of heather and faces a waterfall.

Richard Lamparski

On July 31, 1980, many of the members of the Our Gang *shorts (now televised as* The Little Rascals*) were reunited at the Los Angeles Hilton Hotel. From left to right (standing) are: The late William "Buckwheat" Thomas,[8] Edith Fellows,[8] Eugene "Pineapple" Jackson,[9] Marvin "Bubbles" Strind, Sidney "Woim" Killbrick,[8] Joe Cobb, Ernest "Sunshine Sammy" Morrison,[9] Leonard Landy, George "Spanky" McFarland, Tommy "Butch" Bond,[9] Delmar Watson. From left (seated) are: Dorothy "Echo" Deborba,[9] Verna Kornman (mother of Mildred and the late Mary Kornman), Peggy Ahern, and Mildred Kornman.*

On January 25, 1986, an Our Gang reunion was sponsoored by Sidney Kilbrick at his Desert Shadows Recreational Vehicle Park in Cathedral City, California. All attendees, including Robert Blake (not pictured), signed their names and put their handprints in wet cement in front of the main building.

From left to right (standing) are: Darwood "Waldo" Smith, Mel "Junior" Jasquar, Tommy "Butch" Bond,[9] Sidney "Woim" Kilbrick,[8] Leonard Kilbrick, George "Spanky" McFarland, Gordon "Porky" Lee, and William Thomas, Jr., son of "Buckwheat." From left (seated): Marvin Hatley (musical director of Hal Roach Studios and composer of Laurel and Hardy's theme, "The Cuckoo Song"), Jackie Lynn Taylor, Dorothy "Echo" DeBorba,[9] Ernest "Sunshine Sammy" Morrison,[9] and Eugene "Pineapple" Jackson.[8]

Biographical Notes on Personalities Marked
with an Asterisk (*) in the Text

ADDAMS, DAWN The actress best known for her role in the Chaplin picture *A King in New York* (1973) died in May, 1985.

ANKERS, EVELYN Known as "The Queen of Scream," she had lived for over twenty years in Hawaii with her husband, Richard Denning. She died on August 28, 1985.

ARNAZ, DESI, SR. The former costar and husband of Lucille Ball was living in the guest house of her Beverly Hills estate in early 1986. He was widowed in 1985.

ARTHUR, JEAN The reclusive star lives in Carmel-by-the-Sea, California. She has several cats, gardens, and until recently played tennis. She does not discuss her career, even with friends, and refuses all requests for interviews or autographs.

ARTHUR, ROBERT Known mostly for his portrayal of juveniles in movies. He is single, lives in Los Angeles, and is the head of an insurance brokerage. He is very active in Project Rainbow, a self-help organization for gay senior citizens.

BAKER, KENNY For many years before his death in 1985 the singer lived in Solvang, California, where he recorded hymns and worked as a Christian Science practitioner.

BARRY, DON The actor known for his portrayal of "Red Ryder" on the screen and his relationships with Joan Crawford, Susan Hayward, and Linda Darnell took his own life in 1980.

BARTHOLOMEW, FREDDIE The child star retired in 1985 from the vice-presidency of one of the world's largest advertising agencies. Divorced, and living on the East Coast, he house-guested in 1986 with his longtime friend Jimmy Lydon. [8]

BARTON, EILEEN The singer's biggest hit was "If I Knew You Were Coming I'd Have Baked a Cake." She is single, lives in Los Angeles, and plans to reactivate her career.

BECK, THOMAS Retired from real estate sales, he is single and lives in Miami Shores, Florida.

BENNETT, BRUCE Deals in real estate in and near Palms, California, where he lives.

BERGNER, ELISABETH Died on May 12, 1986.

BLEYER, ARCHIE The musician best known for the years he conducted his orchestra on various programs hosted by Arthur Godfrey lives in Freeport, New York.

BOND, LILLIAN The English actress of the thirties lives in Northridge, California.

BOOTH, EDWINA During the filming of *Trader Horn* (1931) in Africa she was stricken with an ailment that has never left her. Semi-invalided, and a Mormon, she lives with her husband in Long Beach, California.

BOOTH, SHIRLEY The 1952 Academy Award winner as Best Actress in *Come Back, Little Sheba* lives with a companion in Chatham, Massachusetts. Ten years later she won a Tony award for her performances in the title role of the TV comedy series *Hazel*. Her health does not permit her to perform or give interviews. It is impossible for her to respond to fan mail, but she wishes her admirers to know that she is very appreciative of their interest.

BORCHERS, CORNELL The German actress lives in Sternberg, Germany.

BOWERS, JOHN The leading man of silent pictures had been estranged from his wife, Marguerite de la Motte, a leading lady of the same era, when he drowned in November, 1936. Bowers, who had been despondent over his marriage and career, rented a sloop and made good on his threat to "sail into the sunset."

BREEN, BOBBY Married, he lives in North Lauderdale, Florida. He works in nightclubs occasionally and books various acts.

BRIAN, DAVID The leading man to both Bette Davis and Joan Crawford has been inactive due to ill health. He and his wife, Adrian Booth, who was also known as Lorna Gray, live in Sherman Oaks, California.

BRITTON, SHERRY The stripper and actress lives with her husband, an industrialist, in the Gramercy Park area of Manhattan.

BROWN, TOM Almost completely retired from acting, he lives in Sherman Oaks and is actively involved in the operation of gold and silver mines he owns.

BUPP, SONNY The actor who portrayed "Charles Foster Kane" as a boy in *Citizen Kane* is an executive with Ford Motor Company. He lives in Southfield, Michigan, and is married.

CALVERT, PHYLLIS The former British star still acts in England but wishes no publicity in the United States because, "I was a complete flop in Hollywood and would like the world to forget that mistake." She is married and lives in Buckinghamshire.

CALVET, CORINNE The French siren is single and lives in Santa Monica. She is in private practice as a counsellor, treating emotionally disturbed, depressed, and drug-addicted patients.

CARLISLE, MARY The leading lady of the thirties is married to a retired executive of Twentieth Century–Fox. They live in Beverly Hills.

CARRADINE, JOHN Lives in Santa Barbara, California.

CAULFIELD, JOAN Single and living in Beverly Hills.

CLOUTIER, SUZANNE The French actress-producer and former wife of Peter Ustinov has homes in France and Hollywood.

COLBERT, CLAUDETTE The widowed star lives in Barbados.

COLLIER, LOIS The Universal player of the forties is married to an attorney and lives in Beverly Hills. She does not grant interviews.

COLLINS, CORA SUE The child actress of the thirties is married to a businessman. They maintain homes in Beverly Hills and Phoenix.

COULOURIS, GEORGE The character actor, now in his mid-eighties, works occasionally in England. He and his second wife live in a cottage on Hampstead Heath in London.

COURT, HAZEL The English actress lives in Santa Monica with her husband, the former actor Don Taylor, who is now a director.

COURTLAND, JEROME The former actor is married and has a family. He is now a well-established director-producer.

CUGAT, XAVIER The "Rhumba King" lives in an apartment in the Hotel Ritz in Barcelona. In 1985 at age eighty-five he filmed a special program for Spanish television.

DENNING, RICHARD The widower of Evelyn Ankers lives on Maui, Hawaii.

DeWILDE, BRANDON The actor was killed at age thirty in an automobile collision in 1972.

DEXTER, ANTHONY After he retired from teaching speech and drama at a high school in Eagle Rock, California, the former actor moved to Denver, Colorado.

DOMERGUE, FAITH The Howard Hughes discovery is married to an Argentinian businessman. She lives in Switzerland.

DONLEVY, BRIAN At the time of his death in 1972 he was married to the widow of Bela Lugosi.

DONNELL, JEFF Lives in the San Fernando Valley and is single. She appears from time to time as Anna Lee's maid on the TV soap opera *General Hospital*.

DOW, PEGGY Last known to be married to a wealthy oilman and living in Tulsa, Oklahoma.

DOWNS, JOHNNY Married and the father of five daughters, he lives in Coronado, California. In 1986 he retired from the real estate business and now spends his time "gardening, playing doubles with my wife, and studying Spanish."

DRAKE, CHARLES The Universal player lives in East Lyme, Connecticut. He declines to give any details about his present life.

DU BOIS, DICK "Mr. America of 1954" is a married fundamentalist minister, and lives in Santa Monica.

ELAM, JACK The actor best known as a heavy in westerns lives in Tucson, Arizona.

ELDRIDGE, FLORENCE The widow and sometime costar of Fredric March lives in Santa Barbara, California.

FIELD, SHIRLEY ANNE The English leading lady is active on the stage and TV in the United Kingdom. She lives in London apart from her husband, a literary agent.

FRAZEE, JANE The Universal star of the forties and onetime wife of the star Glenn Tryon died in 1985. After retiring from the screen she became a realtor.

FURY, ED The cover boy of fifties physique magazines went to Italy in the sixties where he starred in a number of muscle movies. He lives in North Hollywood with his wife, who was formerly married to Reg Lewis, "Mr. America of 1963." *Thoran, The Avenger* with Fury in the title role was released in Europe in 1986.

GAM, RITA The actress makes an occasional appearance on the stage in New York City where she lives.

GODDARD, PAULETTE The star of forties films and the third wife of Charles Chaplin is the widow of author Erich Maria Remarque. She has residences in Manhattan and Switzerland.

GRAY, NADIA The Continental actress lives in Manhattan.

GRAY, SALLY The British beauty retired from acting when she married into the aristocracy in 1953. She lives in London and is known as Lady Oranmore & Browne.

GREENWOOD, JOAN The pixieish English actress is widowed and lives in London.

GREER, JANE The star of features has recently ended years of retirement by appearing in a movie and on several TV shows. She and actor Frank London live with their menagerie of pets in Bel Air, California.

GYNT, GRETA The glamorous star of British films lived for years on Malta with her husband, who was a surgeon. After his death in 1984 she moved to London.

HALE, GEORGIA She came into prominence as the lead in *The Salvation Hunters* (1925) and played the dance hall girl with whom Chaplin falls in love in *The Gold Rush* (1925). Because of her Christian Science beliefs, her death on June 7, 1985, was not disclosed to the press.

HARAREET, HAYA The Israeli-born actress is married to British director Jack Clayton. She declines all interview requests.

HARRISON, RICHARD The star of Italian-made muscle movies of the sixties is in film production in Rome.

HARRISON, SUSAN Considered one of the most promising young actresses of her generation after she appeared in *Sweet Smell of Success* (1957). She believes that there are "no roles for me anymore." Married to an artist, the couple has homes in Nevada and in the California desert.

HARVEY, LILIAN The English actress who became a star in Continental films died in 1968. In the last years of her life she had a boutique in the South of France.

HATFIELD, HURD The actor lives in County Cork, Republic of Ireland.

HAYDON, JULIE The actress, who is the widow of drama critic George Jean Nathan, is an artist-in-residence at the Roman Catholic College of St. Teresa in Winona, Minnesota.

HAYWARD, LOUIS The South African–born actor died in 1985 in Palm Springs, California, where he had been living in retirement.

HAYWORTH, RITA The "Love Goddess" of the forties and fifties lives in a Connecticut nursing home. Her affairs are looked after by her daughter, Yasmin, who is by her marriage to Aly Kahn.

HEISS, CAROL The skater is married to Hayes Jenkins, another championship skater, and lives in Akron, Ohio.

HERVEY, IRENE The former actress is the mother of singer Jack Jones by Alan Jones. Divorced, she lives alone in North Hollywood.

HILL, CRAIG The American actor best known for his role on *The Whirlybirds* TV series is married to the actress Teresa Gimpera. The couple runs a restaurant in Bagur, Spain.

HOBSON, VALERIE The British star has retired from acting and does not grant interviews. She is married to Anthony Profumo, former member of Parliament.

HOMEIER, SKIP Married, he lives in Palm Desert, California.

HOVER, HERMAN The man who owned and ran Ciro's, the famed Sunset Strip nitery, is a writer and consultant. Single, he lives in Hollywood.

HOWARD, JOYCE After moving to Hollywood she held an executive position with Paramount Pictures. Single and living in the Santa Monica Canyon, the former British star considers herself a photographer and has had a one-woman show of her work. *Letters from Henry Miller to Hoki Takuda,* a book she compiled and edited was published in fall, 1986.

HYDE-WHITE, WILFRED The character actor lives in Cathedral City, California.

HYER, MARTHA Retired from acting, she is married to producer Hal Wallis. They maintain homes in Holmby Hills and Palm Springs, California.

JANUARY, LOIS The leading lady of westerns is engaged in public relations. She is widowed and lives in Beverly Hills.

JENKINS, BUTCH The child actor best known for his appearances in *The Human Comedy* (1943), *National Velvet* (1944), and *Our Vines Have Tender Grapes* (1945) is a land developer living in Greenville, North Carolina.

JOHN, ROSAMUND The British actress is married to a member of Parliament of the Labor Party.

JORDAN, DOROTHY The widow of producer Merian C. Cooper lives in Coronado, California.

KAHN, SAJID The heartthrob of the sixties, best known for playing in the film *Maya* (1966) and the 1967–68 television show of the same title, acts in his native India. He appeared briefly in *Heat and Dust* (1983).

KAYE, NORA The former ballerina works closely with her husband, producer-director Herbert Ross.

KELLY, NANCY According to her brother, she is unmarried, retired, and lives in the Brentwood area of Los Angeles.

KELLY, TOMMY The star of *The Adventures of Tom Sawyer* (1938) is an executive with an educational foundation near Washington, D.C. He does not discuss his career or respond to fan mail. He once declined an interview with the explanation that the years of his career in movies were the ones that held mostly unpleasant memories.

KENT, JEAN Semi-active in England where she lives with her husband, an Albanian-born economist.

KERR, JOHN Practices criminal law in Los Angeles.

KING, JOHN Until recent years he was the proprietor of a waffle shop in La Jolla, California. He is now retired.

KIRBY, DURWOOD Lives in Sanibel, Florida.

KNIGHT, EVELYN The songstress billed as "The Lass with the Delicate Air" declines any publicity. She is the mother of a son and is active in the Baptist church in Phoenix, Arizona.

KNOX, ALEXANDER Best known for playing the title role in *Wilson* (1944) for which he received an Oscar nomination. He is married to the former actress Doris Nolan and lives in Northumberland, England.

KNOX, ELYSE She is married to Tom Harmon and lives in the Brentwood area of Los Angeles. The Harmons are the parents of Kristin and Mark Harmon. The former was for years the wife of singer Ricky Nelson.

KOHNER, SUSAN Married to designer John Weitz, she lives in Manhattan with their two sons.

LAMARR, HEDY The Viennese star maintains an apartment in Manhattan, but has lived since 1984 in Miami.

LAMB, GIL The gangling comedian is widowed and lives in Palm Springs, California.

LAMBERT, JACK Known as "the meanest mug in the movies," he is now retired, married, and living in Carmel-by-the-Sea, California.

LANE, PRISCILLA Widowed, she is living in one of the homes she owns in Derry, New Hampshire. She is the surviving member of the four Lane sisters who became entertainers.

LANG, JENNINGS Formerly Joan Bennett's agent, he is now an executive producer at Universal Studios. His wife is the singer Monica Lewis.

LEE, ANNA The English star of quota films is the widow of poet-novelist Robert Nathan. She lives in West Hollywood and plays a running part on the soap opera *General Hospital.*

LEE, CAROLYN The child actress best known for *Honeymoon in Bali* (1939) is married and lives in St. Louis, Missouri.

LEE, HARPER The author of *To Kill a Mockingbird* is in law practice with her sister in Alabama.

LEWIS, ROBERT Q. The host of radio and TV shows lives in Beverly Hills and is single.

LOCKWOOD, MARGARET The English star does not consider herself retired. She lives in Kingston Upon Thames, England.

LORD, MARJORIE Married to a banker, she lives in Beverly Hills. Her daughter is the actress Anne Archer.

LORRING, JOAN The actress best known for her performance in *The Corn is Green,* which brought her an Oscar nomination as the Best Supporting Actress of 1945, is married to the head of cancer research at Sloan-Kettering in New York City.

LUND, JOHN The leading man of the forties lives in Santa Barbara. He does not grant interviews.

LYNN, VERA The songstress was known throughout the British Empire during World War II as "The Forces' Sweetheart." She lives with her husband in Ditchling, Sussex, and is considered to be one of the closest of the Queen Mother's friends.

MAHONEY, JOCK The actor lives in Sherman Oaks with his present wife.

MARA, ADELE Lives in the Mandeville Canyon area of West Los Angeles with her husband, producer Roy Huggins, and their three sons.

MARTIN, DEWEY The film actor and former husband of Peggy Lee replied in 1983 to a request for an interview thusly: "I have not the slightest interest in any publicity spotlighting my late career in theatre and films. My life, these days, is very private and fulfilled. Please allow me to keep it that way." He keeps a post office box in Beverly Hills.

MARTIN, MARION The spectacular blonde bit actress died in August, 1985. Her brother is the pastor of the famous San Juan Capistrano Mission. According to her husband, she asked to be interred in the mausoleum at Holy Cross Cemetery in Culver City, "so she could be close to the altar where she often heard Mass and near the M-G-M studios where she made *Boom Town* and *The Big Store.*"

MASSEN, OSA The Danish actress is single and lives in Beverly Hills. She declines all requests for interviews.

MATURE, VICTOR Divorced, he lives in Rancho Santa Fe, California. He acts occassionally and is an ardent golfer.

McCALLISTER, LON The "Boy Next Door" of forties movies is single and divides his time between his properties in northern California and Nevada.

McGUIRE, DOROTHY Widowed, she lives in Beverly Hills. She had a running part on the TV soap *The Young and The Restless* in 1985.

MEEKER, RALPH The star of Braodway's *Picnic* (1953) and movie leading man is in very frail health and lives in a nursing home as a ward of the County of Los Angeles. His legal guardian could make no further comment since his case is under investigation.

MILLER, DEAN Known for *December Bride* and as host of *Here's Hollywood!*, he owns and operates a radio and television station in Sidney, Ohio.

MITCHELL, GUY The singing star of the fifties completed a very successful tour of the United Kingdom in 1985. He and his wife live in Las Vegas.

MOORE, JUANITA Nominated for an Oscar as Best Supporting Actress in *Imitation of Life* (1959), the character actress appears in plays presented by a Los Angeles theatre group.

MORGAN, MICHELE The French star lives in Neuilly, a suburb of Paris.

MUNSEL, PATRICE The former Metropolitan Opera prima donna is married to a producer and performs occasionally on stage. The couple lives on Long Island.

MURPHY, DONALD The former actor now runs his own interior design business in Santa Fe, New Mexico.

MURPHY, GEORGE The former senator from California now lives in Palm Beach, Florida, and Washington, D.C. He is a lobbyist.

MURPHY, MARY Brando's leading lady in *The Wild One* (1953) has recently divorced and is again available for screen roles. She works in an art gallery near her home in West Hollywood.

MURRAY, KEN The author-impresario and his wife live in Beverly Hills. His extensive collection of Hollywood home movies is about to be marketed on cassette.

NELSON, DAVID The elder of Ozzie and Harriet's two sons was named executor of Ricky's will. He lives in the San Fernando Valley and owns his own TV production company.

NEY, RICHARD After a brief film career and an even briefer marriage to Greer Garson he became a financial consultant and has written several books on the stock market. He lives in Manhattan.

NISSEN, GRETA The Norwegian-born star was replaced by Jean Harlow when Howard Hughes scrapped the silent version of *Hell's Angels* and remade it as a talkie. According to Ms. Nissen, she was unavailable for the second production because of a prior commitment and has no regrets. She and her husband, a retired businessman, divide their time between their Montecito condominium and ranch in Santa Inez, California.

NOLAN, LLOYD The actor was a widower when he died in 1985.

NORRIS, EDWARD The leading man of the thirties and former husband of Ann Sheridan shares his Malibu home with Jean Dean, leading lady in the serial *Radar Patrol vs. Spy King* and the original Vargas Girl. Norris collects classic automobiles of the thirties.

O'BRIEN, MARGARET The child star of the forties is married and the mother of a daughter. Her husband is in the aluminum business. They live in Thousand Oaks, California.

O'HARA, MAUREEN The Irish actress is widowed and lives on St. Croix in the U.S. Virgin Islands.

OLSON, NANCY After marriage to and divorce from lyricist-composer Alan Jay Lerner and recording executive Alan Livingston, she married a publishing executive. The couple is considered by some to be the most influential social leaders in Los Angeles.

PAAR, JACK The former *Tonight* show host lives in New Canaan, Connecticut. His daughter Randy is an attorney.

PAGET, DEBRA Once publicized as "The Starlet Who Has Never Been Kissed," she was married first to the late singer Dave Street. In recent years she divorced the nephew of Madame Chiang Kai-shek, an oil millionaire who is the father of her son. She lives in Houston, Texas.

PAIGE, ROBERT After leaving acting he became a newscaster on a Los Angeles TV channel for a number of years. He is now retired as executive assistant to Los Angeles County Supervisor Baxter Ward, married, and living in Studio City, California.

PALMER, GREGG Married, he lives in Encino, California. Asked if he considers himself an actor still he replied, "Yes, but what I have been offered in recent years has all been unacceptable.

PALMER, PETER The actor best known for playing the title role in *Li'l Abner* on Broadway and in the 1959 film musical lives in Woodland Hills, California.

PARKER, JEAN The star, who was for a time married to Robert Lowery, has a son by him. She lives very quietly in Glendale, California, and does not wish any publicity.

PARKER, SUZY Married to Bradford Dillman and living in Santa Barbara.

PARKER, WILLARD Semi-invalided for a number of years, the former leading man is married to Virginia Field and lives in Palm Desert.

PAYNE, JOHN Married, he is living in Malibu. The actor-writer underwent quadruple bypass surgery in early 1986.

PERREAU, GIGI She is married and the mother of four children. She teaches acting at a Roman Catholic school near her home in Sherman Oaks, California.

PILBEAM, NOVA In the thirties and forties this actress had a large following throughout the British Empire. In the United States she is best remembered for Hitchcock's *The Man Who Knew Too Much* (1935). She lives in the Highgate area of London and refuses all requests for interviews.

POWERS, MALA The former actress lives in North Hollywood with her husband, a publisher. She has authored two books for children and their parents and is the narrator of *Dial a Story*, a subscription service that allows children to hear recorded stories over the telephone.

PROVINE, DOROTHY The blonde star of Warner Brothers productions is married to the director Robert Day. The couple and their son live on Bainbridge Island in Washington State. At present she is not granting interviews.

PROVOST, JON The boy actor who became known as the master of "Lassie" on television was last known to be in the real estate business in northern California. He does not choose to discuss his career.

PURDOM, EDMUND He has lived in Rome for over twenty years and directs and acts. In 1985 he played a vampire in *Fraccia vs. Dracula* a feature made in Italy.

QUALEN, JOHN The character actor lives in Torrence, California.

QUINN, CARMEL The singing colleen who became one of the "Little Godfreys" is married and lives in Leonia, New Jersey.

REED, PHILIP The leading man of the thirties and forties is married and lives in Bel-Air.

REED, WALTER The screen player of the forties and fifties is retired and lives in Santa Cruz, California, with his wife of forty-eight years. He is the younger brother of Jack Smith.

RETTIG, TOMMY He is divorced and lives in Marina del Rey, California. He is the coauthor of a best-selling book in the computer field and is self-employed as a computer programmer and consultant.

REVIER, DOROTHY The star of silents and early talkies was known in the profession as "The Queen of Poverty Row" because of her affair with Harry Cohn. After they broke up she left the screen to marry a socialite. Widowed, she shares a West Hollywood apartment with her sister and their pets.

REYNOLDS, JOYCE Widowed, she lives in Holualoa, Hawaii.

ROBERTSON, DALE He is living on his ranch in Yukon, Oklahoma.

ROLAND, GILBERT The Mexican-born star lives in the same Beverly Hills house he once shared with his first wife, Constance Bennett. He is a tennis enthusiast.

ROMANCE, VIVIAN The French star, best known in the United States for her appearance in the title role of the film *Carmen* (1946), lives in the South of France.

RUSSELL, ELIZABETH Best remembered for her startling appearances in *Cat People* (1944). Once married to the brother of Rosalind Russell, she lives in Washington, D.C., and is a convert to Roman Catholicism.

RYAN, PEGGY The star of Universal musicals during the forties now commutes between homes in Honolulu and Las Vegas, where she teaches tap dancing. Her husband is a newspaperman and their daughter, Kerry Sherman, is a regular on the TV soap *Santa Barbara*.

ST. CYR, LILI The star exotic dancer is single and lives in the Larchmont area of Los Angeles.

SANDERS, LUGENE Married to a millionaire, she is living in San Marino, California.

SANDS, TOMMY The singing actor of the fifties and first husband of Nancy Sinatra lives in Honolulu. He is married and works as the manufacturer's representative of a line of men's clothing.

SCOTT, LIZABETH Single, she lives in Los Angeles and drives a black Jaguar sedan bearing license plates reading, "S I N."

SEABURY, DAVID The author of the classic self-help book *The Art of Selfishness* died in 1960.

SEARL, JACKIE A prime contender for the title "The Face You'd Love to Slap" is now an audio engineer and the father of five. The resident of Tujunga, California, refuses all requests for interviews.

SHEARER, MOIRA The dancer-actress best known for her performance in *The Red Shoes* (1948) lives in London with her husband, British journalist and broadcaster Ludovic Kennedy.

SILVA, HENRY Married, he is living in Beverly Hills.

SIMON, SIMONE The French actress best known in the United States for *Cat People* (1942) and *Curse of the Cat People* (1944) is single and lives in Paris. In 1985 Jean Marais said of her: "From across a softly lit room she could still pass for mid-twenties."

SMITH, JACK In the forties he was known in network radio as "The fellow Who Smiles while he Sings." On television he was one of the hosts of *You Asked For It.* Smith lives in Westlake Village, California. He is the owner and producer of the TV show *The American West.*

SOSENKO, ANNA The former impresario now buys and sells estates of celebrities. She is single and lives in Manhattan.

SOTHERN, ANN The star of movies and television is single and lives in Los Angeles.

STRATTON, GIL, JR. The actor-turned-sportscaster owns and operates his own radio station in Hawaii.

STUART, GLORIA The widow of screenwriter Arthur Sheekman lives in West Los Angeles. She has had several one-woman shows of her paintings and sculpture.

SUMAC, YMA "The Nightingale of the Andes" is again performing, most recently at the Vine Street Bar and Grill in Hollywood.

TAYLOR, DON Now a director of both features and television, he is married to the English actress Hazel Court and lives in Santa Monica.

TEASDALE, VERREE The widow of Adolph Menjou lives in Beverly Hills.

TERRY, PHILIP The actor best remembered as the third husband of Joan Crawford lives in Montecito, California, with his present wife.

TODD, RICHARD Has been starring in the thriller *The Business of Murder* since 1984 in London's West End.

TOMLINSON, DAVID The British comic actor was de scribed by David Quinlan in his book *The Illustrated Directory of British Films Stars* as "the archetypal 'silly-ass' of his day." He lives in Buckinghamshire, England.

TRENET, CHARLES One of France's most popular singing stars of the forties and fifties. He lives with a companion of over twenty-five years in the South of France.

TRENKER, LUIS The star of German cinema during the thirties has homes in Munich, Germany, and the Italian Alps.

URE, MARY The actress best known for her role in *Look Back in Anger* (1959) was married to and divorced from its author, John Osborne. She died in April, 1975, from a combination of sleeping pills and alcohol.

VALLEE, RUDY The star of recordings, vaudeville, radio, and Broadway lived in a Hollywood Hills home that was once owned by the late star Ann Harding. He died on July 3, 1986.

VALLI, ALIDA Publicized in the United States as "Valli." She is active in Italian cinema and lives in Rome.

VEE, BOBBY The rock star lives in St. Cloud, Minnesota.

WEAVER BROTHERS and ELVIRY The family of bumpkins made their movie debut in *Swing Your Lady* (1938) and went on to star in eleven low-budget features at Republic studios. Cicero died in 1967. Abner died in 1950. Elviry, who was married to and divorced from Cicero and later married Abner, died in 1977.

WHELAN, ARLEEN The manicurist, who bacame a leading lady in movies, is one of Hollywood's "missing" personalities. One of those who would like to be in touch again is her ex-husband, Alex D'Arcy.

WHITING, LEONARD Best known for playing the title role in *Romeo and Juliet* (1966). Divorced, he lives in the outskirts of London with his teenage daughter. "Publicity for the sake of publicity does not appeal to me," was his response to a request for an interview. Recently he produced a recording, *Charlie's Dream*, a musical fantasy which is narrated by Peter Ustinov. Whiting wrote both music and lyrics and plays several characters.

WHITNEY, ELEANORE The leading lady left acting when she married a socialite-lawyer. Last known to be living in Manhattan.

WOOLEY, SHEB The musician best known for his 1958 hit recording "The Purple People Eater" lives in Memphis and performs under the name Ben Coulder.

ZETTERLING, MAI The former star writes, directs, and produces films. She maintains residences in England and France.

ZORINA, VERA The dancer-actress is the widow of the late music critic and recording executive Goddard Lieberson. She lives in Manhattan.